CAMMING

Camming

Money, Power, and Pleasure in the Sex Work Industry

Angela Jones

NEW YORK UNIVERSITY PRESS

New York

NEW YORK UNIVERSITY PRESS
New York
www.nyupress.org

References to Internet websites (URLs) were accurate at the time of writing. Neither the author nor New York University Press is responsible for URLs that may have expired or changed since the manuscript was prepared.

Library of Congress Cataloging-in-Publication Data
Names: Jones, Angela, 1978–   author.
Title: Camming : money, power, and pleasure in the sex work industry / Angela Jones.
Description: New York : New York University Press, [2019] |
Includes bibliographical references and index.
Identifiers: LCCN 2019009085| ISBN 9781479842964 (cl : alk. paper) |
ISBN 9781479874873 (pb : alk. paper)
Subjects: LCSH: Sex-oriented businesses.
Classification: LCC HQ121 .J66 2019 | DDC 338.4/73067—dc23
LC record available at https://lccn.loc.gov/2019009085

New York University Press books are printed on acid-free paper, and their binding materials are chosen for strength and durability. We strive to use environmentally responsible suppliers and materials to the greatest extent possible in publishing our books.

Manufactured in the United States of America

10 9 8 7 6 5 4 3 2 1

Also available as an ebook

CONTENTS

LIST OF FIGURES

LIST OF TABLES

PREFACE

In 2013, when one of my favorite students stopped attending class I became very concerned.[1] Alyssa had taken a couple of courses with me, and we had developed an excellent rapport. She was a highly motivated student who always attended class, completed the reading assignments, and participated meaningfully in class discussion. Alyssa was a self-proclaimed feminist who was never afraid to speak up in class, especially about progressive issues. I sent Alyssa an email. I wanted to see if she was okay and to make sure she knew that if she returned to class that I would be happy to help her catch up on the materials she had missed. Alyssa replied that she was well but asked if we could meet in person because she was considering leaving college. I responded that I would be happy to meet with her, which we did the following week.

Once in my office, she asked to close the door—she wanted to share something personal: she had started camming on a site called MyFree-Cams. She explained that in the last month she had made $10,000.[2] Given these high earnings, she decided to take a break from school. She explained that she could always return to school if the wages she was making did not continue or if she tired of the work. In addition to being profitable, Alyssa described camming as fun, easy, and pleasurable. I congratulated her on her success and we remained in contact for some time.

Alyssa's disclosure struck me—$10,000 a month for being a cam model? I did not think she was lying about her income, but I did wonder if it would remain so high. I wondered, Was there a new online sex work industry that could promise sex workers physical safety and high wages? Alyssa was not the only student who confided in me that they had worked as a cam model. However, it was her disclosure that made me begin this research project and so to Alyssa—I am forever grateful and hope wherever you are now, you are happy.

Alyssa also made me think more about my past as a former sex worker. After dropping out of college, I worked as a stripper for about four years in the late 1990s and early 2000s. I also entered into what is now on the Internet called a sugarbabying relationship, and exchanged emotional labor—a girlfriend experience outside of the strip club with a regular client. There were things I loved about stripping. I loved being naked (and still do). I loved dancing. I loved having people appreciate and compliment my body. I loved that entranced look in a man's eye that told me he was so captivated with me that he'd empty his wallet if I commanded him to. I had never felt this empowered before: I had power over these men and power over my own body, sexuality, and destiny, despite the stigma perceived by friends and family. I loved getting paid to consume alcohol and party, and yes, I loved making money. I will never forget being able to take my friends down to South Beach in Miami, all expenses paid. I lived well and had a beautiful one-bedroom apartment in New York.

But the work was not always pleasurable, and customers were not always pleasant. They were often demanding, cheap, and menacing. My managers were creeps and as an independent contractor who paid "house fees"[3] to work I was conscious of the exploitation I was experiencing. Over time, I stopped making consistently high wages. In the context of a strip club, regulars quickly tire of their favorite dancers and move on. Also, I began finding that I was drinking excessively; for mental health reasons, I had to stop stripping. My decision to stop was about my sobriety and my struggles with drug addiction, not about the industry itself. I eventually got clean and went back to school, but I often still look back on my time in the industry with great fondness.

Thus, when Alyssa animatedly told me her story, it made me recall the good times I had stripping. She reminded me of the excitement and pleasure I often experienced as a dancer. I wondered, Was it possible that the Internet had resolved many of the problems I and other strippers encountered working in strip clubs in the late 1990s? Online, dirty men cannot sexually assault you. Online, there are millions of potential clients—not the regular cast of a hundred customers or so who patronize a strip club during a given evening. Also, I thought, the Internet never closes. In the camming industry, nobody is setting your hours, or charging you fees to work and assessing you penalties for being late. I remember thinking to myself, Under the working conditions Alyssa described would more people from various socioeconomic backgrounds start performing sex work?

As I'd come to learn, the camming industry is not a utopian paradise. It is an exploitative capitalist marketplace that also reproduces White supremacy, patriarchy, heterosexism, cissexism, and ableism. However, it is also an industry where cam models report high rates of job satisfaction and experiences of pleasure. For many cam models in this study, the industry presented an opportunity to earn decent wages. Cam performers, like all sex workers, are motivated to perform erotic labor for a myriad of reasons, many of which are not about money. The physical safety found in online sex work can be appealing to people who ordinarily would not perform offline erotic labor. The bourgeoning erotic webcam industry is part of a rapidly and exponentially growing online global network of sex work industries. These are exciting times, then, to be living in—a period of increased sexual commerce and sexual exploration. I believe the growth of online sexual commerce will continue to push cultural mores forward, challenging hegemonic neo-Victorian discourses regulating sex and pleasure. If my research on the camming industry and my brief background as a sex worker have taught me anything, it is that sex workers have always been on the frontlines of the struggle for human and sexual freedom.

Introduction

Rita's workspace is ready. Music plays softly—a silky baritone voice emanating from a diminutive speaker connected to a smartphone will provide the show's score. Her laptop and webcam are skillfully positioned on the mahogany wood end table that sits at the foot of her bed. Rita turns her computer on, hops onto her bed, and crawls across her white goose-down comforter. She rearranges three sex toys, her Hitachi Magic Wand, VixSkin dildo, and Lovense vibrator, which she had earlier placed on a blue towel. She adjusts the shoulder strap on her form-fitting pink camisole—the soft HD lighting in the room allows for a glimpse of the outlines of her beautiful brown nipples beneath the chiffon. Rita looks intensely at the computer screen, her fans lying in wait; she energetically starts, "Hey guys, are you ready for me?"

In October 2016, Rita needed extra money. She had spent much time thinking about various employment options, especially those in the burgeoning gig economy.[1] Rita wanted quick money and pleasurable work that would also provide her with autonomy. She found this in the erotic webcam industry. She now makes $1,200 per month camming part-time and is one of the millions of people around the world who have turned to online sex work as a refuge from poorly remunerated service occupations in increasingly precarious global economies.

The erotic webcam industry,[2] which emerged in 1996, is an exponentially growing sex industry where workers, called cam models, from all over the globe are finding decent wages, greater autonomy, community, and pleasure. Colloquially called "camming," it is a genre of indirect sex work,[3] in which cam models sell interactive computer-mediated sex online. The camming field, like other sex work industries, monetizes human desires for sex, intimacy, and pleasure.

I believe cam models provide an essential economic service. The camming field functions according to the logic of capitalism, but it stands apart because these workers are selling sex. For decades, sex worker activists and scholars have worked hard to demonstrate that sex work is legitimate labor. These activists and scholars are correct—it is vital to sex workers' lives that societies around the globe accept sex work as legitimate labor, decriminalize sex work where it is illegal, and provide sex workers with all the same protections all workers should have. However, a political strategy that advocates for sex worker's rights using respectability politics[4] has limitations.

Respectability politics involves subordinate groups demonstrating to dominant groups that they are worthy of rights. In this case, to gain access to basic rights, sex workers must prove to political gatekeepers that sex work is honest labor and like any other job in the service economy. Respectability politics glosses over the subversive outcomes of sex workers' labor. Every day, sex workers challenge various overlapping systems of oppression, calling into question discourses around appropriate modes of sexuality and sexual gratification. In the erotic camming industry, a primary motivation for selling sex online, alongside decent wages and autonomy, is to explore sexuality and experience pleasure. A political strategy that hinges upon demonstrating how similar sex work is to other forms of service work unintentionally glosses over the radical and essential labor sex workers do to push social boundaries and make the world a less sexually repressive and more pleasurable place.

Governments around the world craft policies and laws that constrain the rights of sex workers and enact a pernicious form of state-sponsored violence on their bodies. While governments and their law enforcement agencies mobilize moral police forces to govern the lives of citizens, sex workers resist these forces. For centuries, sex workers have resisted the policing of sex, bodies, and the acquisition of pleasure by the state, religious institutions, and various other social institutions; workers in the camming industry contribute to this long history of resistance.

The Camming Industry

In the 21st century, as access to the Internet became more widespread, e-commerce flourished, and sex entrepreneurs and sex workers also started selling sex online. Technology has diversified forms of sex work and the rise of online sex work presents new opportunities for studying and theorizing about sexuality, gender, race, inequality, and labor.

The Internet has helped to create new opportunities for sex entrepreneurs and workers to craft a labor environment that is more appealing to workers across social classes.[5] My research suggests that the increase in online sex work is not a reflection of a unilateral move of sex workers from offline to online environments. Instead, given the improved working conditions of online sex work, erotic labor may now appeal to people who previously were unwilling or unable to perform sex work that occurs offline. More workers may be open to performing sex work because the online context provides physical safety, autonomy, and access to pleasure they could not find in other areas of sex work or the economy more broadly. Workers who were previously unable to secure work in other forms of erotic labor because of their gender, race, sexuality, age, disability, or embodiment have found new labor opportunities in the growing camming industry.

Carl, a 31-year-old bisexual Black cisgender[6] man from the United States, said:

> If this was never an option, I probably wouldn't have done any type of sex work because . . . I'm kind of introverted and shy. . . . But I think with the sex cam stuff, also the stuff that I do on this show, there's no way I could do on a stage, at all. So, I think it's also cool in that sense, that it offers an alternative for people that don't think that stripping is right for them . . . just knowing that you could do this at home and not have to worry about how uncomfortable actually being at the physical strip club can be; so, that's definitely a benefit. And I know it's definitely a benefit to me because, well, my sexuality is well, a little out there, compared to what other available strippers do.

The online environment makes people feel safe and less inhibited. The working conditions appeal to those who would not consider performing sex work that involves physical contact.

Carl is known for his extreme anal shows, acts he couldn't perform in a strip club. When Carl noted that his sexuality was "out there," he was highlighting the point that camming provides a unique space for sexual exploration—whereas strip clubs are generally highly regulated environments. For male performers like Carl, it is challenging to even find employment as exotic dancers. According to cam models, the camming industry has opened up opportunities for people around the world who before the Internet would have never performed sex work.

The growth of the camming industry reflects an expansion of the online market of sexual commerce. The camming industry has not replaced the demand for traditional pornography; it offers sexual consumers an additional way in which to consume pornographic content online. Camming is different from traditional pornography because camming is interactive. Clients,[7] who cam models told me were overwhelmingly cisgender men, are purchasing a live and intimate encounter with a cam model(s), which is substantially different from purchasing a prerecorded and scripted pornographic film. Unlike traditional pornography, cam models use chat rooms to sell a range of erotic fantasies to online patrons—from intimate conversation to erotic striptease to explicit sex acts. The model chooses when, how, and if they climax—a movie producer does not direct the cam model. On some cam sites, cam models perform in public shows and receive tips called "tokens." On other cam sites, cam models perform in private pay-per-minute shows. There are cam sites that offer both public shows and private shows. While many cam models build up a following of regular clients that they perform private shows for on platforms such as Skype, most cam models still perform on one or more cam-site platforms. Despite the rapid growth of the camming industry, there is a paucity of empirical data about the industry and research that explores how the rise of online sex work can contribute to our thinking and theorizing about sexuality, gender, race, inequality, and labor.

There have been many mainstream news media accounts of the camming industry, yet most, like Sean Dunne's 2015 documentary *Cam Girlz*, focus on cis women, called "camgirls," who work as adult webcam models.[8] Even if unintentionally, these stories can erase the lives of all the other erotic webcam models of various genders who work in the industry. Journalists focus primarily on White cis camgirls from Romania, the United Kingdom, and the United States. Mainstream stories about the camming industry have left many questions unanswered about the diverse groups of people who work in the camming field.

Fortunately, new research has emerged that has begun to document the camming industry empirically. Paul William Mathews has published an important study of women who work as cam models in the Philippines.[9] Kavita Nayar has examined the complex ways camgirls use both their professional and amateur statuses in the camming industry to maximize wages.[10] Similarly, although not limited to women, Van Doorn and Velthuis have studied how cam models "hustle" or navigate the competitive economic environment on the cam site Chaturbate.[11] Additionally, there are rigorous studies of online sex work that examine the lives and workplace experiences of cam models. Teela Sanders, Jane Scoular, Rosie Campbell, Jane Pitcher, and Stewart Cunningham recently published *Internet Sex Work*, the most inclusive and comprehensive study of Internet-facilitated sex work to date. However, their extraordinary research covers a wide range of online sex work (not only camming) and focuses exclusively on sex workers in the United Kingdom.

Camming presents a holistic portrait of the contemporary camming industry by drawing from my five-year mixed-methods study of the erotic webcam industry. I use multiple methodologies, which include web analytics, participant observation on cam sites, statistical analyses of data collected from cam-model profiles, content analyses of web forums for cam models, survey data, in-depth interviews, and auto-ethnography. *Camming*, the first book devoted solely to the camming industry, empirically documents the industry's current size, profitability, history, and analyzes the motivations and the experiences of a relatively diverse sample of cam models. This thorough examination of the camming industry uses a transnational lens and, as a result, provides a unique vantage point from which to understand and theorize around sexuality, gender, race, and labor in a time when workers globally face increasing economic precariousness and worsened forms of alienation, and desperately desire to recapture pleasure in work.

Embodied Authenticity

Most customers perceive camming as authentic. Cam models construct what scholars of sex work call "manufactured identities."[12] They perform under screen names in order to protect themselves from doxing[13] and harassment.[14] In addition to these manufactured identities, cam models' shows are performative—models do often have to engage in some amount of acting. However, cam models often spend copious time talking with customers online, and, in many ways, they are being themselves. Their rooms are often their bedrooms, and from the perspective of a consumer, everything about the experience appears real. The model uses a stylized performance to offer an authentic presentation to customers, which is highly valuable in the world of erotic labor. Cam modeling appeals to what cultural anthropologist Katherine Frank has called customers' desire for "realness"[15] or what sociologist Elizabeth Bernstein has called "bounded authenticity."[16] As both have noted, in contemporary sex markets, customers want to feel they are having an authentic sexual encounter that, while bounded by the economic exchange, is also characterized by intimacy. Cam models provide what I call *embodied authenticity* to clients.[17]

While it is no secret to most customers that cam models are working, the appeal of the erotic webcam market is that performers are perceived as amateurs—as real people, who have turned on their webcams. The allure of camming is that a viewer can get glimpses into the lives of strangers from all over the world. According to the popular cam site CAM4:

> CAM4 has been supporting sexual openness, freedom, and equality for over ten years. It provides consenting adults with a place to express themselves on webcam—regardless of sex, race, size, or sexual preference. A community with a strong focus on social networking, CAM4 is much more than a traditional webcam site. People can make global connections and form communities without discrimination—they meet, make friends, explore their sexuality and, in some cases, even get married. CAM4 is translated into 42 different languages and boasts over 23 million members from more than 230 countries. CAM4 allows for genuine interactions of real, intimate and personal moments by adults who all share a desire to connect to form a global society from the comfort of their own homes and beyond.[18]

While CAM4 overstates the likelihood of cam models and clients forming romantic relationships, this marketing material nicely highlights my conceptualization of embodied authenticity, which underscores the importance of clients feeling like they are purchasing authentic experiences with "real" people. The pleasure cam models and clients experience are born out of these intimate social encounters with strangers from all over the world. Given that these interactions take place in real time, online, and are interactive, the client is purchasing a one-of-a-kind experience with an individual(s) whom the client may not be able to interact with intimately and sexually in their everyday life. Webcam modeling has an authentic character that other forms of sex work often fail to deliver to clients.

Throughout this book, I use the term *embodied authenticity* to emphasize the importance of embodiment in effectively delivering authentic performances. Crucially, the online context and interactive experience ostensibly allow clients to verify the authenticity of the performance and the mutual experience of pleasure. In the camming market, the online context and the agency that cam models do have allow them to also experience pleasure while working. Cam models frequently said things to me such as "I get paid to have orgasms."[19] Clients are paying not only for their pleasure—they are also paying to watch the cam model experience pleasure. The online context makes it easier for cam models to deliver embodied authenticity to clients. The computer-mediated interaction between model and client forms a psychological barrier that, for the most part, makes both parties feel safe and more willing to be themselves, which also opens up the potential for more pleasure for the worker.

Pleasure and Online Sex Work

While this book focuses on both pleasures and dangers in the camming industry, my focus on pleasure makes a unique contribution to studies of sex work and to broader theories of labor. The nascent literature on sex work in the digital era has primarily focused on the practical benefits of Internet-based sex work, such as better wages, better and safer working conditions, and a decline in risk exposure.[20] While these benefits are important, with little exception[21] this literature does not highlight the way the online environment fosters a space in which workers have a greater potential to experience various pleasures.

The online context shapes the acquisition of pleasure in the camming industry. Many people adhere to an offline/online binary, distinguishing between the virtual and physical worlds. People often think of the virtual world as an alternative reality or as a realm of social experience that is separate from the "real" physical world. Following this line of thinking, some people may believe that interactions that occur in cyberspace are less "real" than face-to-face interaction in physical space. Like sociologist Christine Hine, I too caution against understanding cyberspace in this binary way.[22] The Internet and the spaces that people have formed and created on the Internet are real spaces. Offline and online spaces are merely different contexts. Moreover, the spread of mobile computers and communications technologies means that increasingly people (with access) are simultaneously immersed in both offline and online contexts. Our offline and online experiences are diffuse and symbiotic.

The online context shapes the acquisition of pleasure in the camming industry precisely because people rely on the virtual/physical world dichotomy. While our actual embodiments do not change in either context, based on my research, many people still see the consumption of *virtual embodiment* differently than they see the consumption of *physical embodiment.* The absence of physical touching and the computer-mediated sexual exchange make many people perceive sexual encounters online as not sex—as something other. The computer-mediated sexual experience may qualitatively shape the cam models' and customers' experiences of the sexual encounter, but the interactions are most definitely still sex. Mutual masturbation online does not cease to be a sex act because it occurred in cyberspace. The online context, like any social space, shapes the ways people experience the sex act. However, given that people adhere to the virtual/physical world dichotomy, camming, for participants, is a more socially acceptable form of sex work than stripping or escorting because they use only virtually delivered projections of their embodiments. Middle-class sex workers and consumers employ this logic as a form of stigma management—to rationalize both the selling and consumption of sex online. Importantly, these contextual elements create the conditions under which people open themselves up to experiencing new forms of pleasure.

Pleasure is not only an initial motivation for camming—it is also often the reason why people continue in the industry. As Rita told me, she became a cam model because she "really needed the easy money . . . [but she] stay[s] one because [she] actually like[s] it." Crucially, the more pleasure performers experience in the field, the more likely they are to continue camming. The pleasure they do experience allows them to effectively deliver embodied authenticity to clients, which increases wages. My case study suggests that sex worker job satisfaction is directly tied to pleasure. Future lines of inquiry in sociological studies of labor, especially research on sex work, should explore the role of pleasure in work.

I hope my focus on pleasure throughout this book will help people better understand the motivations for working in online sex work, as well as the complex social interactions between cam models and customers. The sociological theory of pleasure I offer emphasizes that societal institutions, social norms, culture, and social context all shape how our bodies experience pleasure, and that pleasure is an understudied motivation for social behavior. Pleasure is a social experience. The pleasures we feel in our social interactions reflect a complex interplay, or a symbiotic relationship, between affectual and corporeal pleasures that are conditioned by social context and culture. My goal is to open up an entirely new subfield in sociology—the sociology of pleasure. The sociology of pleasure can provide new insights into the motivations for social behavior and assist sociologists in analyzing social interactions in everyday life.

Critical Pedagogy

My investment in critical pedagogy guided the writing of this book. In traditional positivist empirical research, there is no room for social critique and personal experience. My goal is to educate people about the camming industry, but pursue this goal with a deep commitment to transformative social justice, and I present and incorporate data in ways that I hope inspire readers to think about this capitalist industry in critical ways. In what follows, I discuss my use of progressive stacking, autoethnography, and the pornographic imagination, and I discuss my belief that these choices advance critical pedagogies. I hope that other sociologists will adopt and expand on these critical pedagogies in ways that advance the discipline by not only making sociological research more inclusive but by bringing more critical attention to the social-justice issues the people we study face. This will require that researchers be willing to adopt queer methods[23] and let go of their investments in rigid positivist epistemological and methodological traditions in the interest of advancing transformative social justice.

Progressive Stacking

Activists use progressive stacking during their meetings to structure the flow of dialogue and to ensure that marginalized people's voices are heard and they have a voice in all decision-making. When used by the Occupy Wall Street movement in the United States, activists emphasized that people who have been historically marginalized by the systems of capitalism, White supremacy, cissexism, heterosexism, and ableism should always speak before people who are privileged by these systems. As another example, there are educators who use progressive stacking in their classrooms.[24] I do not doubt that there are also researchers who prepare and publish their data with an eye toward being inclusive. However, the widespread, intentional, and systematic use of progressive stacking is not evident in contemporary sociological research. The use of progressive stacking in the presentation of research is not merely a symbolic gesture—if used widely by researchers, progressive stacking has the potential to transform knowledge.

As the writer of this book, I have an enormous amount of discursive power because I decide whose voices to use, and how and when I use their voices. With this in mind, I used progressive stacking to determine the ordinal presentation of both quantitative and qualitative data. In the social sciences, in the presentation of quantitative data related to gender, researchers generally present data for men first.[25] Often, researchers do not even survey transgender and nonbinary people. This persistent practice by social scientists reifies the social hierarchy created by patriarchy and cissexism; applying progressive stacking resolves this problem via the inversion of hierarchal systems for all demographic variables. Scholars can apply progressive stacking to the presentation of qualitative data, as well.

I applied progressive stacking both to the selection of quotations and to the order in which they appear. The application of progressive stacking prioritized the voices of people of color, people from Latin America, trans people, queer people, and people with disabilities. This strategy does not mean that I do not present the voices of people who came from privileged social locations, but I made deliberate choices to ensure, for example, that the lives of people of color and trans people are prominent and visible. This strategy is crucial because people of color and trans people are underrepresented in mainstream or so-called generalist sociological research.

Progressive stacking is an imperfect system, and its application in research can be tricky. My goal here is not to construct a highly systematized rubric that could be applied by scholars uniformly—doing so would be a misstep. Any attempt to create a standardized instrument for applying progressive stacking will miss the importance of researchers thinking carefully about how intersecting systems and various contexts shape people's social positions, as well as their experiences with inequality. It is difficult to neatly apply progressive stacking because identities are intersectional and overlap. The spirit of progressive stacking and the idea I am advocating, though, calls for researchers to be more thoughtful about how they choose what data to present and to acknowledge that how scholars present data matters. I believe that progressive stacking and inclusive methodologies must become the rule in sociological research—not the exception. I call on more researchers to embrace progressive stacking as a formal research technique because doing so can directly increase the visibility of marginalized people and if adopted on a grander scale can help to disrupt various systems of oppression and their institutionalization in academic research.

Autoethnography

Anthropologist David Hayano refers to autoethnography as the use of ethnography by a researcher to study their "own people." Sociologist Carol Ellis and communications scholar Arthur P. Bochner describe autoethnography as "an autobiographical genre of writing and research that displays multiple layers of consciousness, connecting the personal to the cultural."[26] Autoethnography allows the researcher to use personal narrative constructively, as data, to reveal insights about social institutions and social interactions.[27]

I decided to also use autoethnographic vignettes and stories about my experiences as a former sex worker. As sociologists Orne and Bell note, "Many forms of autoethnography are based in a critical pedagogy, seeking to disrupt the often colonial and powerful 'researchers' with indigenous, post-colonial, and marginalized voices."[28] I push back on what it means to be a scientist and researcher. My voice, along with my participants', can help to push back against positivist sciences that often silence people of color, poor people, trans people, and people such as sex workers whom society too often sees as deviant and whose voices are deemed invalid. As Ellis, Adams, and Bochner argue:

> Those who advocate and insist on canonical forms of doing and writing research are advocating a White, masculine, heterosexual, middle/upper-classed, Christian, able-bodied perspective. Following these conventions, a researcher not only disregards other ways of knowing but also implies that other ways necessarily are unsatisfactory and invalid. Autoethnography, on the other hand, expands and opens up a wider lens on the world, eschewing rigid definitions of what constitutes meaningful and useful research.[29]

Using autoethnography can help to bring an honesty and intimacy to writing that we do not often find in scientific research. I hope using autoethnograhic vignettes and reflections will help to introduce a writing style that my readers find engaging.

The Pornographic Imagination

Researchers often censor depictions and accounts of actual sex from scholarly work. This erasure can cause scholars to miss essential features of people's lives. In "The Pornographic Imagination," Susan Sontag observes that pornography is generally denounced as lowbrow trash and famously makes the case that literary texts that foray into the pornographic are, in fact, literature. She argues that because scholars in the humanities cannot divorce their moral sensibilities from their evaluation of literature, they will never see pornography as valuable art. I would like to raise a line of inquiry similar to Sontag's. What explains the lack of pornographic imagination in sociology? What explains the absence of actual sex in a lot of the research published in the sociology of sexualities? If a sociologist employs material categorizable as pornographic—that is, if they ask explicit questions about sex or if they include graphic narratives from respondents about sex acts or if they dare to accompany a text with pornographic imagery—would these choices call into question the scientific legitimacy of their work?

A sociological imagination is not antithetical to a pornographic imagination. If a sociological text reads pornographically, it does not cease to be sociology. As Sontag notes in her discussion of Bataille, certain works of his

> qualify as pornographic texts insofar as their theme is an all-engrossing sexual quest that annihilates every consideration of persons extraneous to their roles in the sexual dramaturgy, and the fulfillment of this quest is depicted graphically. But this description conveys nothing of the extraordinary quality of these books. For sheer explicitness about sex organs and acts is not necessarily obscene; it only becomes so when delivered in a particular tone, when it has acquired a certain moral resonance.[30]

Sontag's words are instructive. The problem in sociology, not unlike in the humanities, is that the mere sight of pornographic data, language, or imagery triggers concerns around morality, stigma, and legitimacy. Yet, I would argue, and as I hope to demonstrate here, sociologists can write explicitly about sex without compromising the quality and value of their empirical and theoretical contributions. It does not devalue the work, quite the opposite—the use of pornographic questions, the inclusion of pornographic data, and the use of pornographic language and pornographic imagery give us a deeper insight into humanity and human behavior. In this book, I do not shy away from explicit discussion of sex and I present pornographic imagery. The people I studied sell sex online; to hide frank discussions or imagery of sex would do them an injustice and would fail to capture the most radical elements of their work. Only through the presentation of pornographic data can I thoroughly analyze the complex forms of pleasure that cam performers experience.

Analytical Frameworks

The Polymorphous Paradigm of Sex Work

Feminists have written extensively about sex work. Their debates about sex work became known to academics as the Sex Wars.[31] The first charge in this proverbial war was led by culturally conservative radical feminists who focused on only the exploitative characteristics of sex work (particularly misogyny in pornography).[32] Pro-sex feminists fired back by focusing primarily on the agency of sex workers and the empowerment found in sex work.[33] Sex radicals argued that sex work is contingent on both danger and pleasure.[34] Carol Vance argued that the theoretical debates among feminists over whether sex work is inherently exploitative or empowering were problematic because they were reductive. Concurring with Vance, sociologist Ronald Weitzer refers to this as the oppression/empowerment paradigm. As Weitzer argues:

> Both the oppression and empowerment perspectives are one-dimensional and essentialist. While exploitation and empowerment are certainly present in sex work, there is sufficient variation across time, place, and sector to demonstrate that sex work cannot be reduced to one or the other. An alternative perspective, what I call the polymorphous paradigm, holds that there is a constellation of occupational arrangements, power relations, and worker experiences.[35]

My analyses are guided by the polymorphous paradigm, or the theoretical standpoint that the experiences of sex workers are fluid—workers in any field are likely to have varied experiences of exploitation and job satisfaction. The camming industry is exploitative, and workers face other forms of discrimination in the market based on their subjectivities and embodiments—camming is still capitalist labor—but their work also allows them to subvert antiquated ideas about sexuality, and thus also produces empowerment and pleasure.

Intersectionality

As noted above, this project's analytical framework draws from the polymorphous paradigm of sex work and the recognition that adult webcam performers' workplace experiences are diverse and likely to include both experiences of exploitation and empowerment. However, workplaces are not neutral meritocracies. Worker's social identities play a role in how their employers and customers perceive them and remunerate workers' for their labor.[36] The experiences workers have in the workplace are affected by their social positioning in various systems of stratification.

Intersectionality is a critical framework used to analyze the ways that various social markers of identity simultaneously work to condition our all our experiences in society. Beginning in the 1980s, legal scholar and critical race theorist Kimberlé Crenshaw criticized conceptions of discrimination for analyzing subordination along only one single axis. Challenging legal policies regarding race-based and sex-based discrimination lawsuits, she wrote:

> [T]his focus on the most privileged group members marginalizes those who are multiply burdened and obscures claims that cannot be understood as resulting from discrete sources of discrimination. . . . Black women are sometimes excluded from feminist theory and antiracist policy discourse because both are predicated on a discrete set of experiences that often does not accurately reflect the intersection of race and gender.[37]

In subsequent work, Crenshaw used cases of battering and the rape of women to further her astute analysis of the deficiencies within both feminist and antiracist discourses in addressing the marginalization of Black women.

Along with Crenshaw, sociologist Patricia Hill Collins has famously critiqued liberal feminism and gynocentrism[38] by noting that Black women's oppression is experienced along three interlocking dimensions, which she refers to as the economic, political, and ideological realms. All women do not have a core or shared experience of oppression, because other aspects of identity (e.g., race) also affect our experiences of oppression. Black feminists have a strong track record of highlighting the importance of race, gender, class, and sexual identity in conditioning individuals' experiences.[39]

Scholars tend to use intersectionality in studying the lives of people who are situated on the lower tiers of social hierarchies—that is, people who are disadvantaged by capitalism, racism, sexism, heterosexism, cis-sexism, and ableism. However, people have both advantages and disadvantages due to their positions in multiple systems.[40] As with my cautionary note about progressive stacking, in many cases, intersectional identities can be complex and tricky; an individual could receive privilege from their position in one system (e.g., race), but be disadvantaged because of their position in another, overlapping system (e.g., gender).

Intersectionality has now become a standard analytical tool in gender studies. The primary way scholars employ intersectionality has been through the case study method, which is how I use it in this study of erotic webcam performers. Generally, those scholars "who are interested in intersectionality use the case study method to identify a new or invisible group—at the intersection of multiple categories—and proceed to uncover the differences and complexities of experience embodied in that location."[41] McCall identifies this method as the "intracategorical approach," while Choo and Ferree call it the "group-centered approach."[42] Whichever term is adopted by scholars, the point of this intersectional research is to study an invisible or hidden population—one that has been ignored by scholars and social institutions. My intersectional approach aims to demonstrate how cam models' positioning along different social axes conditions their workplace experiences. Since the full range of what can be accomplished via the use of intersectional analysis in sociological research has not yet been achieved, this case study of webcam modeling also contributes to the advancement of intersectional theory.

Overview of the Book

Camming tells a pornographic story about a growing online sex work industry where people find decent wages, friendship, intimacy, community, empowerment, and pleasure. This book is not a utopian tale. Cam models, like all sex workers, must grapple with exploitation, discrimination, harassment, and stigma. It is also crucial that we think transnationally and remember that economic growth is not evenly felt and that the camming industry remains inaccessible to many. The inequality generated by global capitalism means that, for so many people around the world, the costs associated with becoming a cam model are prohibitive and access to the technologies and private space required to cam are not available. The resources required to begin camming can force people to work under exploitative conditions in studios, and can also be a reason why street-based escorts working under deplorable conditions who want to migrate into online indirect sex work cannot. The camming industry can be lauded for creating an opportunity for safe and legal sex work that allows workers to earn decent wages, have more autonomy, work less, find community, and experience pleasure.

However, this opportunity is not open to the most economically vulnerable people around the world and the market privileges White bodies and native English speakers, especially from the US.

This book uses the camming industry as a springboard for an analysis of sexuality, gender, race, and labor in a historical moment when workers globally are facing increased economic instability and alienation, and who under these conditions also desperately want to recapture dignity and pleasure in work. People are not solely motivated to sell sex online because they need a job to pay their bills. Their stories are complex and show that a desire for pleasure and intimacy guide their decisions to become and stay cam models. What makes camming unique and unlike other employment in the gig economy is that it is a capitalist industry that does not require the sacrifice of pleasure. Being successful requires that workers provide pleasure to others *and* acquire pleasure for themselves. In camming, unlike other sex work industries, the safe conditions of labor provided by the online context contributes to the experience of pleasure as a fundamental part of their work.

My theory of pleasure applies not only to sex work or to industries like camming where people say their work is pleasurable. If people say their work is not pleasurable, this raises revealing questions. Why is so much work not pleasurable? Why and how do different aspects of worker subjectivity also compound the experience of displeasure in work? Traditional capitalist labor is rooted in exploitation. As Karl Marx argued, capitalism thrives through the estrangement of labor, through the alienation of workers. Capitalism necessitates the sacrifice of pleasure. For scholars who study work, studying pleasure—even its absence—is essential. By drawing on the experiences of erotic webcam performers, I demonstrate the usefulness of a sociological theory of pleasure.

1

The Pleasure Deficit

Toward a Sociological Theory of Pleasure

Scientific and medical research has focused too much on the nature of desire and sex. Instead, with inspiration from Michel Foucault, I call on sociologists to explore pleasure as a mode of self-exploration. We need a sociological theory of pleasure to unpack the ways that pleasure both motivates human behavior and mediates social interactions. A sociological theory of pleasure asks scholars to focus on the ways in which social forces, social institutions, and culture construct hegemonic discourses, which regulate experiences of pleasure; contextualize pleasure and account for space and location in shaping experiences of pleasure; and examine the complex ways in which hierarchal social systems and individual subjectivities influence people's access to and experiences of pleasure.

To all sociologists, I ask the following questions: How does pleasure shape the social interactions and experiences we have in various social institutions? Conversely, how do various social institutions shape how we understand what is pleasurable? What has been society's role in regulating pleasure? What would it look like for sociologists, generalists, and those individuals in various sociological subfields to place pleasure at the center of their analyses? How would the sociology of pleasure influence scholars who study the family, politics, and so forth? For family scholars, what is the role of pleasure in household decision-making and the division of labor? How does pleasure mediate family dynamics and power relations? Sociologists have already shown us that emotions play an essential role in collective action, and affective and sexual ties can often influence why people join and remain involved in protest.[1] Thus, for political sociologists, how does pleasure motivate and shape political behavior and participation? While I would like to develop a theory of pleasure applicable to all sociological fields, we can learn a great deal from sexualities research about the importance of pleasure.

In the sexualities, while a concrete theory of pleasure is absent, scholars have shown the value of making pleasure a focal point of research. Ruth Dixon-Mueller famously critiques scholars of reproductive health for focusing almost exclusively on risk and disease and not studying pleasure.[2] Dixon-Mueller argues it is vital to people's health and the ability of medical practitioners to do their jobs for researchers to also study sexual pleasure and enjoyment. How pleasure-seeking behavior influences contraceptive choices can help medical practitioners to advocate for effective condom use.

Higgins and Hirsch later revisited this issue and found that the study of pleasure is still largely absent from the literature on reproductive health. In their analysis of "the pleasure deficit," they show that including pleasure in studies of reproductive sexual health helps save people's lives and reveals that gender inequality is built into reproductive sexual health research and applied services.[3] I too, in another study, have shown that contemporary sexual science research ignores pleasure, and instead focuses on risk, disease, and dysfunction and reinforces heteronormativity.[4] Addressing the absence of pleasure is vital because the empirical findings of scientific research often inform political policy, healthcare policies, workplace policies, and broader societal understandings of human life and experience.

Scholars have questioned the exclusion of pleasure in research on drug use and have shown the numerous benefits of placing pleasure at the center of analysis. Pat O'Malley and Mariana Valverde write, "Governmental discourses about drugs and alcohol, in particular, tend to remain silent about pleasure as a motive for consumption, and raise instead visions of a consumption characterized by compulsion, pain, and pathology."[5] They argue that drug researchers and policymakers disregard pleasure because to argue that drug use is motivated by a rational desire to maximize pleasure would make drug use seem legitimate. Liberal governance and capitalism do not want citizens, workers especially, to consume drugs. Doing so compromises their ability to be engaged citizens and, I would argue, dutiful handmaidens to capitalism's ruling class. Pleasure is a reward for the moral, for dutiful workers, for people who deny instant gratification.

The literature on pleasure and drug use has grown significantly in recent years and collectively shows that if we can better understand the role that pleasure plays in drug use, then our society and its institutions, such as the criminal legal system and public health institutions, can more effectively grapple with widespread drug addiction.[6] Borne out of this new drug policy research is a focus on pleasure and the importance of understanding what Cameron Duff calls "pleasure in context." Not only does Duff highlight the importance of studying pleasure, but they[7] also argue that contextual factors influence the experience of pleasure. In Duff's research, they find, "participants described drug related pleasures that [they] obtained primarily in the range of activities and practices that the consumption of these drugs facilitated."[8] Teenagers at a rave party are using drugs as part of the party experience. Dancing enhances the pleasures of drug use. Pleasure is an effect both of the consumption of drugs and of the activities one engages in while high. The use of drugs often drives down inhibitions, and Duff reports that participants are often more ready to engage in intimate conversations, which are also pleasurable. In addition to what one does while using drugs, space is equally important. If drug-using teenagers are in a club, filled with loud music, as spectacular light shows play against the walls, this context sets the tone for pleasure. Drug use, Duff says, also can change people's experiences of their bodies. Drugs create new pleasures for users, leading individuals to experience alternative subjectivities that they find pleasurable. These examples illuminate the need for a sociological theory of pleasure. I am making a call for more empirical research that uses pleasure as its central analytical framework to test and explore just how pleasure is constructed, regulated, accessed, and experienced in various contexts by people across different social locations.

Pleasure as a Sociological Construct

Sociology has had very little to say about the importance of pleasure in shaping social action, the ways that society constructs what pleasure is, and how we experience pleasure. Sociologists such as Adam Isaiah Green have focused on the role of sexual desire in social life, but sexual desire and pleasure are different.[9] The theory of pleasure I am developing is focused not only on what motivates sexual conduct, but on how desires for pleasure are engrained within all social interactions. Pleasure can be found in all areas of our lives, not just in the bedroom. People with asexual (Ace) identities, for example, may not desire sex but have and maintain pleasurable relationships. We need a theory of pleasure that is applicable to all areas of social life, not just sex.

Pleasure is embedded in complex social interactions in everyday life. It is not just that the desire to maximize pleasure and reduce pain drives social behavior. This Freudian idea is too simplistic. Pleasure gives meaning to social interactions and experiences. Echoing Green's theories of desire and sexual fields, I argue that the ways we access and experience pleasure are shaped by our subjectivities or pedigree (habitus), the social contexts in which we act (fields), and the resources (forms of capital) we have. These factors are precisely why pleasure is sociological. To underscore this point, let's turn to antiquity.

Plato liked wine. Plato often references the consumption of wine in his many discussions of pleasure. Well, Dionysus and I are also kindred spirits. I love red wine. I love a rich, big, bold Cabernet. When I drink this wine, it is delightful in my mouth. It arouses my tastes buds. After a few glasses, it causes a dopamine party in my brain. These responses are physiological. However, we should also consider the context in which I am consuming this wine. Say, for example, I enjoy this wine at a five-star restaurant in New York City while on a romantic date. The wait staff brings over the bottle of wine that I have ordered. They proceed with bottle presentation. They show me the bottle. I approve, acknowledging with a nod of my head this bottle is the one that I ordered. They pour an ounce so I can taste the wine. I place the tip of my nose into the large Bordeaux glass and smell the wine's notes of blackberry and licorice. I swirl the wine in the glass to help it quickly oxidize. I finally taste the wine. It is delicious. I, again, grant my approval to pour the wine. The wait staff fills my date's glass and then returns to pour my glass of wine. The story that accompanies my physiological responses to the wine is crucial.

Drinking the wine indeed causes physiological responses, which trigger my experience of pleasure. However, this experience is also shaped by many social factors. First, I was on a date. In what ways is my pleasure enhanced by drinking with another person? The wine is a prop in a romantic social interaction. The consumption of wine would feel different depending on where and with whom we are drinking. Whether we are drinking wine with a colleague, a parent, a friend, or a date is essential.

Are you drinking at your office party, at a bar, or at your grandmother's 90th birthday party? Each context provides individuals with different social scripts that govern our behavior, and hence how we experience pleasure, both affectively and physically. Moreover, while the social interaction I have described may produce corporeal pleasure, my affective state might also involve nervousness or anxiety. Perhaps it is just this interplay between the affective states of the mind and pleasure felt within the body, which also occurs within a particular social context that makes this date feel so pleasurable.

Second, ordering a bottle of wine in a fancy New York City restaurant can be quite expensive. The exchange value of the wine matters. In what ways is access to pleasure, then, also shaped by an individual's capital? My ability to experience the pleasure of this wine is conditioned by both my economic and cultural capital. I need both the money for the bottle and the knowledge of wine to order the supposed right bottle. Sociologists Thorstein Veblen and Pierre Bourdieu have both shown that people take pleasure in consumption.[10] Sociological theories of taste and conspicuous consumption have come closest to developing a distinctively sociological theory of pleasure. Pleasure is often commodified. Our class and pedigree often shape our ability to acquire pleasure and to understand what forms of pleasure are socially recognized and legitimate. For some people, there is pleasure in behaving in socially sanctioned ways. Drinking the right wine is about social-group membership. It is about making visible to others who know wine that I am a wine connoisseur—I know how to pick a good wine, too. There is pleasure in social belonging. In addition, there is also pleasure in abjection—that is, for many people, there is also pleasure found in not consuming or acquiring pleasure in conventional ways.

Third, my consumption of the wine began with a highly performative public ritual. The ritual of wine service is an exercise of power—that is, I exert my privilege and power over the wait staff, who must endure this exercise of power. No doubt, this public display of status feels good to the consumer, not the wait staff. The wages they received for catering to my pleasure surely did not equalize power in this interaction. A sociological analysis of pleasure must then also ask: Who serves pleasure to whom? Who expects pleasure? Who feels entitled to pleasure in various contexts? Experiences of pleasure can reveal complex power relationships. As the writer Sarah Schulman posits, people often derive pleasure from exerting dominance over others.[11] The homophobe, she argues, is not actually scared of gay people but rather enjoys feeling superior. In what ways is exerting superiority over others pleasurable? These are all critical questions for sociologists.

Finally, I am a Black queer woman, who grew up in a working-class family, who is now in this restaurant publicly ordering and consuming expensive wine. What does it mean for me as an individual to acquire pleasure in this way? How am I perceived by others experiencing pleasure in this way? Crucially, subjectivity matters. How we access pleasure and experience pleasure are always reflections of our identities. People's access to pleasure and experiences of pleasure are conditioned by class, race, ethnicity, nationality, gender, age, ability, sexuality, religious identity, and citizenship status.

I am not arguing that people situated at the bottom of social hierarchies do not have access to or do not experience pleasure and that those at the top of social hierarchies have unbridled access to pleasure. People at the top of social hierarchies often have to deny themselves specific forms of pleasure to maintain their status (e.g., the way social rules of endogamy regulate intimate relationships). Moreover, I am not arguing that poor people, people of color, trans people, queer people, people with disabilities or people from the global South do not experience pleasure. Instead, those at the bottom of social hierarchies often face numerous constraints on particular forms of pleasure, especially those that must be purchased. Access to social spaces can often be restricted by race, gender, class, sexuality, and so on, thus people must create alternative spaces in which to acquire pleasure.[12] The point is, pleasure is a regulatory regime.

In the queer feminist Sara Ahmed's brilliant account of how affect plays a role in subjugation, she posits that the affective state of happiness is a regulatory regime of social control. The social pressures to live a good life—to be happy—is pervasive. All pleasures, affective or corporeal, occur in the body and pleasure exists within regulatory regimes. Ahmed astutely writes, "Pleasure or joy might involve not just finding such and such agreeable but the experience of being affirmed *because* you find the right things pleasing. Those around you 'agree' with your agreement."[13] Pleasure acts as a hegemonic force. As readers will learn in my account of utilitarian hedonism, individuals often seek out pleasure that is socially acceptable and acquire pleasure through social belonging. We are granted the right to pleasure by others. Ahmed also argues that happiness is masked as freedom, but the compulsory desire to be happy actually constrains our freedom—leading us to question in what ways our desire for pleasure is also constrained by societal pressures to acquire pleasure in normative ways.

By critically examining happiness, Ahmed provides a new framework through which to study happiness that is also applicable to the study of pleasure. Ahmed says we fetishize happiness—well, we also fetishize pleasure. We commodify pleasure. We build entire industries, like camming, devoted to helping people acquire pleasure. Social systems regulate access to pleasure and shape experiences of pleasure. Pleasure is a social experience controlled by regulatory forces, and these mechanisms of control create a system of inequality that can limit human freedom.

Defining Pleasure

I define pleasure as infinitely different sets of gratifying social experiences. Pleasure is always subjective and contextual. Scholars must recognize that pleasure is a social experience, in which the body is caught up in what anthropologist Clifford Geertz calls "webs of significance." Geertz famously says that culture is "a system of inherited conceptions expressed in symbolic forms by means of which people communicate, perpetuate, and develop their knowledge about and attitudes toward life."[14] Geertz uses the example of a wink to explain his thesis. In one context, a wink could be a gesture used to signal another person furtively. A wink could be a romantic gesture. A wink is a gesture with infinite sets of possible meanings given the cultural context. Drawing from Geertz, I argue that our bodies are bound up within intricate systems of meaning, which define for us how we experience pleasure.

All pleasure, including affective states of pleasure, occurs within the body. Scholars have already well theorized positive emotions, and so there is a well-established theory of affective pleasure, but scholars have failed to theorize corporeal pleasure with the same precision. I want to account for the dynamic role of *both* the affective and corporeal in shaping social experiences of pleasure. Pleasure has traditionally been seen as either *corporeal pleasure*—pleasures of the body—or as *affective pleasure*—pleasures of the mind. Corporeal pleasure is traditionally seen as the extreme enjoyment of bodily practices. Examples include sex and the consumption of beverage and food. Affective pleasure, on the other hand, relates to feelings and emotions. For example, if you listen to delightful music, and it causes you to feel happy, then this pleasure is an affective one. People frequently use the word "pleasure" to describe affective pleasures in everyday life and it is most often associated with feelings of happiness, joy, contentment, or satisfaction.

Like all dualisms, the affective/corporeal pleasure dualism is limited for two reasons. First, the dualism fails to capture the complex and dynamic relationship between affective states and corporeal pleasure. Therefore, I do not treat affective states and corporeal pleasures as separate entities, but rather as forces bound up together within the same body. Second, the affective/corporeal dualism is also limited because it does not account for the complexity of social experience and the ways social forces shape the total experience of pleasure.

The relationship between affective and corporeal pleasure is symbiotic, not linear. It is not always easy to distinguish between affective pleasures and corporeal pleasures. A pleasurable experience within the body does not always produce a pleasurable affective state, and conversely, pleasurable affective states do not always produce corporeal pleasure. Pleasures of the body, for example, can cause a range of affective states. Precisely because pleasure is a social experience, people may have pleasurable bodily experiences that also cause them to feel anxious, sad, guilty, or disgusted.

Pleasure is not a direct route to happiness. The consumption of food and alcohol can be a pleasurable experience, but due to societal norms that pathologize overindulgence in food and drink, a person may simultaneously feel corporeal pleasure, but still feel disgusted. An individual may take off from work to go to the beach—the lulling sound of crashing waves and the warm rays of the sun make their body feel relaxed and at peace, until that pleasurable cathartic moment is interrupted by feelings of guilt brought on by the insidious spirit of capitalism, which makes people feel duty-bound always to be working.

Also consider this: a person is ill, and their body is in pain. A family member brings them soup, caresses their back, and plays them their favorite music—this experience of tender love and care from a family member can produce a pleasurable affective state. The introduction of a pleasurable affective state does not necessarily assuage their physical pain, yet they still experience pleasure. The affective pleasure they experience occurs precisely because they are ill, their body feels displeasure, and a family member nurses them. Affective and corporeal pleasures are symbiotic—not binaries, they are shaped by social scripts, and they occur within complex social interactions.

As a final example, when writing this book, I was frequently reminded of my days as a stripper. Here is one specific recollection:

> One of my regulars was an accountant, and so it went that during tax season, we both did well. For example, he'd generally pay me between $800 and $1,200 a night (not including the money showers[15] I'd demand on stage) just to sit with him and drink alcohol and talk. We developed a friendship as a result. I'd occasionally leave him to perform dances for other customers, which I usually found pleasurable—gyrating against another human to pulsing music. One night, I was sitting with the accountant, and Bianca called me into the back. She was an incredibly gorgeous caramel-skinned Puerto Rican dancer with long thick curly dark hair that always tickled her nipples when she danced. I knew what she wanted. Bianca and I fucked in the bathroom while the accountant waited. I spent the remainder of the evening chatting with the accountant and having tipped the DJ well, I'd only occasionally dance on stage and always to my favorite songs.

My reflections on nights like this one remind me of how vital pleasure is to understanding sex work, and human social interaction more broadly. As a social experience, pleasure is much more than just an immediate corporeal response to compounded stimuli. This night at the strip club was pleasurable because I had sex with Bianca. However, the context where we had sex also matters; we had sex at work—in the backstage bathroom as my client waited, and while we were under panoptic surveillance. Also, dancing can be euphoric. The alcohol pulsing through my bloodstream enhanced that feeling of euphoria. The dim lighting, the vibrations from the DJ's speakers playing music felt throughout the space, the sexual gaze of others, the exchange of money, and gyrating bodies all create a context for pleasure. The intimate conversations I had with the accountant were also pleasurable, especially because other patrons and dancers gazed at and evaluated our relationship. I was in my early 20s, and the account was 30 years my senior. I am a woman of color, and he is White. At the time, I weighed no more than 120 pounds and the accountant likely weighed 250 pounds. Our embodiments and the cultural lens through which others viewed us shaped the intimacy we shared and the pleasure I experienced during our time together in the club. Finally, between the accountant, my stage work, and other customers I made excellent money that night. There was pleasure in simultaneously fulfilling the capitalist imperative to work and make money, yet doing it in a way deemed socially unacceptable by society. Pleasure is often characterized by feelings of satisfaction that result from demonstrating social membership *or* when we successfully defy social conventions. The pleasures we experience in our social interactions reflect a complex interplay between affectual and corporeal pleasures that are conditioned by social context and culture. Pleasure is also not bound or restricted by time—that is, pleasure is an experience that can linger within our bodies long after the initial pleasurable stimuli have disappeared. Pleasure is a complex social experience, and our desires for pleasure drive human behavior.

An Intellectual History Pleasure

The sociological theory of pleasure that I am developing here draws ideas from biology, psychology, neuroscience, and philosophy. While scholars in these disciplines have written extensively about pleasure, I show how sociological analysis will complement and enhance these existing theories.

Evolutionary Biology

First, in establishing a sociological theory of pleasure, I draw from a biological model of pleasure. I agree with biologists that pleasure occurs in the body. However, I depart from this perspective because the motivation for seeking pleasure cannot be reduced to evolutionary destiny. Traditionally, pleasure has been seen as a biological force, as an evolutionary tool to ensure genetic fitness—to maximize the potential for reproductive success and survival. Humans need food and water to survive, so people devote time to priming their culinary and mixology skills because if eating and consuming beverages is pleasurable, we are more motivated to ensure our survival. If humans must reproduce, the clitoris, for example, was designed to ensure that sex would be pleasurable—to encourage sex for procreation. As Gene Wallenstein notes, "all of our emotions, including the experience of pleasure, have been shaped by natural selection to cope with challenges and opportunities that have recurred over the course of hominid evolution."[16] From this perspective, pleasure is an evolutionary strategy.

The primary limitation of biological models of pleasure is that culture is treated as a footnote in a broader story of human evolution and survival. Biologists do mention the importance of culture in defining pleasure and experiences of pleasure, yet they often gloss over and underestimate the importance of culture. As Wallenstein explains:

> The feeling of pleasure can be elicited by a wide range of experiences, each involving disparate sensory systems. Likewise, the expression of pleasure in terms of overt behavior or verbal descriptions varies considerably within different contexts and cultural norms. Although each of us has unique likes and dislikes, there is a common core of sensations that the vast majority of humans label as pleasurable. Our preference for these core sensations arose through natural selection to ensure that we experience key sensory events during our early years that are *required* for normal brain development.[17]

Consider that eating is not pleasurable merely because it satisfies biological needs. We often eat and drink when we are not hungry and thirsty. We snack on appetizers at a friend's party. We toast with champagne in celebration of family members' achievements. Pleasure does not only arise in our quest to fulfill biological needs. The social contexts in which we eat appetizers or drink champagne influence how we experience pleasure. Our social identities shape how these occasions make us feel and what emotions they conjure up. As we learn from psychology, humans have essential psychological needs, and pleasure is a psychological phenomenon, as well.

Psychology

Psychology has also played a significant role in our scientific under-standing of pleasure. In Freudian psychoanalysis, the pleasure principle drives our id. Humans are innately hedonists who are motivated by a desire to increase pleasure and minimize pain. We do so in the interests of both biological and psychological needs. According to Freud, children cannot delay instant gratification. The pleasure principle and their ids drive their behavior. As humans grow older and become socialized, and if proper socialization is successfully accomplished, they learn to sup-press certain desires and impulses in the interests of the greater good. Mastering this reality principle means conforming to social norms. Civilization and society are the forces that keep the id in check. It is civi-lization, with its extensive mores, that shapes how we seek out pleasure.

Societal institutions and mores restrict our ability to experience plea-sure. Attempts on the part of the individual to push back against norma-tive regimes of social control are motivated by their desire to procure pleasure for themselves, their families, friends, and communities. Freud says civilization makes us unhappy because our conscience makes us feel guilty for putting our pleasure before the needs of society. He says, evoking Hamlet, "our conscience makes us all cowards."[18] Freud, no doubt then, laid the groundwork for a sociological theory of pleasure. Sociologists need to explore his original thesis through qualitative stud-ies focusing on experiences of pleasure that show how civilization—or more specifically, social institutions—regulate pleasure and how indi-viduals seek out pleasure in the social world.

Almost 80 years after Freud, Paul Bloom, also a psychologist, made another call for a nuanced understanding of pleasure that is not just biological, not just psychological, but sociological as well. Bloom posits that pleasure is not caused merely by a Darwinian imperative to procre-ate or seek nourishment. Our attractions to certain foods or objects, for example, are caused by what he calls essentialism. Bloom asserts, like many evolutionary psychologists, that essentialism is part of the human condition:

> But isn't it weird that we enjoy things—like a dead man's shirt—not be-cause of anything that they can do for us, and not because of any tangible

properties that they have, but rather because of their histories, including the invisible essences that they contain.[19]

Bloom submits that we attach essences to cultural artifacts. Why would a person find pleasure in antiquing? Bloom says because we are also purchasing the history of the antique. Take, for example, a broken antique clock. Bloom argues we find pleasure in having it on our mantel because it may have also sat upon a famous historical figure's mantel. Although the clock cannot be used, by purchasing it, we are participating in the history of the clock and capturing a piece of its possibly famous owner.

Bloom uses the term "essentialism," but he is gesturing toward how society, social institutions, and people have constructed meanings and social systems that condition how we experience pleasure. Bloom describes, for example, how a person who spends thousands of dollars on John F. Kennedy Jr.'s tape measure finds this purchase pleasurable because it is the essence of the item purchased that is the source of pleasure. What brings the customer joy is that they believe they have purchased a piece of history. The Kennedy family has enormous political, cultural, and economic capital, and JFK's assassination was a world-historical event. Purchasing JFK's tape measure is the outcome of a desire to acquire this essence. Bloom's salient point is that a tape measure has no value until society assigns it a value. However, he fails to explore that commodity fetishism is an outgrowth of capitalism. Political economy and status systems shape people's perceptions of value. A sociological analysis would show how society historically and culturally constructs the essences that people attach to objects, and thus, shapes the pleasure they experience consuming those objects.

Neuroscience

Neuroscientists have also been on the cutting edge of the scientific study of pleasure. Psychologists James Olds and Peter Milner were the first to write explicitly about "pleasure centers of the brain." When we have pleasurable experiences, our brains produce endorphins, oxytocin, serotonin, and dopamine. Dopamine has long been understood as the pleasure chemical in our brains. The production of dopamine triggers our reward circuit. Our amygdala regulates emotions, and our nucleus accumbens regulates the release of dopamine in our bodies. Pleasure is a sensory experience. Neuroscientists have helped to uncover the complexities of pleasure by upsetting the affective/corporeal pleasure dualism. Music, for example, can complicate our understanding of pleasure. Listening to our favorite song causes affective pleasure; it makes us happy. However, it also stimulates our bodies—our pupils may dilate, and our hearts may race. These bodily sensations can be pleasurable. Importantly, neuroscientists recognize the dynamic relationship between affective states and corporeal pleasure.

Neurological theories are useful, but they still fail to theorize how social forces influence pleasure. Again, the importance of a sociological analysis of pleasure is often mentioned, but not pursued in depth by biologists and neuroscientists. Kringelbach and Berridge write:

> Further, in social animals like humans, it is worth noting that social interactions with conspecifics are fundamental and central to enhancing the other pleasures. Humans are intensely social, and data indicate that one of the most important factors for happiness is social relationships with other people. Social pleasures may still include vital sensory features such as visual faces, touch features of grooming and caress, as well as in humans more abstract and cognitive features of social reward and relationship evaluation. These may be important triggers for the brain's hedonic networks in human beings.[20]

Scientists repeatedly note the physiological and biological underpinnings of pleasure. They also acknowledge, albeit briefly, that pleasure is not just a physiological response to external stimuli but also the ways that complex social systems shape the ways pleasure is experienced, beyond the reactions in our brains. By and large, though, it is the sociologist's job to explore the social nature of pleasure.

Antiquity

Ancient Greece is too often romanticized as a bastion of sexual freedom and hedonistic delight. The ancient Greeks were indeed less restrictive of sexual behaviors than many societies in the contemporary world, which have come to intensely regulate sexual practices such as queer sex or intergenerational sex. When we turn to classical Greek philosophy, however, we see a much more reserved sexual ethos than popular convention holds. In *The History of Sexuality, Vol. 2: The Use of Pleasure*, Michel Foucault examines how the ancient Greeks understood sexuality, desire, and pleasure. He is attentive to their concerns regarding unbridled desire and pleasure:

> setting oneself against pleasures and desires, not giving into them, resisting their assaults, or on the contrary letting oneself be overcome by them, defeating them or being defeated by them, being armed or equipped against them [were matters of great importance]. . . . [Their concerns were] expressed, too, by such themes as that of the untamed forces of desire that invade the soul during its slumber if it has not had the foresight to take the necessary precautions. The relationship to desire and pleasures is conceived as a pugnacious one: a man must take the position and role of the adversary with respect to them.[21]

Foucault's analysis is acutely on point. Take Plato for example—while Plato argues that humans are driven by a desire to maximize pleasure and minimize pain, he also expresses concerns about desire being unregulated. In both the *Symposium* and *Phaedrus*, Plato argues that seeking out pleasure is natural, but, that how people seek out and experience pleasure are matters of concern for society. Unrestrained pleasure is like a noxious gas emanating from a smokestack, which makes both the individual and the society sick.

Greek philosophers believed people should submit to social and moral restrictions. Reason can save us from ourselves and protect the individual's soul. The soul/body dualism was important in antiquity. In *Phaedrus*, Plato's character Socrates says:

> Let us note that in every one of us[,] there are two guiding principles which lead us wither they will; one is the natural desire of pleasure, the other is an acquired opinion which is in search of the best; and these two are sometimes in harmony and then again at war, and sometimes the one, sometimes the other conquers.[22]

Plato highlights an important fact—people feel conflicted by their own desires and the needs and expectations of society. In contemporary societies around the world, people are just as concerned with preserving their souls and denying pleasures of the flesh as philosophers were in antiquity.

In the *Symposium*, Plato also posits that pleasure is corporeal and experienced through the body. However, he regards corporeal pleasure as a lower form of pleasure. Humans will continuously be presented with opportunities for brief sexual flings and momentary dalliances and have urges toward sex and drunkenness, but they must use their rational powers to set aside these bodily desires. For Plato, to delight in art and to inspire one's mind are far higher levels of pleasure. The mind must always come before the animalistic desires of the body. To put it another way, for Plato, if the mind and body were kinky, the mind would always hold the flogger. I argue, in contrast, that there is no inherent hierarchy of pleasure. The prevailing hierarchy of pleasure exists because society creates a social hierarchy of pleasure as a mechanism of social control.

Utilitarian Hedonism

The Greek philosopher Epicurus laid the groundwork for the hedonistic perspective of pleasure. For Epicurus, pleasure drives human behavior. In *Letter to Menoeceus,* he writes, "Pleasure is our first and kindred good. It is the starting-point of every choice and of every aversion."[23] While pleasure motivates all human behavior, Epicurus warns people about the harms of overindulgence in pleasure. Like Epicurus, in *Utilitarianism*, John Stuart Mill advances a utilitarian theory of pleasure in which individuals should try to acquire pleasure that is good for everyone, not just themselves. I, too, have no interest in advancing a theory of pleasure based solely on an egoistic pleasure principle. Mill provides the example of money that underscores his point. Why do people desire money? Mill observes that it is intrinsically no more valuable than a pile of rocks. We want money because society tells us to desire money. The laws and logic of capitalism dictate money's value. Everything that we desire—everything that gives us pleasure—has no essential value or character. We tend to think that universal bodily pleasures, such as eating and sex, exist. However, Mill also recognizes that pleasure is heterogeneous and always varies among different people. A note to biologists, not everyone desires sex or food. Many people living with anorexia do not derive pleasure from eating. Asexual people do not desire sex in the way many scientists suggest we all do. How we desire and experience pleasure is culturally defined.

While I draw from Mill to advance a hedonistic theory of pleasure, which places pleasure at the center of analysis, I depart from Mill's hierarchy of pleasure. Like Plato, Mill distinguishes between higher and lower pleasures. Higher pleasures relate to affective pleasure—pleasures of the mind—and lower pleasures relate to corporeal pleasures such as sex and quenching thirst. Mill famously says, "It is better to be a human being dissatisfied, than a pig satisfied; better to be Socrates dissatisfied, than a fool satisfied."[24] Mill argues that it is better to deny oneself bodily pleasures and pursue higher pleasures of the mind. Crucially, this moral evaluation, which has been made by philosophers for centuries, may explain the continued lack of theorizing of corporeal pleasures and the emphasis placed by scholars on pleasures of the mind and affective states. Happiness experienced while listening to music is generally socially acceptable. Gorging food, excessive drinking, and fucking strangers for money are most often not seen as socially acceptable behaviors, and therefore are not seen as legitimate topics of scientific inquiry. Moreover, placing affective pleasures above corporeal ones also misses what neuroscientists have already empirically shown us—affective pleasures are corporeal pleasures. All pleasure is a social experience derived from the interplay between human affective states and physiological reactions. Mill is correct that people do not experience pleasure in the same ways, and not all pleasure is valuable. It is of sociological interest to examine the social construction of pleasure. How has society come to construct discourses of pleasure, and in what ways do we construct hierarchies of pleasure? Finally, we must not underestimate the importance of the desire for pleasures in driving human behavior.

Philosopher Jeremy Bentham builds on Mill and offers a utilitarian theory of pleasure, which recognizes how pleasure is an innate drive of the individual, but also a drive that is conditioned by society. As Bentham says:

Nature has placed mankind under the governance of two sovereign masters, *pain* and *pleasure*. It is for them alone to point out what we ought to do, as well as to determine what we shall do. On the one hand the standard of right and wrong, on the other the chain of causes and effects, are fastened to their throne. They govern us in all we do, in all we say, in all we think: every effort we can make to throw off our subjection, will serve but to demonstrate and confirm it. In words[,] a man may pretend to abjure their empire: but in reality[,] he will remain. Subject to it all the while. The *principle of utility* recognizes this subjection, and assumes it for the foundation of that system, the object of which is to rear the fabric of felicity by the hands of reason and of law.[25]

This utilitarian ethical theory focuses on the outcomes of individual choices; our choices must take into account the needs and desires of others. Bentham's work is vital for thinking about pleasure sociologically because he demonstrates that our acquisition of and quest for pleasure is subjected to the social rules delineated by society.

Bentham's work is also instructive for sociologists because he argues that pleasure can be studied empirically. Bentham posits that we can measure pleasure in four categories: intensity, duration, certainty/uncertainty, and nearness/farness. Mill, on the other hand, argues that because there are higher and lower pleasures, pleasure should be measured qualitatively. While in my work, I see pleasure as a social experience that is highly contextual and subjective and, therefore, best studied qualitatively, room still exists for both quantitative and qualitative sociologists to systematically study pleasure.

Pleasure, Sacrifice, and Social Control

Societies construct sexual taboos as a means of normative social control. Sexual taboos are used to defend and maintain existing social boundaries and institutions.[26] Anthropologist Gayle Rubin argues that society regulates sexual practices in ways that deny people human freedom and pleasure.[27] In figure 1.1, the inner circle represents what she calls "the charmed circle." As Rubin's charmed circle suggests, sex has been too often idealized when it is between similarly aged cis women and cis men in married monogamous relationships, which presumably serves the interests of procreation. If sex is primarily about procreation, then sexual behaviors that are non-procreative (see the outer limits of the circle) are seen as taboo. While these standards have certainly changed in important ways, many such norms remain.

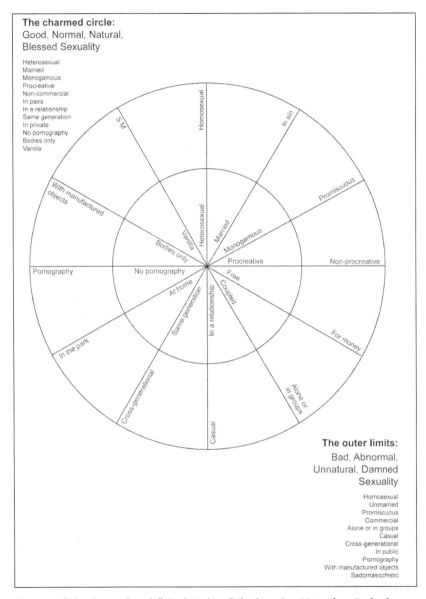

Figure 1.1. "The charmed circle." Gayle Rubin, "Thinking Sex: Notes for a Radical Theory of the Politics of Sexuality" (1984).

Intergenerational sex remains taboo in many global contexts. Sex for money is criminalized in most parts of the world. According to the International Lesbian, Gay, Bisexual, Trans, and Intersex Association, around the world, relationships between females are illegal in 45 countries, and relationships between males are illegal in 72 countries.[28] The point is that sex is still highly regulated, and how and why it is regulated varies based on geographical and cultural context.[29] Crucially, the task of the sociologist is to empirically document the power regimes and social institutions that regulate sex.

Sociologist and post-colonial feminist Jyoti Puri has theorized the relationship between sexuality and the state. In *Sexual States: Governance and the Struggle over the Anti-Sodomy Law in India*, she argues that the regulation of sex is central to state formation and the persistence of states in an increasingly post-colonial and transnational global landscape. Importantly, whether scholars are examining Section 377 of Indian penal law, Section 53 of the Belize Criminal Code, or Sections 76 and 77 of the Offences against the Person Act in Jamaica, for example, I argue that such analyses must also examine how transnational structures of power seek to control access to pleasure. Scholars and activists must critique colonialism and imperialism in various contexts and the laws that birth homophobic, transphobic, and racist policies, but to those studying transnational sexualities, I also ask: What role do global and local regulatory forces play in controlling access to pleasure?

Scholars have focused too much on the regulation of sex, and have missed the point that the underlying motivation for sexual regulation is a fundamental desire on the part of societies to control pleasure. Throughout history, although in different ways, societies have sought to control all of our desires of the flesh. In premodern societies, religious institutions played a significant role in controlling human desires. Over time, modes of social control changed. As Foucault has shown us, modernity ushered in a new age of social control dominated by medical discourses and medical authorities.[30] In any period, a fundamental belief exists in societies that humans cannot control their urges and desires to maximize pleasure, and, thus, only experts external to the individual can help individuals help themselves. Specialists develop strategies for protecting individuals from the dangers of the flesh and body. Doctors and political pundits use the frame "obesity" to mark all fatness as a social problem caused by individual pathology—an inability to control one's desire for food. Doctors, politicians, and religious leaders frame sex as dangerous. Overindulgence in sex will lead to disease and punishment. Society regulates pleasure.

The central task of major social institutions has been to control people's pleasures of the flesh. Religious institutions, the family, the government, medicine, and the media all function in various ways to control our desire for pleasure. Each institution exerts control in interesting ways. Religious institutions promise salvation in exchange for the sacrifice of pleasure. Medical institutions tell us our bodies and our survival depend on the sacrifice of pleasure. Patriarchal families are built upon the standard of monogamy, which tells people to sacrifice pleasure in the interests of the effective maintenance of the structure of the family. Parents must sacrifice pleasure for their children, and partners must sacrifice pleasure for one another. The economy tells us to sacrifice pleasure in order to be successful. Our political institutions require the sacrifice of pleasure for citizenship. The media provide us with scripted pleasure so that we can live vicariously through performers in films, television, and music. As we learn from utilitarian hedonism, the point is that societies are built around sacrificing pleasure. The routine sacrifice of pleasure is a hallmark of social life. The sacrifices of pleasure provide structure and order to society and its institutions; yet the sacrifice of pleasure is embedded with power, and in this process, human freedom is limited, and people are subjugated.

Conclusion

As I show through my case study of the camming industry, camming is appealing to a wide range of workers because the industry provides a unique opportunity to fulfill the capitalist duty to work while experiencing pleasure. Instead of sacrificing pleasure, they experience pleasure as a fundamental part of their labor. For cam models, there is pleasure in simultaneously being good capitalist entrepreneurs and sex workers who also have orgasms for a living. As Foucault famously notes, "Where there is power, there is resistance."[31] While societies have continued to enact social control over pleasure, people will push back against these discourses, which can give birth to new forms of pleasure, and communities will develop that are built around pleasure, especially sexual pleasure.[32] I hope my focus on pleasure throughout this book will help people better understand the motivations for engaging in online sex work, as well as the complex social interactions between cam models and customers. However, the implications of these analyses are not limited to sex work markets. A sociological theory of pleasure can provide new insights into understanding motivations for social behavior and assist sociologists in analyzing social interactions in everyday life and in a range of complex social institutions. This book is an invitation to sociologists to open up an entirely new subfield in sociology—the sociology of pleasure.

2

Introduction to Camming

Technology, Embodied Authenticity, and the
Demystification of Porn

The camming industry moved the strip club into people's homes. Like exotic dancers, cam models sell sex, intimacy, and pleasure, but the Internet allows cam models to sell sexual performances to customers online, where they are free from physical touching. A customer seeking an interactive erotic experience can now log onto one of thousands of cam sites from the privacy of their own home—where there are no bouncers, drinks are free, and they can request and receive sexually explicit shows. By logging on to a cam site, a customer can virtually step into the bedrooms of strangers located in countries throughout the world.

Figure 2.1 is an example of what a customer sees when they log onto a typical cam site. It features the home page for Chaturbate (CB), a popular cam site. When a customer logs onto CB or a similar site, they will find categories of different models. On CB, an incredibly diverse site, customers can select a tab on the top left of the page if they would like to narrow down the number of active cams displayed and browse through the cams of exclusively trans, female, couple, or male models. Like CB, most erotic cam sites feature rows of small thumbnail pictures of cam models. Under each photo is a short message; cam models use this space to attract customers to click on their rooms. Models write things such as "anal play with big glass dildo" or "squirt @goal." These messages also make customers aware of what acts the cam model is engaged in and will eventually perform if the customers in the room collectively tip a designated amount, called the goal.

Each picture also features the cam model's age. Customers need to click on the model's page to get access to their profile, which contains more personal information. Clients can also use the "tags" at the top of the page to see the rooms of cam models who have tagged themselves with one of the respective labels (e.g., #asian, #bigboobs, #bbw). On the right side of the webpage, cam sites generally run ads for other sexual products available for purchase online. Camming is not an isolated industry; it has become interwoven with other sexual markets such as those for sex toys and pornography.

As shown in figure 2.2, once logged into a cam model's room, a customer can look to the top left side of the page, directly over the cam model's live streaming video and find the model's tip goal and a brief description of the show in progress. Customers purchase packages of camming currency that they use to tip models. On almost all cam sites, the currency used for tipping is called a "token." (On Streamate, members tip with a currency called "gold.") On cam sites with public chat, very often cam models will post a topic. This topic might say, for example, "1500 tks/anal, 1000 tks/cum show, 500/strip, 100tks 3 VIDS." This means the model has initiated what is called a "countdown"; after members have collectively tipped the number of tokens (noted above as "tks") charged by the model, customers will see the associated show. In the example above, this would mean once members tipped 500 tokens, the model would perform a strip show; at 1,000 tokens the model would masturbate (often with sex toys); and the model would perform an anal penetration show with toys once 1,500 tokens have been tipped. Models perform a wide range of acts; some models will perform only

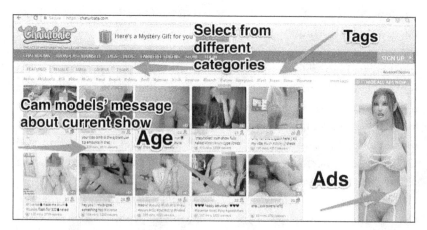

Figure 2.1. Popular cam site Chaturbate.

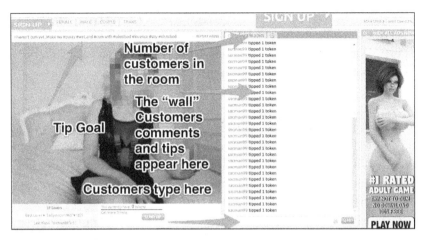

Figure 2.2. Sample of a cam model's room.

erotic dance, and no sex acts, and some will perform more explicit sex acts. The topic and countdown are individualized and set by the model according to what acts they will and will not perform. Models also sell pornographic videos of themselves (e.g., "100tks 3 VIDS") and will often reward big tippers with videos.

Customers' tips and comments are displayed on "the wall." In figure 2.2, a customer has given this model a "yellow wall" or a constant stream of tips. When customers tip or comment, the username the customer selected when they registered will appear on the wall to the left of their tip amount or comment. Customers can also choose to tip privately, while the cam model will usually still publicly thank such customers using the term "ninja tipper." In the figure above, there were over 4,300 people in the room; normally, given this size crowd, the wall would also be filled with customer comments and dialogue. How much cam models also type on the wall varies, but because everyone in the room can generally hear the cam model's audio, the wall is primarily filled with clients' comments. Cam models will often post a more detailed tip menu on the wall, as well. While I was conducting participant observation during a popular girl-on-girl show, the models posted the following tip menu:

Tip Menu: Spank Each other 10x (51) | Paddle Each Other 10x (52) | Spank Each other 15x (61) | Both Show Pussies (62) | Both Show Feet (63)

| Spread Asses (76) | Rub Asses Together (81) | Shake Asses (91) | Play with Each Other's Boobs (92) | Both Deepthroat (94) | Both Finger Pussies (95) | Both Finger Assholes (96) | Makeout (97) | Suck on Each Other's Nipples (98) | Makeout while we Finger Each Other (201)

Models use tip menus to instruct customers on how much they need to pay in order to see particular sex acts performed. Depending on the structure of the cam site, models can also perform private shows with clients. While some cam models prefer sites where the model performs only in public, other models prefer pay-per-minute cam sites where they do only private shows.

Cam models are selling intimacy, not just sex. In public performances, cam models often begin a show by talking with customers in their room. Conversation is an integral part of camming and a primary way that cam models sell embodied authenticity. If clients only want to watch someone cum, they can watch porn. Cam models repeatedly said that a high-energy personality is what makes a model successful. Matt, a 23-year-old straight White cis man from the United States who is currently living in Mexico, said:

> I'll be a little bit vain here and say . . . I'm somewhat good looking. But the main reason people tip me and I get the money that I do is just because of my personality and how I talk to people and the fact that I talk with everyone. So, I would say that looks do have a big part in the camming industry—but, in my personal opinion, personality is key, like that is the biggest aspect . . . the people who are quiet, like I don't get it personally, if customers want porn, they can go to Pornhub or any other porn site and get free porn. . . . They're not necessarily what they are paying for—to see your dick—to see your ass—to see your tits, it's more; they're paying for the connection, the personality and connecting with them. Like— that's the difference between like camming and porn, is the connection between the cammer and cammee.

It is vital to a cam model's success that they are willing and able to sustain an upbeat conversation with customers. Matt is correct; a high-energy personality and engaging presence will keep clients in the room and coming back for more. However, it is also crucial to analyze what brings customers to particular rooms in the first place. A neoliberal perspective that attributes success only to individual personality glosses over the importance of appearance and how various overlapping systems of oppression shape how clients determine who is attractive and desirable.

While this neoliberal perspective ignores the complex ways that race, nationality, gender, age, sexuality, and ability shape cam models' market outcomes, cam models' emphasis on the importance of individual personality and motivation does underscore the importance of embodied authenticity. It is crucial that cam models be prepared to engage in conversation and perform emotional labor for their clients by asking about their lives and showing interest in their desires. Given that clients from English-speaking countries dominate the camming field, cam models that are not fluent in English are at an extreme disadvantage because it is harder for them to deliver embodied authenticity and intimacy effectively.

Embodied Authenticity

I spoke with cam models about the importance of embodied authenticity and the client desire for authentic intimate experiences. Naomi is a 38-year-old queer White trans woman from the United States. She explained her approach to her shows and in doing so highlighted the importance of embodied authenticity.

> NAOMI: I've tried a lot of different things. Mostly what I do is . . . if the crowd comes in early, I'll look at what they're doing and I'll bounce off them and I'll just kinda go in that direction. Otherwise if it starts off slow, I'll usually just kind of go with my music and I'll dance, or sometimes, I've actually found that some of my best nights are when I just do my makeup and they like that; they love it.
>
> AJ: Who's got it better? Right? Folks just wanna pay to watch you do your makeup. Wonderful!
>
> NAOMI: Right?! I used to . . . every morning, [broadcast] my morning routine . . . on cam. I would get dressed. I'd do my makeup, all my stuff, and they loved it.

The fact that clients love to watch Naomi perform her everyday routine is evidence of the client desire for embodied authenticity. For some, there is pleasure in voyeurism, and camming provides a consensual space for clients to peer into the bedroom or home of a cam performer.

Amelia, a 29-year-old straight White cis woman from England, has cammed sporadically for six years. Amelia, too, highlighted the importance of embodied authenticity in our interview.

> Ya know, guys don't spend all that money because they want something fake. I mean, they come because they want to believe that it's a real woman they're taking to and it's a real person. And that they can tell you what to do; they can get exactly what they want. . . . For them, it's about the realism; it's about the interaction . . . it is genuinely about the interaction. Some of them I think could care less about the sex. It's just having somebody pay them interest, ya know. 'Cause you can end up having a long conversation and you're flirting with them and you're making them feel good about themselves. And I think that means more to them than seeing you bend over and spread your butt cheeks.

Amelia's comments pointed to the ways that in the camming industry, like phone sex but unlike traditional pornography, clients can articulate their fantasies and needs directly to a cam model in an environment where there is no physical contact and where the virtual context lowers social inhibitions and simultaneously makes people feel safe. The computer-mediated exchange also provides clients with visual access to the cam model. Importantly, this visual component shapes the participants' experience of pleasure because the added visual component heightens the sensory experience of the encounters.

Ronnie, a 35-year-old straight polyamorous White cis man from the United States, performs with various women in the couples' category. We discussed how cam models design the spaces where they cam. He emphasized that overproduction of a space compromises a performer's ability to deliver embodied authenticity:

RONNIE: Ah no, no, none of that, because when you see that [well-designed cammed rooms], it's like, oh this is all a production; this is all a show. You just wanna see two young people really just fucking like rabbits, pretty much, ya know?

AJ: That's really interesting. So, you think that's part of what people are coming for, right?

RONNIE: Right, it's more so for the real-life sort of thing. It's not so much for the . . . whole production—this is a whole, set-up, ya know—very meticulously planned and everything.

Naomi, Amelia, and Ronnie's comments all highlighted the importance of my conceptualization of embodied authenticity. As Ronnie noted, customers want to see real people authentically "fucking like rabbits." The development of online porn tube sites has created a space for amateur pornographers to post videos of themselves. Market demand for amateur porn has increased, and in today's visual sex markets there is higher value placed on pornographic imagery perceived as authentic.[1] When porn stars shoot a pornographic film on a set, read lines, and fuck under the direction of a production team, it *is* real sex. However, viewers often perceive recorded sex as inauthentic sex. Porn is scripted sex. Porn may not be the reflection of real people's desires.

Customers perceive camming as authentic because the client can participate in and interactively shape the content of a show. Moreover, because the cam show is interactive, the client can ostensibly confirm the pleasure the cam model experiences, which the client perceives to be a direct reflection of their presence, direction, and tipping. Therefore, based on what models said, the client experiences pleasure because they believe they played a role in providing the cam model pleasure. Cam models, too, often experience pleasure camming, not only because they have orgasms—there are also great affective pleasures for cam models in knowing that the pleasures they experience simultaneously pleasure others. This example highlights the utility of a sociological theory of pleasure. It is not only that the desire for pleasure motivates participation in the market—this is too simplistic. Crucially, the experience of pleasure had by all participants is a complex social phenomenon. Many people derive pleasure from participating in the camming market because of its interactive component, its authentic aura, and the mutual giving of pleasure.

History of the Camming Industry

The creation of a distinct new online sex industry called camming emerged in 1996 because of two converging social phenomena: the introduction of the Internet and the popularity of non-erotic camgirls in the United States in the mid-1990s.

The Internet

Before the Internet, the market for consumers seeking interactive, yet indirect sexual services was largely limited to phone sex. Phone sex was a huge industry in the 1980s and 1990s and is still available to clients who for myriad reasons do not desire direct or physical sexual services.[2] While the Internet and the introduction of camming did not displace the phone sex industry, the Internet did open new spaces for the sale of indirect sexual services. Technology has continued to open up opportunities for individuals to have new sexual experiences. Porn studies scholar Feona Attwood writes:

> The relationship between sex and technology is an old and established one; technologies have always been adapted for sexual purposes, and it is regularly claimed that sex drives technological development. Yet changes in technology do introduce new ways of doing things and create new environments in which to do them.[3]

Like other communication technologies before it, the Internet created new spaces for sexual exploration and experiences of sexual pleasure.

The Internet went live in 1990 and was made publicly available in 1993. In 1993, there was very little content on the web. There were only approximately 130 websites and 14 million global users. In 1996, the year that the first erotic cam sites launched, most of the world did not yet have access to the Internet. The cam industry grew as more people gained access to the Internet and high-speed connections. While there are cam models and customers from all over the world, five countries are considered hubs of the industry: Colombia, Romania, the United Kingdom, Canada, and the United States. Since 1996, people in the UK, Canada, and the US have had superior access to the Internet (see table 2.1).

In Colombia and Romania, home and personal access to the Internet remained low as the industry was growing between 1996 and 2006. This meant that models in Colombia and Romania began working for physical camming studios where they could get access to computers with fast Internet connections, whereas many models in the United Kingdom, Canada, and the United States had the opportunity to cam from home.

TABLE 2.1. Percentage of Population Using the Internet in Camming Industry Hubs

Country	1996	2006	2015
Romania	0.2	24.6	55.7
Colombia	0.2	15.3	55.9
Canada	6.7	72.4	88.4
United Kingdom	4.1	68.8	92.0
United States	16.4	68.9	74.4

Source: World Bank—World Development Indicators.[4]

As access to the Internet and fiber Internet services grew, bandwidth increased, and speed improved, the camming industry became more prominent and more globalized. As shown in figure 2.3, since 1990, North Americans have had the highest percentage of people using the Internet. This explains why most models told me that, regardless of their location in the world, customers from the United States were their primary audience. The economic wealth and access to the Internet enjoyed by most North Americans initially made the United States and Canada the primary centers of the camming industry. As more individuals in Europe, Central Asia, Latin America, and the Caribbean gained personal access to the Internet, more people from these regions were able to participate in the camming industry. In particular, the United Kingdom quickly joined the United States and Canada as the nuclei of the industry. Unfortunately, even 20 years after its inception, people in South Asia and sub-Saharan Africa still have inadequate access to the Internet, and thus there are not many models from these regions, and those models that do camming work from these regions are most likely to work in physical camming studios.

While there are clients from countries in South Asia and sub-Saharan Africa, those from the global North grossly outnumber those from the

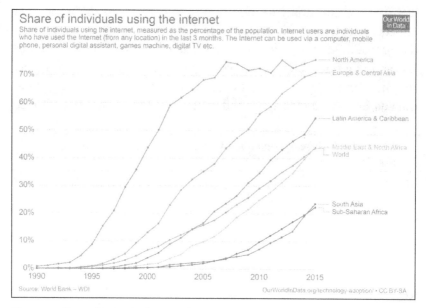

Figure 2.3. Share of individuals using the Internet.

global South. Sexual racism often means that models will see customers from the United States, Canada, and the United Kingdom as the most ideal, and assume clients from outside these areas will be what cam models call "freeloaders"—cheap clients who do not tip and do not spend money. The perception that only clients from the global North are ideal and clients from the global South are freeloaders perpetuates racist discourses. In this regard, it is crucial to remember that access to global communication technologies has remained uneven throughout the world.

The Rise of Camgirls

In the 1990s, camgirls began broadcasting video of themselves to public audiences on the Internet. In 1996, Jennifer Ringley famously launched what she called the JenniCam from her college dorm room. The JenniCam was a direct lens into the authentic life of a young woman from the United States. As feminist media scholar Theresa M. Sneft argues, Ringley was one of many camgirls who used the Internet "to broadcast themselves over the Web for the general public, while trying to culti-vate a measure of celebrity in the process."[5] Ringley, like many camgirls, used live webcams, which in the late 1990s meant either broadcasting still images or poorly streamed video of her daily routine and activities. This popular genre of camming functioned to bring women's "real" lives to the public sphere and laid the groundwork for the camming field's emphasis on embodied authenticity.

The first generation of camgirls primarily broadcast their lives for ce-lebrity and status—not as work. As Senft notes, during this period some women used camming to disseminate their art, form online communi-ties, and promote and sell commercial pornography. However, camming from home was expensive. At the time, even a low-end, low-resolution webcam cost a lot. Broadband connectivity was still not widely available and, where it was, cost-prohibitive for most people around the world. According to Ringley, the JenniCam cost $15,000 per month to run.[6] As a result, in 1998 she implemented an annual fee, which gave mem-bers access to new pictures within minutes.[7] While a small cohort of camgirls like Ringley hosted personal cam sites in the mid-1990s, most people lacked the funds and the knowledge to create, run, and host their own cam sites. These conditions created a propitious moment for sex work entrepreneurs to begin creating and hosting webcam platforms for camgirls.

The Birth of Erotic Cam Sites

As depicted in table 2.2, Flirt4Free (F4F) and Cams were the first major cam sites in the industry. After a few years of their dominating the bur-geoning camming industry, other platforms emerged such as Streamate (SM), LiveJasmin (LJ), ImLive (IL), MyFreeCams (MFC), CAM4 (C4), and Chaturbate (CB). These pioneering cam sites still dominate the con-temporary camming market.

When cam sites first emerged in 1996, they operated as premium sites, which meant that customers could purchase a private interactive online erotic show with a cam model using a pay-per-minute model. SM is an excellent example of a premium cam site. Later, cam sites such as MFC adopted a token-based system where clients could view and tip perform-ers in a public space without necessarily purchasing private shows. In

TABLE 2.2. Overview of the Early Major Cam Sites

Cam Site	Launch Date
Flirt4Free (F4F) *originally called Video Secrets	1996
Cams	1996
iFriends (IF)	1998
Streamate (SM)	1999
LiveJasmin (LJ)	2001
ImLive (IM)	2002
MyFreeCams (MFC)	2004
CAM4 (C4)	2007
Chaturbate (CB)	2011

addition, on sites such as MFC customers can pay to watch other customers' private shows. When CB was launched, it became trendy among models who were unhappy with premium, pay-per-minute sites. On CB, models perform in a public room and make money through tips—there are no private shows. While early camgirls like Jennifer Ringley can take part of the credit for the birth of these erotic cam sites and the erotic camming industry in general, the camming industry and its exponential growth were made possible by the growth of the World Wide Web and other technologies.

The Growth of the Camming Industry

Online Pornography Sites

The proliferation of online pornography has also facilitated the growth of the camming industry. As feminist media scholar Susanna Paasonen has noted, the rise of online pornography, which is increasingly amateur porn, has changed the form and content of porn, and crucially these technological shifts have caused changes in the resonances and experiences of porn users (and producers).[8] The growth of websites known colloquially as tube sites—sites devoted to sharing and disseminating amateur porn—have created a profound cultural shift in the types of pornography that are valued both culturally and economically. In 2007, RedTube was launched. Like its predecessor, market giant YouTube, individuals can use it to post to the Internet and publicly share videos.

The explosion of amateur pornography on the Internet has led to what we can call the *demystification of porn.*

In this historical moment, beginning profoundly in 2007, porn was becoming something that anybody could star in, produce, and sell. Porn was demystified because it was no longer restricted by embodiment and starring in it no longer required auditioning. The Internet created new spaces for the distribution and sale of pornography, but tube sites created a new distribution channel for pornography that was free and open to all individuals with access to the Internet. Importantly, the demystification of porn and the growing number of amateur pornographers posting videos of sex online ushered in a new cultural trend, where consumers of pornography began to demand embodied authenticity in their pornography. Put another way, as more people began to consume free homemade pornography, consumers began not only to get used to amateur porn but came to value pornography with low production values and nonprofessional performers. The growth of homemade porn created a market demand for embodied authenticity—people started wanting to see "regular" people having sex. In short, a demand emerged for authentic sex.

As more tube sites developed, the camming market and cam models had to make adjustments. Sites like Clips4Sale and ManyVids provided a new space for amateur pornographers to sell their homemade pornography. Cam models, too, found that there was an increasing demand, as well an opportunity to make an additional stream of revenue selling pornographic material of themselves. Many cam models initially did not see themselves as pornographers but over time began to adapt to the changing market and sell pornographic videos of themselves, as well. Rebecca, a 34-year-old polyamorous White cis woman from the United States, has been camming for over seven years. We discussed how shifts in the market affected her labor:

> Yeah . . . things have changed. . . . When I first started you didn't have to produce your own videos and sell them in order to make money. Like that wasn't a thing. Like, being a content creator, a video content creator and a cam model wasn't the same thing. I know girls who started . . . around the same time [I did] and they still refuse to make content. Some of them still make money, some of them don't, but most of the time they

end up making content to sell to clients because that's kind of the way things, you know, are going.

As Rebecca noted, initially the camming industry was different from the traditional porn industry. Cam models made money solely by logging online and performing interactive erotic shows for paying clients. Over time, demand for recorded content emerged. Clients began requesting that their favorite cam performer sell them recorded videos that they could watch when the performer was not online. Clients began recording cam models shows without their permission ("capping"). In addition to capping models' shows for their private viewing, customers also began uploading these capped performances to free tube sites and trying to sell the capped shows. Given the prevalence of being capped and growing consumer demand for pornographic images and videos, many cam models also started selling pornography on sites such as ManyVids and Clips4Sale.

As Rebecca suggested, many cam models did not initially sign up to make traditional pornography, but they have grown to realize that if you want to make money, you must be willing to answer the calls of the market. Cam models who refuse to make and sell recorded content can still be successful, but as Rebecca noted, most will not be. After over two decades of exponential growth, the camming market is saturated with cam models, and models must continually find new strategies to market their brands and remain competitive. Selling pornographic images, videos, and even things such as used panties has become a popular strategy for cam models to make money in an increasingly competitive field. The camming and pornography industries increasingly overlap—a trend that will likely raise legal issues for cam models who are now also sell pornographic videos on the Internet.

Skype

The introduction of telecommunication applications such as Skype also contributed to the growth of the camming industry. Skype, launched in 2003, initially allowed people to video chat between computers and later between tablets and other mobile devices. Many cam models use mainstream cam sites to build a loyal following of clients that they can book private shows with off those cam sites. The introduction of Skype meant that cam models now had a place to service regular clients. On Skype, models can set their prices and make 100% of the profit from their shows, using third-party billing sites to receive payments from their clients. Some clients will pay top dollar for private shows because they want a cam model to perform erotic acts that may be prohibited on a cam site. In private Skype shows, models do not have to follow cam-site rules and have more agency and control over the content of their performances; they may find themselves not only making more money but experiencing more pleasure as a result. However, models told me that while Skype shows can be lucrative, many issues arise when performing on the app.

First, many models do not trust Skype's security and have had problems with technologically savvy clients figuring out their identity and location. Second, it is easy to record or cap Skype shows. Given that Skype shows are often used to perform kinky requests, some models have more significant concerns about client capping. Third, scheduling Skype shows can be an issue for cam models. A client may cancel a scheduled appointment at the last minute, not show up, or even do an illegitimate chargeback (i.e., cancel a credit-card payment right after a show's completion). Fourth, many mainstream third-party billers such as PayPal will not work with sex workers. If PayPal learns that a cam model is receiving money for a private show, it will suspend the model's account. In addition, many on- and offline money-transfer services require names, addresses, bank account numbers, and other personal details. Receiving money offline can thus compromise a model's anonymity, which can be dangerous. In response to these issues, Skype launched Skype Private in 2013. Models generally receive a 75–80% payout when using Skype Private. For some performers, this cost is well worth it because the platform has added measures to protect models' anonymity and to prevent capping. The fact that Skype created a platform for cam models and camming studios is a testimony to the growth and economic impact of the camming industry.

If cam models do not want to use Skype Private, there are third-party billing sites that work with sex workers, but they also are not free. On IndieBill, the model pays a 15% charge to receive money. On GiftRocket, the client pays a fee of $2 plus 5% of the gift amount. Moreover, if

GiftRocket learns that the gift is for sex work, they reserve the right to implement higher fees. These costs can be prohibitive to clients. Finally, many third-party billing sites have payment delays. For example, a model negotiates a price of $200 for a one-hour private show. If the model performs the show and the client issues a chargeback, the model will receive nothing. Models need to request payment in advance, but many clients are afraid of sending money without having received the service first. While doing private Skype shows allows cam models to recoup profits taken by cam-site sex entrepreneurs, performing on the app also has disadvantages. For many cam models, private shows on Skype are reserved only for regular clients they believe they can trust.

Social Media

The introduction of social media platforms also changed the camming market. Specifically, Facebook (2004), Twitter (2006), Instagram (2010), and Snapchat (2012) had a significant effect on the burgeoning cam industry. Social media has become the primary mechanism that cam models use to market themselves online. In our interview, Matt said, "Social media is a big part about camming and it's the biggest [and] the best way to get your name out there. . . . Like if you, if you want to be like a successful cammer, you need Twitter, you need Instagram, you need the Snapchat."

Adult webcam performers use "tagging" strategies to market their brands. Performers often use tags on cam sites that help customers find them. These tags often include references to acts that they are willing to perform such as "masturbation," "anal," "penetration," "kink," or "fetish." Performers also use social media platforms such as Twitter to market themselves to clients. On Twitter, examples of popular tags include #webcammodel, #camgirl, and #camboy. Tags such as #bbw (big beautiful women), #ssbbw (supersized big beautiful women), #bigtits, #fatass, and #hugecock describe performer embodiment. Performers often tag the web platform that they are performing on: #myfreecams, #chaturbate #livejasmin, #cam4, #flirt4free, #bongacams, #streamate. Many cam models also engage in strategic branding and use hashtags such as #ebonycammodels, #asiancammodels, and #Tgirl, just to name a few.

Cam models also turn professional social media accounts into additional streams of income in two primary ways. First, many cam sites also pay commissions to "affiliates"—people who drive traffic to the site. While you do not have to be a cam model to be an affiliate, many cam models choose to because it is easy and requires no additional labor. For example, CB has a built-in affiliate program that pays cam models for referrals. If a cam model is marketing an upcoming show on Twitter and they use the hashtag #chaturbate, they can earn a 20% affiliate commission. For the model to receive the commission, a customer is required to navigate to CB with the model-provided link and also purchase tokens. Given that most models now use social media to promote their rooms and brands, cashing in on these affiliate programs is an easy way to boost their wages.

Second, cam models can also generate income by selling subscription access to a social media account. Some cam models sell monthly and yearly subscriptions to their Snapchat accounts. Other cam models sell access via messaging apps such as WhatsApp, Kik, or Netchat. Many models believe that the drawbacks of selling these subscriptions far outweigh the benefits of doing so. Take, for example, what Naomi told me about selling a subscription to her Kik account.

> NAOMI: I've thought about that and for a while and I [decided] to [sell] monthly access on Kik. [However], 'cause I'm super busy and a lotta guys just wanna chat and I'm like, I have a lot to do. So, I tried to sell [it] where they could buy for several months at a time, like, I would try to prioritize them, but . . . I don't know . . . that one ended up bothering me.
>
> AJ: Why's that—like, too invasive? Too much time?
>
> NAOMI: Well, it became the same as my day job. It's a consistency thing. Like, I felt like I had to and that started to get to me.

The use of social media platforms is great for branding, but managing and curating their accounts adds to cam models' workload. For their use of social media to be effective, performers must communicate regularly with fans—not just by posting or tweeting, but by answering DMs (direct, or private, messages). A client who purchases a subscription to Naomi's Kik wants to chat while they are both offline—that is, while she is not working. As I explore in chapter 4, a primary motivation to cam is autonomy and an escape from the alienation of capitalist labor. As Naomi said, she disliked selling access to Kik, because communicating with clients offline began to feel like her day job. If customers grow to expect communication through Twitter and other web-based communication applications, then the freedom and autonomy cam models once felt will lessen—as will the pleasure they experience from camming. Many of the cam models I interviewed noted that communicating with fans has now become part of the work for successful models. Whereas models used to log on only for a show, and log off, now many models find themselves doing hours of labor marketing and communicating with fans.

Smart Phones and Teledildonics

The increased use of smartphone technologies has also contributed to the growth of the camming industry. In 2007, the first iPhone came to market and in 2008 Apple launched the App Store. As more people gained access to mobile smartphones, more people could also access cam sites while not at home.

Figure 2.4 demonstrates that, once again, the digital divide privileges models and clients from the United States, Canada, and various European nations. In countries with the most substantial access to smartphone ownership, clients can purchase services online from cam models in virtually any location. Cam models can update their professional social media accounts and communicate with clients from anywhere. The integration of smartphone apps and the new genre of sex toys called "teledildonics" into the cam industry has been significant.

While the sex toy market had flourished long before the camming market emerged,[9] teledildonics—sex toys that are accessible remotely— now play a major role. In 2006, OhMiBod a pioneering sex toy company based in the United States, created the first vibrator that can be operated remotely through an app. This means that clients can remotely access a vibrator being used in real time by a cam model. When a customer tips, a pinging sound alerts everyone in the room of the tip and the toy vibrates. The cam model can set the time of vibration to correspond with a tip amount. The bigger the tip, the longer the vibration. OhMiBod is now only one company of many producing teledildonics. These toys are shaping the experiences both models and clients have in the contemporary camming industry.

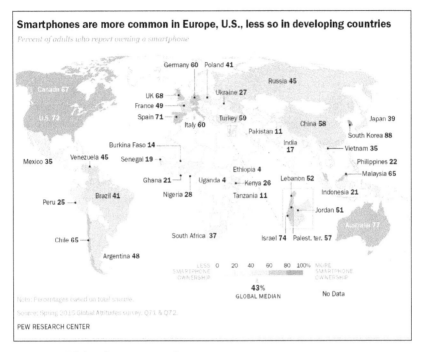

Smartphones are more common in Europe, U.S., less so in developing countries
Percent of adults who report owning a smartphone

Germany 60 Poland 41
Russia 45
Canada 67
UK 68
Ukraine 27
France 49
US 72
Spain 71
Italy 60
Turkey 59
China 58
Japan 39
South Korea 88
Pakistan 11
Burkina Faso 14
India 17
Vietnam 35
Mexico 35 Venezuela 45 Senegal 19
Philippines 22
Ethiopia 4
Malaysia 65
Ghana 21 Uganda 4 Kenya 26 Lebanon 52
Nigeria 28 Tanzania 11
Indonesia 21
Brazil 41
Peru 25
Jordan 51
Australia 77
Chile 65
South Africa 37
Israel 74 Palest. ter. 57
Argentina 48

LESS 0 20 40 60 80 100% MORE
SMARTPHONE   SMARTPHONE
OWNERSHIP   OWNERSHIP

43%
GLOBAL MEDIAN

No Data

Note: Percentages based on total sample.
Source: Spring 2015 Global Attitudes survey. Q71 & Q72.
PEW RESEARCH CENTER

Figure 2.4. Adults who own smartphones, 2015.

Aron, a 31-year-old bi-curious White cis man from Hungary, and I talked about the effect teledildonics have had on the industry. Aron said:

> The teledildonics, like, skyrocketed a few years ago. You know, [there are] all kinds of dildos . . . that you can connect to your smartphone. . . . When I'm using mine, I make the most money because people love it. Because you know, they can use a few tokens and then they control something in you or on you or something, and they're just crazy about it. . . . It makes a huge difference actually. . . . Or you can [use it] when you are not even online. . . . For example, you can sell a package where you are saying, Okay, I am in this or this public place or whatever, I have my plug in, send me X dollars and I'm gonna give control for ten minutes, and then you can control, and [I will] post videos on Snapchat that you can check out or something.

Models are continually searching for innovative ways to offer erotic cam shows and thus maximize their profits. The use of teledildonics is one new way cam models do this. In figure 2.2, which depicted a sample model's cam room, that cam model was using a teledildonic made by another popular company, Lovense. Every time the customer tipped the model creating that yellow wall, the model's vibrator, which was inside her vagina, went off. The connections between sex-toy companies and the camming industry are incredibly important. CB, for example, now offers several apps that are compatible with teledildonics. Cam models frequently use sex toys ranging from vibrators to floggers in their performances, which are often bought for them by clients through Amazon Wishlists. The interconnectedness of the camming industry with the sex-toy industry and the online porn industry helps them all to make a profit and continue to grow.

Conclusion

As more new technologies emerge, the camming industry will continue to adapt and experience growth. The camming industry is a multibillion-dollar industry and has become a significant engine of economic commerce and growth.[10] However, it is also crucial that we think transnationally and remember that economic growth is not evenly felt and that the camming industry remains inaccessible to many. For a cam model to begin working, they need to spend a substantial amount of money (computer, webcam, lighting), and they must have access to the Internet. The inequality generated by global capitalism means that, for so many people around the world, the costs associated with becoming a cam model are prohibitive and access to the technologies described in this chapter are not available. The resources required to begin camming can force people to work under exploitative conditions in studios, and can also be a reason why street-based escorts working under deplorable conditions who want to migrate into online indirect sex work cannot. The camming industry can be lauded for creating an opportunity for safe and legal sex work that allows workers to earn decent wages, have more autonomy, work less, find community, and experience pleasure. However, this opportunity is not open to the most economically vulnerable people around the world.

3

The Contemporary Camming Market

Moral Entrepreneurs, Sex Entrepreneurs, and Cam Models

Camming is a capitalist industry, not an economic utopia. As sociologist Michel Dorias observes, sex workers are not free agents; how workers and clients interact and negotiate sales is conditioned by rules and terms set by moral entrepreneurs and sex entrepreneurs. Moral entrepreneurs dictate the legal policies that regulate the camming industry. Paralleling other gig economies, sex entrepreneurs own erotic cam-site platforms and employ performers as independent contractors. The structure of cam sites and the policies enforced on them condition the experiences and wages of cam models.

Sex entrepreneurs exploit cam models—all cam sites take a substantial portion of models' sales and pay relatively low commissions. Various overlapping systems of oppression shape the industry and affect the wage outcomes and experiences of cam models. Cam models must work hard—but those who are thin, White, cisgender, in their 20s, able-bodied, from the United States, and do not work for studios are privileged by various systems of inequality that they have no control over. What I show in this book is that external structural conditions— neoliberal capitalism, White supremacy, cissexism, patriarchy, hetero-sexism, and ableism—shape the wage differences, overall success, and workplace experiences of the cam models in my study.

Moral Entrepreneurs

Moral entrepreneurs include an array of politicians and political pundits, as well as agents within the rescue industry,[1] who, drawing from religious and neo-Victorian ideas about appropriate sexuality, collectively construct policies that harm and stigmatize sex workers. Cam sites and cam models are not free agents in an open capitalist market. Both operate within the broader global network of pornographic industries, which moral entrepreneurs regulate.

The entire online adult website network generally abides by US laws regarding the creation and distribution of pornographic materials. Given that almost all major cam sites have IP addresses located in the United States, these companies must abide by US law. Additionally, pornography is illegal in many places around the world, and US policies on pornography and obscenity are clearly defined under the law. As a result, US policy provides the default guidelines for the camming industry.

As Larry Walters, who specializes in Internet law, writes, "While the borderless technology of the Internet is not amenable to effective legal regulation by any particular country, US law has become the de facto, Gold Standard for webmasters to achieve."[2] The interconnectedness of the online adult industry makes it hard for adult website owners all over the globe to not rely on one another for various goods and services. Even if US law structures the camming market, it is crucial for all sex entrepreneurs to be mindful of all laws regarding the distribution of pornography in a global marketplace. Pornographic content online is shared across countries and human-made boundaries. While the location of an IP address establishes what laws directly govern a website's practices, the situation is complicated given that the content is being consumed globally. Sex entrepreneurs outside of the US, in places such as Colombia and Romania, for example, must also be careful to abide by the laws in their nations, which are less clearly defined than US regulations and can carry punitive sanctions for violations.

In the United States, adult websites are protected under the Constitution. The creation, publishing, and dissemination of adult content is protected under the First Amendment. However, the issue of whether the production of adult content on any adult website site violates prostitution laws is not clear. Only New Hampshire and California legally recognize adult content production as not in violation of prostitution laws.[3] Moreover, as I discuss further in the book's conclusion, the politics of trafficking and the political mobilization of the rescue industry have thrown a magnifying glass on adult content producers, especially with the April 2018 passage of the Fight Online Sex Trafficking Act (FOSTA).

The moral entrepreneurs have become increasingly alarmed about the prevalence of sex trafficking. All adult website operators must be vigilant in complying with age verification procedures and record-keeping laws. In the camming industry, all cam sites must ensure that all users, both models, and clients are 18 years or older. Cam sites post warnings that they contain pornographic material and that users must be 18 or over to view the content. Figure 3.1 is an example of the sort of message users receive when logging on to a cam site. Chaturbate's prompt provides a brief description of legal terms and conditions, and users must affirm they have read this description, along with an additional 14 terms and conditions. As also shown in figure 3.2, users must affirm their age whether they log in from a desktop or a mobile device.

While users must click a link that affirms their age, there is no way actually to confirm that a given user is 18 years old or older. Some cam sites take extra precautions to ensure that minors who log into their sites do not view overtly sexual material. Streamate's code of conduct says:

> In order to prevent minors' exposure to below the waist nudity and adult material, no below the waist nudity is allowed in "free chat." Below the waist nudity is only allowed in age-verified areas, which are also known as "private" or "paid chat." Below the waist nudity in free areas will result in temporary suspension or permanent closing of your account.

By creating public and private spaces, many cam sites can further protect themselves from government censure and litigation for age violations.

Cam sites also take precautions when registering new cam models. In compliance with US law—specifically, the Child Protection and Obscenity Enforcement Act of 1988—when a cam model registers or applies to work, they must provide government-issued identification, and the cam site must keep records on all performers. Cam sites take these laws seriously and regularly screen models' accounts and rooms to ensure that the person performing is the person registered. Cam models said that Chaturbate was especially known for flagging models for age verification and obscenity.

While pornography is legal in the United States, obscenity is illegal. *Miller v. California*, 413 US 15 (1973), declared that the First Amendment does not protect material deemed obscene. It is often difficult, however, to know the difference between pornographic materials that are legal and materials that are obscene, and therefore illegal. The Miller test was de-

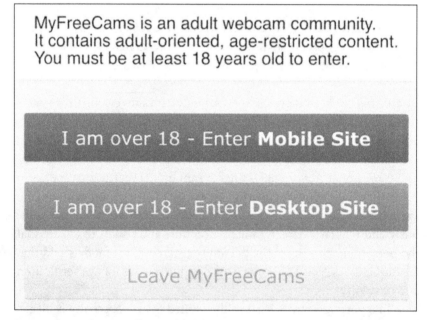

YOU MUST BE OVER 18 AND AGREE TO THE TERMS BELOW BEFORE CONTINUING:

This website contains information, links, images and videos of sexually explicit material (collectively, the "Sexually Explicit Material"). Do NOT continue if: (i) you are not at least 18 years of age or the age of majority in each and every jurisdiction in which you will or may view the Sexually Explicit Material, whichever is higher (the "Age of Majority"), (ii) such material offends you, or (iii) viewing the Sexually Explicit Material is not legal in each and every community where you choose to view it.
By choosing to enter this website you are affirming under oath and penalties of perjury pursuant to Title 28 U.S.C. § 1746 and other applicable statutes and laws that all of the following statements are true and

THIS SITE ACTIVELY COOPERATES WITH LAW ENFORCEMENT IN ALL INSTANCES OF SUSPECTED ILLEGAL USE OF THE SERVICE, ESPECIALLY IN THE CASE OF UNDERAGE USAGE OF THE SERVICE.

I AGREE

Exit this site

Figure 3.1. Sample age verification, Chaturbate.

MyFreeCams is an adult webcam community.
It contains adult-oriented, age-restricted content.
You must be at least 18 years old to enter.

I am over 18 - Enter **Mobile Site**

I am over 18 - Enter **Desktop Site**

Leave MyFreeCams

Figure 3.2. Sample age verification (mobile), MyFreeCams.

veloped to help make this distinction as it set guidelines for evaluating obscene material. In assessing pornographic material, the Miller test poses three questions: (1) Would the average person, applying contemporary community standards, find that the work, taken as a whole, appeals to the prurient interest? (2) Does the work depict or describe, in a patently offensive way, sexual conduct specifically defined by the applicable state law? (3) Does the work, taken as a whole, lack serious literary, artistic, political, or scientific value? The Miller test is problematic. Online, it is unclear what local community standards are or what a work "as a whole" is.

Cam models get flagged for obscenity easily. While models design their own performances, cam sites create rules to safeguard themselves from obscenity violations. For example, all cam sites prohibit bestiality. Cam shows are live, and performers must be sure that their camming space is secure. If Fluffy the cat happens to get in the room, a performer could be flagged or banned, and potentially have their account terminated. Cam sites also regulate the type of objects performers' can insert in their bodies. While performers regularly use dildos, inserting a bat into a performer's anus would be flagged as indecent. Cam sites often err on the side of caution when it comes to obscenity laws.

In addition, cam sites take these obscenity laws seriously because they do not have "safe harbor" protections from obscenity. "Safe harbor" refers to section 230 of the Communications Decency Act (1996), which prior to its amendment under FOSTA, protected internet service providers from being held responsible for what people publish on their websites. Specifically, section 230 stated, "No provider or user of an interactive computer service shall be treated as the publisher or speaker of any information provided by another information content provider" (47 USC § 230). Section 230 protected sites such as YouTube and Twitter from a range of intellectual property and copyright disputes. If a cam model committed copyright infringement during a recorded broadcast, the cam site was not held responsible—the model was responsible. Camsites (or any adult website), meanwhile, have never been protected or given safe harbor from obscenity violations or age violations. This is why cam sites take these two policies very seriously.

The policies that regulate pornography and adult websites have been enacted by the US government under pressure from moral entrepreneurs. Under the guise of thwarting sex trafficking and child pornography, moral entrepreneurs craft policies that harm voluntary sex workers, restrict free speech, and police sexuality using neo-Victorian and religious ideas about normative sexuality. This underscores the main theoretical point of this book: the regulation of pleasure is a central task of major social institutions, and society forces people (often violently) to sacrifice pleasure. It is essential that sociologists of law grapple with the ways in which political actors often weaponize the law to regulate pleasure in order to preserve political power and exercise social control. Despite existing in the capitalist free market, sex entrepreneurs' businesses are subject to intense regulation and are governed by laws that sex proprietors have little control over.

Sex Entrepreneurs

In the camming industry, sex entrepreneurs are the companies that own major cam-site platforms and networks, physical studios, and online studios/agencies. There has been a proliferation of sex entrepreneurs looking to cash in on the growing adult-webcam industry. In 2013, CNBC reported that the webcam industry had grossed over $1 billion in revenue.[4] Based on my research, the camming industry is now a multibillion-dollar industry, from which cam-site owners and studios reap the most rewards.

Cam Sites

As in most contemporary capitalist markets, the camming industry is an agglomerated industry dominated by a small cohort of companies. There are approximately 13 major cam-site companies that are industry leaders (see table 3.1), though an even smaller number of cam sites have historically dominated the industry. Since the development of the pioneering cam sites, thousands of new ones have emerged. Many of these are clone sites (also called white-label sites) that exist within a cam network. The Streamate (SM) network hosts approximately 2,000 smaller cam sites. If a model cams for SM, they will appear on these smaller clone sites as well. Many other industry-leading cam sites such as Chaturbate (CB) and LiveJasmin (LJ) also have thousands of clone or white-label sites. The Donamins Group owns Camster, Naked, and Bangbroschat, which are all clones of each other. MyFreeCams (MFC), which has no clone sites, is an exception.

In addition, many new cam sites cater to specific audiences around the world. The popular cam site BongaCams (BC), launched in 2012, is often called the Chaturbate of Europe by market participants. Many new cam sites also feature cam models of only particular nationalities and races. SakuraLive (SL) features only Japanese cam models. EbonyCam (EC) features Black models from around the world. BBWcam (BBWC) and justbbwcams.com (JBBWC) were created for fat cam models. The cam site TSYUM (TY) features only trans women and BuckAngelCams is a cam site for transmasculine cam models.[5]

TABLE 3.1. Major Cam Site Traffic Scores

Cam Site	Traffic Score
LiveJasmin	69*
BongaCams	75
Chaturbate	112
MyFreeCams	807
CAM4	848
Flirt4Free	968
Camster	1444
Cams	3054
CamSoda	5307
ImLive	8686
Streamate	9597
FreeWebcams	39511
iFriends	92474

Source: Alexa Website Analytics.[6]
*A low traffic score indicates a website has high traffic.

TABLE 3.2. Popular Niche Cam Site Traffic Scores

Cam Site	Traffic Score
SakuraLive	48593
EbonyCam	926074
justbbwcams.com	406369
TSYUM	660053
BBWcam	1525693

Source: Alexa Website Analytics. (BuckAngelCams does not appear in the table because the site launched only one month before this writing and there was no available Alexa data on it yet.)

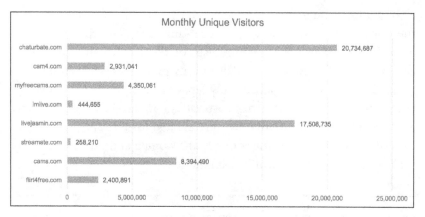

Figure 3.3. Monthly unique visitors to major cam sites, May 2018. Source: Alexa Website Analytics.

The structure of individual cam sites shapes the cam models' performances and experiences, which sites cam models have access to and are willing to work on, and their wages. LJ has steadily been the most trafficked cam site (table 3.1), and this is appealing to many models. However, LJ is a premium site (pay-per-minute for private shows) that caters to the European market. It is used most by European models working in physical studios. LJ has excellent traffic, but models reap only 35% of total sales. The low commission for performing premium private shows is a significant limitation of LJ, despite the site's great traffic. Moreover, it is structured around a binary gender system and forces trans women who have penises to perform in the male model section. Despite LJ's high rates of traffic, trans women that I spoke with refused to work under these transphobic conditions. Adeline, a 25-year-old polyamorous White trans woman from the United States, said:

> Skype is what I mostly do now 'cause I have kind of a large clientele built up. But I first tried Jasmin, and that was just the worst experience. I was immediately turned off. I mean, they tried making me perform under a male tag. So, it was like, oh, I have to be male if I'm gonna cam here, and I just thought that . . . you can't like change it to any other word besides that. They wouldn't and they'd be like, no, we wanna be honest to our viewers, and I'm just like, oh, fuck you.

Many cam models like Adeline use cam-site platforms to build a clientele and then use services such as Skype to book independent sessions with clients, allowing them to recoup profits taken by sex entrepreneurs. In addition, Adeline resists transphobic cam-site policies by performing on Skype. Unfortunately, LJ is not the only gender-exclusionary cam site. MyFreeCams, for example, employs only cis women.

As another example of how cam-site structures influence cam models' workplace experiences, which sites cam models choose to work on, and wages, consider CB, which is structured as a public cam site. This means there are no private shows; models perform and receive tokens exclusively in a public space. Cam models said that the public structure of CB led to having to regularly deal with freeloaders, an issue on every cam site. As a cam model on a web forum succinctly put it, "All cam sites will have their flavor of freeloaders, even private-based ones." In general, pay-per-minute sites have fewer freeloaders because there are no displays of full nudity and explicit sex acts performed in public chat. On cam sites such as SM, clients must pay for private shows to see sexually explicit content. As a result of CB's public-chat structure, performers on the site have to deal with more freeloaders because customers can log on and watch public shows without paying.

On the other hand, CB has excellent traffic and the most unique monthly visitors of any cam site (figure 3.3). Cam models consistently told me that CB was the most inclusive cam site in the industry—the most diverse and the most "trans-friendly." CB, in my observation too, generally had the most racial and ethnic diversity among cam models. Naomi, a 38-year-old queer White trans woman from the United States, said, "I like Chaturbate specifically because . . . they're friendlier to trans cammers than other sites. They seem to be welcoming." In addition, most cam models perform in solo categories, but cam sites also feature couples. Models also saw CB as the most welcoming to couples.

CB is also popular because models are allowed to purchase or code apps and bots through its application programming interface. As Aron discussed in the previous chapter, a favorite CB app connects to the performer's vibrator. Other apps allow models to initiate interactive games and reward systems for generous tippers. While many models frown on the practice, they can employ bots on CB to make it appear as if there is a large audience in their room—thereby drawing in even more customers. Thus, while CB most often ends up taking a 50% cut of models' earnings (CB pays models $0.05 for every token earned), these other incentives make it incredibly popular. CB's public model, high traffic, and decent payment structure create a highly competitive environment and models reported that, to remain competitive, they were needed to deliver more sexually explicit performances.

As a final example, MFC uses both a public and private model, although many models on the site perform in public only. As my examination of LJ and CB above suggest, while major non-niche cam sites were ostensibly open to all models, respondents explained that sites' design can be exclusionary. MFC employs only cis women and thin White able-bodied cis women dominate the site. Models who can access MFC often earn high wages. Members buy token packages that they use for tipping models, who take home $0.05 per token, $3.00 per minute for a private show, $0.50 per minute for a group show, and $4.00 per minute for a True Private Show. Models earn an additional $1.00 per minute for each client who pays to "spy" on one of their private shows, and they receive bonuses for outstanding sales. MFC was popular among many models because of this payment structure and its relatively good traffic. It was also known among models for having fewer freeloaders than sites such as CB. Despite being independent contractors, cam models' workplace experiences, the sites they choose to work on, and their wages are shaped by the structures and policies of cam sites.

Physical Studios

While many cam models broadcast on cam sites from home, many also work in spaces owned by sex entrepreneurs called studios. Physical studios, most prevalent in Colombia and Romania, are buildings that have individual rooms for models to cam equipped with a computer, HD webcam, and quality lighting. Studios are popular in regions where access to technology is limited. While many advertisements make camming seem accessible to all, the reality is many people around the world do not have access to stable Internet connections at home, and many do not have the money for proper lighting, a computer, and webcam. Studios are appealing to people who do not have access to these resources or private spaces in which to work. There are thousands of physical studios throughout the world, and most have partnerships with cam sites. A model who signs up with a popular studio such as Studio 20 can enjoy preferential treatment when camming on LJ, F4F, SM, IM, Cams, and the new FreeWebcams site. Studio 20, a franchise, has physical studios, mostly in Romanian cities, and also in Cali, Colombia, and Los Angeles, USA.

Working in a studio has both benefits and limitations. Self-employment takes discipline. Some models may benefit from having scheduled work hours and even quotas set for them. Tiffany is a 23-year-old lesbian Black cis woman from the United States. In our interview, we talked about why she chose to work for a studio and not from home.

> Well, I'm gonna be honest, [there are] a lot of pros and cons [to working for a studio]. The pros of working for a studio is, you have a space . . . if a guy wants to be a creep and wants to check your IP address, and just be all types of weird, he [will find] the studio, he won't find your actual home. . . . I can say that I felt safe. I like being around other girls who are doing this—it kinda helps giving tips and tricks . . . what the hell, it's a slow-ass night, let's go talk! The cons: I mean, they be taking a lot of our money. That sucks. Every time I make 100 bucks, I only get 20 out of it—that sucks! . . . And them owning my name. So if I wanted to start over, I would have to make a whole account, I couldn't take [NAME] with me, and that sucks.

Tiffany outlined what many models said were the pluses and minuses of working for a studio. First, models have access to a space in which to perform. Second, camming from a studio provides protections that models who cam from home do not always have. Third, when people work in a physical workplace with other workers, they can find support and camaraderie. The creation of community can be a potential benefit to performers working in studios.

The drawback of working for many studios is that models often make low wages and the payment structures are exploitative. Cam models in this situation receive a commission only after both the cam site and the studio get their cuts. Second, if you start camming with a studio, you sign a contract, and if you choose to separate from that studio, you can no longer use the cam name you registered with. For models that build a following, this limitation can cost them a lot of money. Finally, it is important to note that Tiffany worked in a studio located in the United States and English was her first language. These factors likely influenced her experiences working for a studio. The studios I profile in this chapter are high-end. However, there are studios (to which I had no access) where I suspect cam models work under deplorable conditions of labor, potentially even against their will.

I spoke with a Maria Fernanda Duque from H&M Studios in Colombia. I asked Maria why she thought the country was a hub of the camming industry. She said:

> In Colombia . . . [the] main reason is the investment that a model needs to do in order to have a good transmission technology: a modern PC, lights, fiber optics, furniture, training, and so on. Not all the models have the money; so they start in a studio to get money and then work at their home. Finally, not all the models want to work on their houses because they need the discipline of a studio.

Maria and I also discussed how studios support models who do not speak English well or at all. Again, given the importance of embodied authenticity and cam models' ability to engage in conversation with clients, models who do not speak English are at a significant disadvantage. Maria told me:

> Speaking English is a powerful tool for the models because they can communicate easily with customers and understand a lot of information that the pages provide to them. We have a person who's always helping the models in case they don't understand something, they also have a translate tool on the computers, and in our specific case we have a professional teacher who teaches them specific things they can use on their shows and life.

Studios provide cam models with English lessons and have staff onsite to assist models with translation. Without these services, it is hard for many models to compete. While there are clients who only seek quick sexual performances, most clients are also seeking conversation. Studios train cam models in the art of effective communication.

Figure 3.4. Glamour Studio in Romania. In this advertisement, a woman with red hair is kneeling on a bed. Wearing a corset with spaghetti straps and black panties, she smiles while playing with the heel of one of her stilettos.

Figure 3.5. Glamour Studio in Romania, sample model room. This cam room features a twin bed with four large white pillows and two smaller embroidered throw pillows.

Figure 3.6. Glamour Studio in Romania, sample model room. This extravagant cam room features a large circular bed with green velvet throw pillows. There is also a white pedestal bathtub in the room.

Figure 3.7. Glamour Studio in Romania, sample model room. This cam room features a large bed with a gold-trimmed headboard. There is also a beige chaise longe chair in the room.

Figure 3.8. Glamour Studio in Romania, sample model room. This cam room features a large bed with beige and white linens. There is a large mirror on the right-hand wall; the image of the bed can be seen in the mirror.

I interviewed Qanadilo Bashir, the owner of Glamour Studio in Bucharest, Romania. There are thousands of cam studios in the country. Bashir told me that some are fronts for prostitution, which is illegal in Romania. This reality makes operation harder for operations like Glamour that are strictly cam studios—one of the top three in the country, as a matter of fact. Glamour launched in 2008 and by 2017 it commanded a 2,000-square-foot workplace with more than 30 rooms to host cam models and each room is approximately 30 square feet. The studio employs only solo cis women.

The studio offers many services to the cam models it employs. Bashir said the studio sends models on free trips and will pay for plastic surgery such as lip injections, rhinoplasty, and breast augmentation. I talked with Bashir about cam models in Romania. He said:

Romania is a beautiful country, but the salary is very low and as a student, [for example, many women] can't afford to pay a rent, university and to

try to have some fun. After the revolution in 1989, Romania is a big consumer of . . . everything new. . . . If you work normally in a company you
may get $350 per month, while in the cam industry you can make $1,000
in a day if you know how to sell. That's why we have ten trainers to teach
the girls, to guide them, to show them how the money comes, [and] how
to talk with the members, how to treat them, and how to listen to them.

We also talked about the difficulty many models from Romania have
competing in a market dominated by English-speaking consumers.
Bashir continued:

English has a big role in the industry, probably the most important asset.
If you speak perfect English, you can make a lot of money. We had a lot of
girls, with breast implants, lips implants looking like Barbie but their English
was not so good. So a spending member doesn't want only the naked girl;
they want to chat, they want to feel that someone is listening to them. So,
without English [it] is very hard. We had normal girls with good pronuncia-
tion and they stayed in [the] top three on a lot of websites. Nowadays, we
have a problem with new models. Five out of ten don't know English. The
new generation doesn't make school as we did. They don't know that English is the most important language in the world and you have to know it
like your parents. So, we have three teachers that teach them [English]. They
come [for] a month for free lessons and then they can start working. In a
month they see how we work, how is the team, managers, and so on. We are
dealing with a lot of girls that doesn't know the international language and
we try to do our best efforts to provide them the best training in all ways.

As Bashir noted, many Romanian models work for studios such as
Glamour in part because they provide English lessons. A model can
look like "Barbie" and fulfill US-centric normative ideals of beauty, but
if they cannot hold a conversation, they cannot fulfill the client demand
for intimacy. Bashir and I also discussed why Glamour employs only cis
women. Bashir said:

It's true that 98% of men models are visited by gay [men].[7] So, rarely you
see a woman in a man's model camera feed. There are a lot of studios that
have both man and girl models, but . . . in Romania pornography is not well

defined as a law and it's a little bit illegal to have sex online, like a couple if they don't have papers to attest that they're married or something . . . girls make 90% more money than boys do. Plus if they're a couple with no papers, as 95% of them [are], they have to split their money. Studio get[s] 50% of the income and then the others get the rest of 50%, so 25% plus 25%.

Bashir explained that hosting only cis women in the studio was more lucrative and was also safer as a business owner. As in other display industries, women dominate camming and earn more money than men (see chapter 7). Also, Bashir suggested that hosting male cam models at the studio might raise what sociologist C. J. Pascoe calls the "specter of the fag."[8] Bashir implied that, given the prevalence of homophobia in Romania, if people thought the studio was facilitating sexual encounters between men, Glamour might face sanctions. While he did not comment specifically about trans women, I suspect that given his other comments, he was also motivated by cissexism and transphobia in Romania in his decision to employ only cis women. In addition, given that prostitution is illegal in Romania, having couples perform from the studio could raise suspicions with law enforcement. These factors highlight the complex ways that the business decisions of sex entrepreneurs are affected by the actions of moral entrepreneurs and shaped by cultural context.

Online Studios

Many online studios, also called "agencies," purport to help models by providing training and support. Internet Modeling (IM), a well-known cam-modeling agency, took a percentage of their earnings, but did not do any promotion for them, according to models I spoke with. Leah, a 37-year-old straight White cis woman from the United States, told me, "I kind of think of studios like a pimp"—a sentiment shared by many models I spoke with. Others described online studios as scams that deceptively sign up new cam models who believe they are signing up for a cam site, when in fact the model is signing up to an online studio. In 2017, when I typed in "webcam modeling" in the Google search engine, IM's website was one of the first results to appear on the page.

People who are considering camming often begin by searching the Internet for information about the industry. Cam models who sign up for a cam site online without having done extensive research may be lured into an online studio. When I asked Rita, a 26-year-old straight Black cis woman from the United States, if she ever considered working for a studio, she said, "Oh no! Studios are scams. They take a huge chunk out of your money. So happy I did my research—I almost signed up for one." This is what in fact happened to Rachel and Robin. Rachel, a 36-year-old straight White trans woman from the United States, said:

> I started with Internet Modeling, which is a studio, and also a huge scam. They have their own internal camming service, but it's so rarely visited— traffic is nonexistent. They also sign you up for Big Box sites such as Streamate (which you can sign up for independently) and then take a cut of what is already a paltry amount of commission from that site. I would never recommend a studio unless it's a physical studio that provides all your equipment, etc. if you don't have the capability to purchase said equipment.

In an interview, Robin, a 40-year-old straight White cis woman from Canada, described how she also started with IM. Similar to Rachel, she told me:

> I signed up with Internet Modeling, not knowing, whatever. And didn't realize that they were also skimming off 5% of my already low 35% earned from Streamate. My Streamate was really busy when you first start. Like, extremely busy when you first start. So, I'm like, oh, why did it say I'm making this much, but I'm only getting this much.

As a result, Robin switched to another online studio, called Boleyn Models.

Boylen Models (BM) was the only online studio that received overwhelmingly positive reviews from models. BM was their favorite because it offers daily payouts. Lucia, a 22-year-old queer Hispanic cis woman from Spain, also switched from IM to BM because:

> I worked with Internet Modeling and it was horrible! They was taking so much money and they didn't help at all. Now, I am with the studio Boleyn Models because [it] is comfortable for me on the payments . . . because I can be paid everyday if I make at least $20. Also . . . they don't

take so much percentage. The token value on cam4 is 0.10 and working with them I earn 0.09. And on Chaturbate, the token is 5 cents and with them I earn 4.5 cents. So not bad at all!

Models such as Lucia use BM because the site gives them access to fast daily payments, has only a $20 minimum payout, and the service charge is very low. Chloe, a 25-year-old bisexual cis woman from France, told me, "I only recommend Boleyn Models as virtual studio. I use it as a payment processor mainly." BM caters to performers who need money quickly. Unlike IM, which purports to provide training and support, BM does support models by providing expedited payment processing. The increase of online studio agencies has been a part of the growth of the camming industry. As the camming industry continues to expand, there will likely be more sex entrepreneurs who will find ways to provide services to cam sites and cam models.

Cam Models

Cam models, like various other sex workers, are independent contractors. They log onto cam sites and Skype Private to work, but neither are legal workplaces. As independent contractors, cam models have no worker protections and no benefits. As Naomi said, "Sex work—I always joke, there's no dental plan!" We both chuckled when she said this during our interview, but it is crucial to recognize that as independent contractors cam models receive no benefits such as healthcare or retirement plans. They must set aside money on their own to pay taxes, which can be hard if a model needs their camming wages to pay bills and survive. Cam models also deal with frequent harassment from customers. They are not legally protected from discrimination or harassment because cam sites are not legal workplaces and, in general, they do not have the protections that some workers in non-erotic economies have. Of course, some models have worked in manufacturing and service markets around the world where they receive no protections or benefits at all. For those workers, the decent wages and autonomy in the camming industry are a welcome change from the deplorable working conditions they regularly endure.

As with all gig economies, an additional challenge of being an independent contractor is that wages can be sporadic and precarious. The structure of the camming market and overlapping systems of oppression condition the wages cam models earn. Mainstream articles about the camming industry and cam-site advertisements frequently say that cam models can earn wages as high as $10,000 a month. While wages this high occurred in my survey sample, they were infrequent. In my sample (though it is not representative), there were only 12 models who had ever earned $10,000 or more in a month—just 11%.[9] As shown in table 3.3, only 3 models out of 105 earned $10,000 a month. It is likely the case that advertisements which claim that cam models earn $10,000 a month are grossly misleading.

TABLE 3.3. Top Earners in the Survey Sample

Name	Age	Gender	Race	Nation of Origin	Sexual Identity	Primary Cam Site(s)	Years in Industry	*Top Monthly Income	*Average Monthly Income
Candice	23	Cis woman	Biracial	US	Bisexual	MFC	3	$10,000	$2,000
Alicia	32	Cis woman	White	Canada	Queer	MFC, SM	7	$54,000	$11,000
Quinn	25	Cis woman	White	US	Bisexual	MFC, CB	5	$50,000	$5,000
Missy	27	Cis woman	White	US	Bisexual	CB, SM, Naked/Camster	1	$13,000	$4,500
Allison	20	Cis woman	White	US	Bisexual	MFC, CB, SP	1	$10,000	$6,000
Rebecca	34	Cis woman	White	US	Poly-amorous	SM, Naked, MFC, Cams	7.5	$12,000	$7,000
Tanya	27	Cis woman	White	US	Poly-amorous	MFC, Cams SM, IM, BC RealTouch	8.5	$25,000	$10,000
Lucille	36	Cis woman	White	US	Straight	NF, JB	3	$10,000	$2,000
Anca	31	Cis woman	White	Romania	Straight	SM, LJ, F4F, IF, IM	11	$16,000	$5,000
Marissa	29	Cis woman	White	US	Straight	CB, SP +**	3	$10,000	$4,000
Taryn	26	Cis woman	White	US	Straight	MFC	4	$18,000	$10,000
Lukas	21	Cis man	White	Germany	Straight	CB, CS	2.5	$10,000	$3,000

*All amounts are presented in USD.
**Model indicated, "I am on way too many to name niteflirt cammodeldirectory talktome, Skype Private chaturbate etc. They are all good in different ways."

Cam modeling is hard work, and it often takes over a year to build a following and to make large amounts of money. Building a successful brand requires active marketing on social media and building social capital in what cam models call "the camily" (the camming community). Most cam sites give performers who are just starting out a "new model" status that publicly displays their thumbnail picture prominently on the webpage. When new models start working, customers are signaled. The "new model" status increases their visibility on the cam site, which has a positive effect on their wages. Once the "new model effect" wears off, models are often surprised because their thumbnail picture is now only one among a sea of a thousand models' pictures. It often takes cam models months to begin to figure out what shows earn them money, which clients they appeal to, what types of shows/sexual acts they are willing to perform, and how to perform those shows effectively.

As table 3.3 shows, of all the models in the sample who have earned $10,000 in any month camming, there was not one who had been camming for less than a year. Alicia once earned $54,000 in one month and averages $11,000 a month; she has been camming for seven years. Quinn, who one month earned $50,000 and averages $5,000 a month, has cammed for five years. Tanya once earned $25,000 in a month and usually makes $10,000 a month; she has worked as a cam model for over eight years. Anca, who once earned $16,000 in a month and averages $5,000 a month, has been working in the camming field for 11 years. The point is, extremely high wages occurred but disproportionately went to full-time cam models who have worked in the industry for long periods of time and who labored incredibly hard to build popular brands. In addition, none of the models in the top-earning cohort of the sample worked for studios.

Almost all the models who earned the highest wages cammed on multiple cam sites. Only two models cammed exclusively on one site—in both cases, MFC. In addition, seven of these 12 cam models worked on MFC in addition to other sites. Quinn, who used MFC as her primary site, explained her rationale for this strategy:

> Flirt4Free was my first site because it advertised heavy model support, and I didn't know what I was doing. MFC has [the] highest earning potential, and Chaturbate has high traffic. I would use MFC regularly for income, and then cam on Chaturbate occasionally to get waves of exposure to social media.

The models in the highest-earning category suggested that strategically working on multiple cam sites has helped them to be successful.

While cam models can be successful working on various cam sites, working on MFC may create the greatest opportunity to earn top wages in a low-pressure environment. Consider what Alicia told me:

> MyFreeCams has higher income potential and is more social. Streamate is more financially consistent but less high-income potential. Streamate is more transactional and doesn't foster a community environment, so members/clients/customers are more likely to treat camgirls as a sex doll—in an objectifying way. On MFC, I still am objectified, but I have more ability to control the way I present myself and create a dialogue about my own sexual interests. On MFC, what is most profitable is creating a community vibe in a room and making members feel important; on Streamate, what is most profitable is being highly sexual.

As Alicia and other cam models said, MFC is "more social" than many other sites, meaning that models engaged in more conversation with clients on MFC. They suggested that working on cam sites such as SM and CB required more frequent explicitly sexual activity. Good wages can be earned on almost all cam sites, but the labor performed and the models' experience will be qualitatively different based on the sites the model performs on and the models' embodiment. Some cam models who were not thin, White, 20-something cis women from the United States did earn high wages (even if not in the top 1%). To earn such wages, models whose embodiments did not adhere to US-centric idealized notions of beauty described engaging in strategic branding and crafting shows differently than their thin, White, 20-something cis female counterparts from the United States.

Candice's comments to me were similar to Alicia's, but she added another important layer to the analysis:

> I like MFC because it's just what I know, but there are a lot of issues other girls have on the site . . . there is a huge diversity problem. Most guys who can tip a lot of tokens only want to see young White girls.

Candice identifies as biracial and is light-skinned. The "diversity problem" was not one she experienced. Colorism is an essential factor that shapes the success of cam models. The system of colorism that results from the system of global White supremacy privileges light-skinned cam models and disadvantages dark-skinned cam models. Candice's remarks also underscored the importance of intersectional analyses in examining workplace outcomes. Her success was influenced by her talent, but her high wages were also a reflection of the fact that she cams on MFC and of her embodiment and subjectivity.

While this sample of cam models is too small to support broad generalizations about the entire market, it is suggestive that in this cohort of top-earning models, 11 of the 12 were cis women. There were no trans women and only one cis man. Only one of these models, Candice, was a person of color. Of the 12 top-earners models, ten identified their nationality to me as "American" (US). Furthermore, the one cis man in the group, Lukas, identified his nationality to me as German, but he too now lives in the United States. Anca was the only top-earning cam model who lived outside of the United States. In addition, eight of the 12 cam models were in their 20s, and the other four were in their 30s. Finally, only one of these models, Lucille, cammed on a BBW (big beautiful women) cam site. This group of high earning cam-models was diverse in just one area—sexual identity. Overall, relatively thin White cis women in their 20s from the United States were overrepresented in this sample of top-income-earning cam models.

Many workers in the industry may never earn $10,000 a month, but for marginalized people, camming does create better alternatives to the low wages and often discriminatory workplaces they have access to in the nonsexual labor market. Many cam models work part-time and use camming to supplement income from other full-time and part-time jobs. In my study, the median earned wage was $1,000 a month.[10] For cam models in many countries in the world, $1,000 is more than they'd make at any of the jobs available to them. An extra $1,000 month can help families in nonsocialist democracies acquire healthcare. These wages can help people pay rent, pay tuition, afford groceries, pay off debt, and so on. The wages earned camming allow people to take a vacation, to go out to dinner, and have a little extra money for leisure.

While the money people earn camming can help them survive and breathe easier, cam models' wages are not just a reflection of hard work and ingenuity. Median monthly earnings for trans women were $1,000, cis women averaged $1,250, and cis men earned $350. People from outside of the United Kingdom, Canada, and the United States had lower median wages than people from those three countries. Cam models' identities affected both their experiences camming and their wages. Far from a feminist, queer, or economic utopia, the camming industry provided decent wages to workers in the sample, but the industry operates via and reproduces the same inequities that exist in any capitalist workplace.

Conclusion

The contemporary camming market has grown exponentially. It is essential we ask: How will the continued growth of the camming industry affect workers? How will market saturation affect the camming market? When any capitalist market is saturated with workers, overall wages tend to go down. Performers that I spoke with who had been in the industry for long periods helped me gauge the impact of market saturation on workers. Luiza, a 32-year-old straight White cis woman from Brazil, has been camming off and on for 14 years. She said, "Back in the day—in the past, it was so much easier to get money . . . and [now] there are lots of girls because of recession[s] . . . all over the world; so, there are more girls trying to live." While the camming industry has helped workers all over the world "live," as more workers turn on their webcams competition will increase.

Andres, a 20-year-old pansexual Hispanic cis man from Colombia, highlighted the neoliberal idea that market saturation will force cam models to work harder:

> That phenomena [market saturation] actually pushes everyone to be better. And well, if first there were a hundred web cam models, and now there are tens of thousands, then you got to put up a better show to attract those clients. And you gotta be more creative. For instance, when I started camming . . . you used to see a couple of HD broadcasts. . . . Now most of the broadcasts are being broadcast in HD, and some of them are broadcast in 4K and 2K [resolutions], and that's because we need to . . . keep innovating in order to keep being relevant. So, I think that's both a negative and positive in that respect and that's something you just cannot stop.

While Luiza told me market saturation had a direct effect on her wages over time, Andres argued that the influx of cam performers has improved the quality of the services delivered in the industry. The increased market competition requires that performers innovate to remain "relevant." The "positives" that Andres outlined were benefits for sex entrepreneurs and clients. Market saturation means cam models must work harder and spend more money on their brands. Thus, while increased market competition has significant benefits for sex entrepreneurs, market saturation will lead to decreased wages for many workers, an increase in the amount of labor performed, and qualitative changes in workers' experiences of labor.

Amelia, a 29-year-old straight White cis woman from England, reflected on the current camming market and why she had recently taken a break from camming:

> [There are] just so many girls. . . . And . . . I think they were just doing more and more crazy things. Like people were breaking more and more rules . . . urination, like water sports [and] types of things that they weren't supposed to do. . . . Like you have girls in public libraries . . . using the free WiFi to masturbate and like you can't really compete with that. So, it was getting to be so ridiculous. So, I was like, I wasn't making as much on there anymore, and I thought, I'm gonna take a break from this until they start making the rules a bit more strict again.

Amelia highlighted that increased competition not only generates more creativity from models, as Andres said, but forces them to perform "crazy things." Increased competition requires that models design and craft shows that can set them apart. It is plausible that cam models will engage in sex acts that make them uncomfortable, or that do not bring them pleasure, in order to remain competitive. For Amelia, she'd rather take a break than perform acts that are degrading to her or are illegal. Some models may not have the economic privilege to cease working during these ebbs and flows, which could mean they may need to charge lower prices and/or perform in ways that they'd rather not. Market saturation can lead to models' having less agency, experiencing less pleasure, and earning lower wages.

Due to market saturation, some cam models may seek out work in other burgeoning online sex industries such as sugarbabying. Sugarbabying involves women finding men online willing to pay for their living expenses and luxury goods and services in exchange for emotional labor.[11] Unlike escorting, these arrangements do not (usually) involve sexual relationships—sugarbabying provides a girlfriend experience minus the sex. Websites such as SeekingArrangement and Sugardaddie.com have emerged to facilitate these relationships.

Adeline explained that she was pulling away from camming and was currently

> [m]ostly sugarbabying. But that's kind of what I'm mostly doing lately, that's why I don't cam as much and stuff. . . . I kind of like sugarbabying more because it's a guaranteed income and it's usually less work and, if I like the person, it's almost—it's like another relationship to be in.

My research suggests that the Internet has expanded and helped diversify forms of sex work. Like camming, the sugarbabying trend raises interesting questions about how the digital age is transforming our understanding of what constitutes sex work. Is sugarbabying sex work? Do sugarbabies identify as sex workers? Given that the Internet can facilitate these commercial relationships online, and that these jobs require no physical contact, just like camming, these conditions will have mass appeal to those who desire work that provides access to decent wages, autonomy, less and easier labor, and pleasure.

4

Global Motivations to Cam

Challenging Alienation and Recapturing Pleasure in Work

The sex workers rights organization Call Off Your Old Tired Ethics has said that 85% of prostitution is voluntary.[1] Despite this reality, stories of sex trafficking are pervasive, and the mainstream news media inundate us with stories and images of young children, usually girls, who are forced to sell sex by ruthless pimps. No human should be forced into sex work, and governments and NGOs should work collectively to stop forced sexual labor. The mainstream focus on trafficking is misleading, however, because it ignores that most sex work is voluntary. Journalists and politicians only exacerbate the stigma that sex workers face by creating moral and sex panics through sensationalistic news coverage and paternalistic governmental policies.

Anthropologist Laura Agustín argues that the "rescue industry," which is composed of a range of anti-trafficking activists, politicians, and social service agencies, misses the crucial point that many sex workers have no desire to be saved.[2] Many do not see themselves as victims. People around the world make rational choices to sell and trade sexual services. By casting all sex workers as victims, the rescue industry deprives sex workers, particularly poor migrant workers, of dignity, power, and agency. While I do not doubt that there likely are cam models performing in studios who are forced into camming by traffickers, this topic is not the focus of this book because most cam performers are selling sex online voluntarily. Advocates and activists should investigate the small population of cam performers who may be working in cam studios against their will, but again, this help must come in ways that genuinely aid people who want and need help—not in ways that satisfy moral, political, and economic actors whose motivating interest is in social control.

When agents of the rescue industry recognize sex work as voluntary, they perpetuate discourses that depict sex workers as pathological—

either too sick from past trauma, too strung out, or just too lazy to find legitimate labor. My respondents said these were discourses they hoped my work would address. I ended all my interviews by asking performers what they thought was the most crucial thing readers should know about the camming industry. Most said something about wanting to transform public perceptions of camming and sex work more broadly. Naomi is a 38-year-old queer White trans woman who cams and escorts. She told me that people need to understand better the complex economic and social reasons people choose sex work and that her motivation, like that of so many others selling sex, is not rooted in pathology:

> I'm not doing it 'cause daddy hit me [sarcastic and chuckling]. I'm not doing it 'cause momma didn't love me . . . because of trauma or because of alcoholism or because of other past traumatic experience. . . . I'm not strung out on anything . . . and even if I was, if I did have addictions, that wouldn't be why I'm in sex work. It's just an old stereotype of, oh, she just needs to feed her habit.

Framing motivations for sex work as driven by pathology is a convenient political strategy that absolves societies from remedying the broken social institutions that play a significant role in shaping motivations for participation in erotic labor. By framing the choice to perform sex work as motivated by pathology, the rescue industry also ignores the ways that various overlapping systems of oppression, including neoliberal capitalism, White supremacy, patriarchy, heterosexism, cissexism, and ableism, shape entry into the field.

Decades of sex work research and sex work activism have shown that sex workers are motivated not by pathologies but rather that people trade sex because they desire decent wages.[3] Carol Leigh, also known as Scarlet the Harlot, coined the term "sex worker" in 1978. Sex workers are service professionals who perform erotic labor in a highly competitive capitalist marketplace. Traditionally, sex work, especially street-based sex work, such as prostitution, has appealed most to populations of people who have been historically and systemically deprived of access to the resources they need to survive and live comfortably. However, what I learned from cam models was that the motivations to cam were far more complex than just needing to find stable employment.

As an example to highlight the complexity of people's motivations to cam, I turn to Liam, a 24-year-old gay White cis man from Canada. He explained all of the overlapping reasons why he began to cam:

I did need to make money. After trying out webcamming, I realized I could make a fair amount of money in a short period of time. I can make anywhere from 50 dollars to 150 dollars for one show, which usually doesn't last longer than 1 [to] 2 hours. A waged job in my city on average would offer less than this for a full day's work. Working this way allowed me to stay in control of my time, which is important to me. I began web-camming regularly after art school. I had worked hard in school, and was being offered many opportunities to continue my art career, but I did not have the money to support these. If I took a regular job, I would need to trade my time and miss out on opportunities in front of me. I decided that maintaining control over my time and being able to make money while travelling were priorities in this stage of my development. So, web-camming was a practical solution. I also justify webcamming, by saying that it is also for the experience, in its uniqueness and its contemporane-ity. I grew up in the time of "manhunt" and "Grindr" and other online platforms. Most of my sexual exploration was online since the beginning. Performing on webcam was in some ways a progression from the sexual persona I developed as part of my coming out on Grindr, Facebook, and messaging local and Internet boyfriends. It was a creative challenge, to embody and perform a side of myself I had previously only developed through text and images and surprisingly used a lot of the skills I devel-oped in art school [such as] lighting, camera angles, fashion, sometimes even sound tracks and set-design. I considered a lot of these things when I first started out. I am also a person interested in questioning the es-tablished way of things and interested in how technology is being used to explore new sides of people and relationships. Webcamming, when I started, seemed like an extreme example of that. Though it doesn't seem so extreme to me anymore.

Liam suggests that he started camming for money, but again, recog-nizing why he needed money is an integral part of understanding the motivation to cam. In considering camming, Liam realized he could earn a living wage working very short periods of time. Liam wants to

Figure 4.1. Elizabeth in front of her computer. Wearing a long blue wig that hangs down to her cleavage, she holds a mug in front of her face that reads, "If we all work together we can totally disrupt the system."

have time to travel and create art. Camming allows him to do that. He also described how camming was an extension of an online persona he developed in online gay social networks such as Grindr. Camming allows him to explore his sexuality. Selling sex online opens up new opportunities for human intimacy, sexual encounters, and sexual pleasure. Finally, as Liam noted, camming can be a way to challenge "the established way of things"—to crack various oppressive social systems.

In *Crack Capitalism*, John Holloway proposes that workers can challenge capitalism in quotidian ways that have the potential to cause fissures in the system.[4] Holloway uses the metaphor of a lake to explain this thesis. Picture a lake that becomes frozen. As workers refuse to work or make minute challenges to capitalist labor practices, cracks begin to appear in that lake. Now, these challenges in no way cause all the ice to melt, nor do they dismantle capitalism, but they do help the worker to feel dignity again. Those cracks not sustained through constant political agitation will likely refreeze. Cracking capitalism is thus not a political movement to destroy capitalism. Instead, attempts at cracking capitalism are individualized efforts to resist alienation. Here, I argue that cam performers' work creates such fissures. They work within the logic of capitalism not to challenge the system itself, but to challenge the alienation they experience and recapture the experience of pleasure in work.

Global Motivations to Cam

The desire for decent wages motivates most webcam performers. It is the failures of global capitalism and capitalist industries to provide workers living wages that drive people to cam. Martina, a 27-year-old bisexual White cis woman from Spain, explained that she needed money and job security: "In Spain everybody is afraid to lose their jobs because we haven't recovered from the [economic] crisis." Martina's comments underscore the importance of place and geography in conditioning economic motivations. Aron, a 31-year-old bi-curious Hungarian White cis man, similarly noted:

> [M]oney was a huge issue because, ya know, the average job in Hungary pays around less than $1,000 a month. If you're working in retail, you make $400 a month. . . . And then you turn on your webcam, and you can make thousands of dollars, from home, with a few hours a day, so there's a huge difference.

Aron explained that he can earn more money camming than he can working in other service professions in Hungary.

For people already engaged in sex work, camming is an additional stream of income and can help them expand their existing brands. Especially in countries where prostitution is legal, camming helps certain sex workers market escorting services. Lenny, a 34-year-old polyamorous Black cis man from the United Kingdom, said:

> I created an online persona, a profile for the purpose of offering escort services, selling homemade porn video clips, and an additional feature is

webcamming, which I utilise by creating live sex shows to replicate what customers could experience during escort meetings face-to-face.

For cam performers like Lenny, camming is a mechanism to promote his escorting business, but his motivation to cam is financial.

There are also performers who began camming because of a specific incident that caused them to need money quickly. Sofia, a 22-year-old White Greek cis woman living in the United States who chose not to disclose her sexual identity, said, "I was in a major auto accident, and I had to pay bills. The doctor wasn't going to sign off on me working at my regular job. I decided that [camming] is a route for me." For many working-class people like Sofia, the costs associated with both auto and health insurance can be crippling, especially in countries without universal healthcare. One accident can send someone into a spiral of debt; camming offers a way out. Bridget, a 29-year-old straight White Scottish cis woman, said she began camming not only to "have a better quality of life with extra income, and because it's fun," but "to pay off debts."

Among survey respondents, 56.2% said money was not their only motivation to cam. Even performers who did begin solely out of economic necessity or for supplemental income often noted that there are other motivations to cam. Gia, a 26-year-old queer White trans woman, said, "I had started to [cam] out of necessity, but as I got better at producing, it became something I love doing." Like Gia, other participants in my study also expressed a desire to find work that is not mundane, is exciting, fun, pleasurable, and flexible, and is accommodating to the complexity of their lives and needs, as well as paying decent wages.

Economically determinist theories of motivation for entry into sex work are a much-needed corrective to the discourses of trafficking and psychological theories. However, even economically determinist theories are limited. It is crucial that scholars examine what people need money to purchase. Various costs of living have increased dramatically, while wages have largely failed to keep pace. Consider, for example, the following stories about the cost of education in nonsocialist democracies and how the market demand for college degrees in industrialized nations is a factor in why some people choose to cam.

Education Costs

Camming provides decent wages to college students, but what is crucial is that cam performers do not have to work long hours. In most cases, performers told me they made more money camming in far fewer hours than in other jobs they've held. This situation is perfect for working- and middle-class college students who often struggle to balance work and school. When I asked about motivations for camming, Kaya, a 23-year-old straight Black cis woman from England, told me:

> It was primarily income and being able to work from home/my own hours, especially as I'm a student, so it balanced perfectly. It's hard being able to juggle studying and bringing in a decent income; plus this way on AdultWork in particular, I can study and cam at the same time, when the room is quiet.

Many performers shared similar stories with me. Allison, a 20-year-old bisexual White cis woman from the United States, said what a "great gig" camming is for college students. This sentiment was especially prevalent among performers whose identities also compounded their financial concerns. Jen is a 25-year-old bisexual White cis woman from the United States whose comments also demonstrate the importance of thinking about global motivations to cam intersectionally. She explained:

> As someone who is in school, and also has struggled with both mental (anxiety and depression) and physical issues, being able to work when I feel able and take time off when I'm not has been priceless. Weeks that I have multiple tests, I can scale work back. Coming from more team-based work environments, it can be really nice to take a sick day without feeling like you're letting your team down or making someone else pick up your slack. The money, too, is an obvious draw. It's entirely in the realm of possibility to have a good day and make more in that one day than I was in a week working retail.

Jen is a person with disabilities and we discussed how camming allows her to manage her coursework effectively. The accommodations schools and employers make for people with disabilities are often limited.

Students' class backgrounds, races, nationalities, genders, sexual identities, ages, and abilities all shape access to and experiences within institutions of higher learning.

Concerns about money, the cost of education, and debt were among the most salient variables in my discussions with college students who cam. Crista, a 27-year-old polyamorous White cis woman from the United States, echoed Alison's and Jen's remarks. She said, "I just kind of wanted more freedom; and I wanted to be able to go to school, and I wanted to be able to pay for things and, like, not put myself in debt— that's the main reason, but also, it just seemed like I could work less and make more." People around the world who have the privilege of attending college often do so at high costs. Cam models' comments also point to the education and student loan crisis as a structural problem for which camming offers a solution.

Childcare Costs

Childcare costs are another example of the structural forces that shape the motivations for entering into the camming field. Many parents, especially mothers, find it hard to balance work and parenting. Depending on one's location in the world, the costs of childcare can be exorbitant. In many industrialized societies, working mothers are required to perform the second shift—that is, once they've come home from their jobs, they still must do housework and are primarily responsible for childrearing activities.[5] Moreover, poor women may be doing a third or fourth shift because they are working multiple low-wage jobs just to get by. Camming provides flexibility for many working mothers. For decades, the mainstream press published stories about how women can have it all— the career and the family—and all it requires is that they learn how to balance work and family strategically. Here is the problem: the work/ family balance narrative is a lie. There can be no balance under patriarchy and capitalism. Period. It is no surprise that not one of the men in my survey sample or on the web forums I examined discussed flexible parenting as a motivation to cam.

For the mothers I spoke with, they cam because it enables them to be more available parents. Elizabeth, a 38-year-old bisexual White cis woman from the United States, asked rhetorically:

Why didn't I do this sooner? I make in ten hours what I would've made working 40 [hours] slaving my ass off, begging for time off to go see my kid's Christmas concert. Like, why the fuck-why? Right? . . . And it's funny because a lot people would look at me as, oh, she's a bad mother—she's a sex worker. It's like, are you kidding me? I'm doing this for my family!

Many cam performers who are also parents were drawn to camming so that they could be better parents. Camming allows many parents to make money while having more time to spend with their children and save money on childcare expenses. Erica, a 28-year-old White polyamorous cis woman from the United States, said she began camming for "flexibility and money." She continued:

I can spend time with my kids during the day and work at night (2–4hrs) and make very good money without childcare expenses and commuting costs. I am also my own boss, which is important to me since I am in control of what I do, don't do, and how I choose to work and conduct myself.

Mindy, a 46-year-old straight White cis woman from the United States, similarly said her primary motivation for choosing to cam was that she "was able to work without paying for childcare." Taryn, a 26-year-old straight White cis woman from the United States, said, "I chose camming because it was something I could do while staying home with my kids and not sending them off to daycare to work a 9–5 and barely get by." The mothers I spoke with all highlighted that they wanted to be more available to their children and save money on childcare services.

Some mothers must choose work based on location. Specifically, selecting a job that is close to home is crucial because it allows them to be close to their children's school in case of an emergency. This proximity is also essential because long commutes can require that parents pay for childcare for hours before and after the regular school day. Such situations are even harder for individuals who depend on (and are lucky enough to have access to) public transportation.

Robin is a 40-year-old straight White cis woman from Canada. She said, "We live in a very rural area; there aren't a lot of jobs unless you want to work night and weekends. With children, one vehicle and living far from town, this wasn't an option." She continued:

I started because the small little place I live in Canada has no jobs! So, it was either go out and work nights and weekends, and I have a nine-year-old and a 13-year-old now; but four years ago, they were much younger and [I was] paying for afterschool. . . . I would've been paying more out [than] I would have been getting in.

Robin, like the other parents above, had trouble finding work near her home, and, as with so many working-class parents, childcare costs were higher than what she could plausibly earn. Unemployment in such circumstances is thus an outgrowth of an economic system that pays workers low wages and yet expects those same workers to pay for expensive services so that they can work. High childcare costs disincentivize work. Robin enthusiastically told me how she believes camming solves this all-too-familiar problem for working mothers:

This is the most amazing, rewarding, make-you-feel-good job. It would be perfect for the single mom that has kids in school and can't find a job. . . . I mean, it would be an excellent choice for so many. There's so many people, so many women, particularly where I live, they're on welfare because they have kids at home or they can't get a job. And ya know, if you can, you can pick what you want to show to people, too. . . . Do what you're comfortable with and go from there and really, hey, I get to have fun and play with myself.

Camming allows workers to work around their family's schedule, instead of asking their families to live around their work schedules. Robin describes both the freedom she acquires camming and the actual labor as fun. She gets to be a better parent and enjoy her work—that is pleasurable.

These stories demonstrate that people choose to cam not only because they need money. Economically determinist theories of motivations to perform sex work are reductive, often failing to explore the structural conditions related to education, housing, healthcare, and so on that push people into sex work. Yes, people trade sex because they need money, but they need money because in far too many countries throughout the world capitalism constrains people's access to every resource they need to live and survive. Additionally, another limitation of economically determinist theories of sex work participation is that many such analyses of why individuals choose to perform sex work do not take an intersectional perspective. People trade sex because they face marginalization under various overlapping systems of inequality.

It's Complicated: Intersectional Perspectives on Workplace Motivations

Trans women face multiple forms of discrimination in the economy and society at large and as a result were the group most likely to begin camming purely out of economic necessity. Given this, I use their stories to highlight the importance of combining intersectional analysis with economically determinist theories of sex work market participation. According to the 2016 National Transgender Discrimination Survey (NTDS), 26% of trans people have lost a job due to discrimination, and 50% of respondents reported being harassed on the job. Per the NTDS, trans people were almost four times more likely than cis people to have a household income of less than $10,000 and live in extreme poverty. For these reasons, some trans people turn to trading sex in deplorable working conditions.[6] The conditions of labor in street-based sex work are often incredibly dangerous, especially for trans women and even more so for trans women of color. Jimena, a 33-year-old gay Hispanic trans woman from Colombia, told me that a primary motivation to cam was that, unlike escorting, there is "no physical contact with any client." Bodily autonomy is important, especially for people whose bodies are already vulnerable. Overall, camming provides a relatively stable source of income in a safe environment for people who face rampant and legally sanctioned discrimination in the economy, as well as in other institutions.

Michelle is a 21-year-old straight White trans woman from the United States. When I asked her why she started to cam, she said, "I have a learning disability that prevents me from doing well in conventional settings, and good paying jobs for trans girls are hard to find." As Michelle's case highlights, employment discrimination most often results from overlapping forms of oppression and is always conditioned by context or location. As another example, Rachel is a 36-year-old straight White trans woman, also from the United States:

> As a trans girl from the South and in a rural area . . . I found it hard to find any kind of work. . . . I was let go from my position as a supervisor at a marketing research firm because the company decided they wanted to go in a more "family-oriented" direction, and a trans woman in a supervisory position was not part of their vision. I have always been a highly sexual person, and, honestly, it was a last-ditch attempt at making some sort of income that turned into the best career for me.

Natalie, a 26-year-old demi/asexual poly-romantic White trans woman from the United States, told me, "[I]n my state, it's hard to find full-time work even at a fast food place as a full-time trans female who is pre-op and not on hormone replacement therapy." Note, both Rachel and Natalie also link their experiences of discrimination to location. Their stories also speak to the vast differences trans women face in labor based on their embodiment.

Embodiment and Economic Marginalization

Examining worker embodiment and its relationship to economic marginalization is essential to fully understand why people choose to enter the camming industry. Marginalization occurs because employers (and other institutions) see specific embodiments as not productive—certain bodies have little to no value to capitalist production. To provide examples of people whose marginalization prompted them to cam, I turn to several cam performers with mental health conditions, chronic health issues, and disabilities. These performers explained that their bodies often bar them from traditional employment because most capitalist workplaces are not supportive of workers with these health profiles. Kim, a 33-year-old straight White cis woman from the United States, explained that camming is "easier to work with my bipolar disorder." People with a range of mental health profiles often require work that is flexible. People with chronic illness, like Amelia, want to work. However, her Crohn's disease often makes it difficult, if not impossible, to follow a rigid work schedule. Amelia, a 29-year-old straight White cis woman from England, explained her reasons for entering the camming industry:

I had no other options. I have Crohn's and was unable to hold down a regular job. I didn't have a degree [and] I dropped out of college due to the disease. My parents had no money, and I felt guilty asking them for help. So I decided to research ways to earn money from home. This worked well.

In our interview, I asked Amelia to tell me more about working with Crohn's disease. She explained:

I used to work in a call center before I started working as a cam model. And I was kind of forced to resign because they were just getting fed up with me having to take time out for hospital appointments. Ya know, with Crohn's, you can't have surgery; you have to have a lot of treatments to get yourself into remission, and they just weren't very understanding about it. And it got to the point where I was, like, I'm going to have all these gaps in my employment. It's going to be really difficult to explain to future employers. Do I really want them to know my health history, 'cause that's probably going to prevent me from getting hired . . . and I thought, what am I gonna do? So, I began thinking about things you could work from home, and most of them were just pyramid schemes. So it was just sell makeup, sell whatever, or vitamin supplements, and I just thought, I can't do that. I can't actually make any of that work—these pyramid schemes.

People with chronic illness face myriad career barriers.[7] Chronic illness can lead to gaps in employment history, and most capitalist industries value steady employment history. Amelia also highlighted the problems with other available work-from-home jobs. Many such jobs involve highly gendered, low-wage, precarious, network-marketing sales of products from companies such as Avon and Pampered Chef. These multilevel-marketing companies require consultants to purchase inventory and supplies to do presentations and demonstrations. In many at-home sales jobs, workers still report to network managers. Camming is an excellent option for people with chronic illness, and the industry does not involve pyramid-structured network-marketing sales, which have high rates of individual failure.[8]

Crucially, many people with disabilities are also highly motivated to work, yet because society marginalizes them they often cannot find employment. Whitney, a 28-year-old bisexual White cis woman from the United States, explained what it has been like living with spinal muscular atrophy:

> I have a physical disability . . . and had recently moved from the city to the rural area where I currently live. I wasn't working, and, honestly, I spent a lot of time at home bored and lonely. I started posting nudes on a social site and fell in love. I can remember being younger, watching porn, and thinking no one would want to see *me* doing that. They'll immediately know I'm disabled, and there's nothing sexy about that, even though it was the only career I could see myself enjoying. With the support of my husband, I started camming. People did want to see me, and I really did love it.

Accounting for how workers' intersectional identities influence their motivations to choose sex work is essential. This finding is relevant not only to scholars of sex work. People's motivations to choose any job are a reflection of their identities and embodiments, and labor scholars must always employ intersectional analyses in their examinations of job choice.

Challenging Alienation

Cam performers, like so many other workers in a range of markets, do not want to feel alienated.[9] Many workers are sick of feeling like employers do not value their work or their lives. Halona, a 32-year-old queer Native American woman from the United States told me how camming compares with other jobs she has held:

> My [camming] schedule is very flexible, which is part of why it appeals to me. If I miss a shift because I'm in a garbage mood or am busy running errands around the city I live in, I don't get a call where I'm yelled at and made to feel guilty. Also, it's the job I feel least exploited for my labor. There are some weeks where I only have to work two hours because that one shift becomes so lucrative. At any other job I've worked, I have to give the majority of my waking hours to some unappreciative employer who

doesn't care that I'm struggling to pay my rent and bills, while he's going on random vacations all over the world.

Naomi and I also talked about how camming compares with other work she has done:

[Camming is] infinitely better than day jobs. Like, I'm not a schedule person. Like, the freedom of this, of any kind of sex work, is infinitely better than any day job I've ever had. . . . [S]ome people need that structure, that, like, knowing that they have a place to be every day. For me, the longer I'm in a day job, the more painful it gets. I just can't stand it.

Chloe, a 25-year-old bisexual White cis woman from France, said:

I have been harassed during job interviews and vanilla jobs too. I had to quit [non-sex work] to preserve my integrity. Webcamming allows me not to sell my soul or body, but just an illusion of what I am.

Carl, a 31-year-old bisexual Black cis man from the United States, told me:

The benefits of cam work [are] much the same as most independent jobs. You work at home on your own schedule, and avoid the 9-to-5 daily grind that makes most jobs a grind. You get to express your sexuality, and some creativity forming your sex cam show. Getting to masturbate for a paycheck is still pretty cool.

Audrey, a 24-year-old straight White cis woman from the United States, said:

I am not good with authority and as such have a hard time maintaining a regular job working under someone else and being told what to do and when to do it. I had an office job at the same time when I started camming, so I wasn't hurting for money; but I was unhappy with my vanilla work and wanted to pursue something more entrepreneurial and creative.

When people toil in jobs that provide them with low wages, no dignity, and no autonomy, work, as Naomi put it, is a painful experience.

While many options for workers now exist in the gig economy, which ostensibly provides access to decent wages and autonomy, there is a reason the folks in this book cam and don't drive for Uber or Lyft. As respondents said to me, name another job that pays you to dance, have orgasms, talk, laugh, and meet people from all over the world. As sociologist Elizabeth Bernstein points out, we are witnessing more middle-class, highly educated workers selling sex.[10] This is because workers are not merely seeking better wages, but also a resolution to various forms of alienation. By choosing to be cam models, people are trying to escape the drudgery of labor by working fewer hours, while making decent wages in safe, convenient, and boss-free working conditions. They are reconciling pleasure with work by going back to an older model of work that emphasizes craftsmanship, where the worker is connected to rather than alienated from the product and the labor process. As a result, instead of being miserable at work, cam models have a good time. Their stories cannot be reduced to false consciousness—they take charge of the product and process of labor rather than being subjected to it; they seek to restore their connection with their humanity, as well as their connections with peers. Thus, while their work cannot eliminate alienation—only the destruction of capitalism can do that—their work does challenge and resist alienation. In camming, workers feel like their humanity is restored. The result of this restorative process is pleasure.

Recapturing Pleasure in Work

Pleasure is a mode of self-exploration and a social experience through which we learn about our subjectivity and explore ourselves—our bodies, our spirits, and our humanity. The motivation to cam for many performers arises from the basic human desire for pleasure. While marginalized people and people in the most precarious social locations perform various forms of sex work out of economic necessity, the camming industry has created a space where people from various, often economically comfortable social locations feel safe to explore their sexual desires while making money. Many performers, especially cis men, in this study said that exhibitionism and a thirst for sexual pleasure led them to cam. Sexual needs and pleasure are underdeveloped themes in understanding the motivation for work in erotic labor. Carmen, a 19-year-old queer Black cis woman from the United States, said, "I became a camgirl in order to make money, yes, but also boost my self-confidence, and become more sex and body positive." Sex positivism is an essential motivation for sex work.

Developing sexual agency is another crucial motivation for selling sex online. For many sex-positive people, though, traditional forms of sex work are off-limits. The cost-benefit analysis proves too risky for many privileged people. Milena, a 28-year-old polyamorous German cis woman living in the United Kingdom, told me she was "interested in working in sex work but not the real-life experience." She continued, "I have a high interest in psychological and philosophical matters regarding fetishes and social interaction. I love dealing with people. For me, it's the adventure that I love." The porn industry is often hard to break into, and performing in strip clubs or working as an escort involves risks that many economically, politically, and socially privileged people are not willing to take. Meanwhile, cam models like Milena derive pleasure not just from the sex acts they perform but from the "adventure" they experience interacting with strangers from all over the world.

The camming industry is an exhibitionist's playground. Tanya, a 27-year-old polyamorous White cis woman from the United States, exemplified this position. She told me:

> As an exhibitionist, I found the idea of webcamming exciting when I started. In fact, I used to post nude photos on the net and chat with people for free before I started. When I found out I could make money doing what I was doing for free, it naturally made sense to pursue it as my career.

I communicated with many performers like Tanya who identified as exhibitionists and saw camming as an exciting opportunity to escape the monotony of work and the sexually constrained social life. Here's how Vanessa, a 34-year-old straight White cis woman from the United States, described why she began camming:

> To expand my sexual horizons [and] a bit of exhibitionism. . . . I was [already] giving away pics and videos to guys for free and felt used, so I could be doing the same for money. [I was also motivated by] a bit

of loneliness; I love to connect with guys from the safety of behind my computer screen; I've been on bad dates where I've felt threatened or was sexually taken advantage of.

It was typical for performers who identified as exhibitionists, like Tanya and Vanessa, to say that by camming they were getting paid for actions they were already performing. Vanessa's comments also highlighted that part of her motivation was a desire to interact with men sexually, but feeling increasingly unsafe to do so in her offline life. Sexual violence against women is pervasive, and camming allows sexually agentic women to explore their desires and acquire pleasure in a way that feels safe. Exhibitionism is a motivation to cam, while individual performers' life circumstances also shape that desire. Abigail, a 33-year-old bisexual Canadian cis woman, told me about how she started camming to satisfy her sexual desires, but that it was also a way to save her marriage. She opened up:

> I am an exhibitionist and crave attention. I used to cheat on my husband, emotionally and physically, because I craved the taboo attention so much. Camming, sexting/phone sex, and content making was our compromise. I get to have my online presence and talk to as many people as I want, as long as I only have sex with him.

Interestingly, Abigail and her husband do not see the sexual encounters she has with customers as "real" sex. The Internet creates a space where people see their online sexual encounters as substantively different from ones that occur offline. Many people see the consumption of virtual embodiment differently than they see the consumption of physical embodiment. In this case, drawing this distinction allowed for a compromise between Abigail and her husband, and Abigail is happy because she can use camming to explore her desires for sexual attention from others, and thus experience pleasure.

Tayna's, Vanessa's, and Abigail's perspectives were not marginal among participants in this study. Just listen to these male cam models:

> I found camming as a safe space to express and explore my sexuality.
> —Francisco, a 21-year-old queer Hispanic cis man from Mexico

I've always been intrigued by the world of adult webcam performers. I decided once to try in order to satisfy my curiosity and considered it as a funny way to get some extra cash.
—Alvaro, a 32-year-old straight White cis man from Spain

I wanted to experience my sexuality . . . getting extra money and learning more about my sexuality.
—Daniel, a 32-year-old straight White cis man originally from
  Spain and currently living in Poland

The webcam job helps me to fulfill my affection for exhibitionism. [I am] making money while exploring my sexuality.
—Gian, a 55-year-old straight White Swiss cis man living in Germany

I'm an exhibitionist. I enjoy camming. The money was an added benefit.
—Rick, a 27-year-old bisexual White cis man from the United States

I like to masturbate, and I like to be watched.
—Samuel, a 70-year-old straight White cis man from the United States

As these performers suggested, a desire to explore sexuality is an essential motivation to cam, one highlighted most often by cis men. Historically, patriarchal systems have demanded chastity and purity in women, while at the same time they have empowered men sexually.[11] Given the extensive social regulation of sex in societies across the globe, it is no wonder some models said sexual exhibitionism and desire motivated their decision to cam.

In what follows, I explore the complexities of sexual motivations for camming by examining in-depth my interview with Luiza, a 32-year-old straight White cis woman from Brazil who works as an accountant during the day. Luiza has been camming off and on for 14 years. She told me that when she started camming again a few years ago, after a break, it was for exhibitionism and to satisfy her own sexual desires. She said, "I already have a full-time job that supports me. My husband also has a great job. I webcam because I'm an exhibitionist. But the money is also very good." When she first started camming at 18, however, her motivations were different. Luiza reflected on her early days in the industry:

I started when I was 18. I'm 32 right now; and I was 18 years old looking for a job, and I saw an ad in the newspaper looking for "a young good-looking girl that could speak English"—not so many people [in Brazil] speak English. So, I went there and I realized what it was, but it was very nice, like, you would think it was a shady environment, you know, but no. They explained the website and [that] I would have to talk to people on my cam, and I could do something sexy or not; it was up to me. . . . I could take pictures of myself and put [them] online; they just told me how to use the site and [how to do] live shows in the studio, and . . . I would make a lot of money, but they were paying me so little. It was like a minimum wage, which was like around, back then, it was around, $100, and I was making over $1,000 for them . . . and then I was like, oh my God, I should just do this at home. I talked to my mom, and she bought me a computer; it was very expensive back then, especially here in Brazil. . . . I started doing it at home, and I worked on webcam for like two years, one year and a half, more or less; but then I got married with my boyfriend. . . . He was very jealous. So I stopped it.

Out of respect for her husband, Luiza did not cam for years. However, after years of marriage, Luiza became bored:

I stopped, and we are together since; we have a very long marriage, and I was bored—ya know—I was very bored. I have a job; he has a good job too. And I wanted to explore . . . he's a very serious vanilla person. [chuckles] . . . I was like, let's go to the swinger's club place, and let's have sex in front of people; and we went once, but we didn't do anything. He didn't want to, and he said, we can do [it] online, like you did before; and I said, OK, I'm gonna research and see how it is nowadays. And I was very interested [because] it's so different nowadays. It's much more sexual than it was before, and [there] were couples that are fucking online and getting money on places like Chaturbate; and I thought, oh my God, I wanna do that! [chuckles] . . . But he didn't want to do it. . . . I set up, and I was ready, and he was like, oh, I don't wanna do it, and I said, OK, that's fine, I respect you. . . . But I wanted to, and he said, OK, go for it; he's not jealous anymore.

Luiza, like Abigail, renegotiated camming with her husband as a compromise. Luiza is a sex-positive woman who wants to explore her sexuality, but who describes her husband as "vanilla." Camming became a compromise that Luiza is very pleased with. Her motivations were not just a reflection of her feeling bored in her marriage; her boredom with her accounting job also shaped them. Luiza said:

> I'm not that good at my real job. . . . I am an accountant. I just do my job, over there, my accountant job. It's boring. . . . But I'm not like, a super good accountant, I know that. I don't get home, and I'm like, oh my God, I'm gonna read those accountant books because I'm gonna be a great accountant. I don't . . . but when I'm on webcam [or shooting] porn videos all by myself, and it's just solo, I love it. And I put my videos online and . . . guys buy my videos, and they just make comments; and I love to read my reviews. I feel so proud, and I wanna do more. I love the attention. I love the feedback I get. I get to know people. I like to talk to people. So it's fulfilling. . . . My dream is maybe in the future, I can stop my other job, my accountancy job, and do only webcam. I think I'd be like strapped [for] money, [but] I'm saving—I'm saving it all, and when I have a good amount, that I'm investing always, I hope to stop my accountancy job and do only webcam and videos for fun.

Camming provides Luiza with both corporeal and affective pleasures that she cannot find in her job as an accountant. Her final comments above were incredibly powerful. Her dream is to quit her respectable job as an accountant and cam full-time. Performers like Luiza are trying to crack capitalism by saying no to work that is alienating and unfulfilling. Luiza is trying to reconcile pleasure with work. She highlighted the potential for camming to fulfill her sexual desires and her economic needs simultaneously. To anyone who cannot understand why someone would dream about leaving their job as an accountant to sell sex online, understand this—camming for Luiza is a profession that does not deny her humanity or access to joy and pleasure.

Conclusion

The development of capitalist production stripped the fun and joy from work. As described by the Marxist William Morris, in the Middle Ages there were craftsmen who enjoyed, were enriched and fulfilled by their work. Beginning as early as the 16th century, workers were stripped of the ability to create commodities themselves; with the rise of capitalist production and industrialization, by the late 18th century joy had been almost completely stripped from labor. According to Morris, precapitalist craftsmen were artists, and the products of their labor were expressions of joy.[12] The modern laborer does not produce art, and finds no joy in work—workers are machines producing private property for the bourgeoisie. Since capitalist production strips the joy from labor, people search for occupations where they can still be artists or masters of a craft, and through their artistry can find pleasure in work.

The lack of joy and fun in work may explain why people often seek vicarious or ephemeral moments of freedom in the consumption of culture. Sociologist and labor scholar Kristen Lawler, who has studied the cultural imagery of the professional surfer in the United States, writes:

> The surfer is American culture's most prominent and most consistent archetype of freedom—freedom *from* alienated work and the clocked time, repressed libido, and material scarcity that this work depends on, and freedom to live spontaneously, within a pleasurable ecological and subcultural connection. And the surfer image has always signified the transcendence of the imperatives of modern instrumental rationality in favor of a more "primitive," libidinal relationship with the world."[13]

Lawler argues that the surfer image symbolizes a refusal to work—a rejection of capitalism. People may cling to the surfer image precisely because surfers' lives embody the lives they can only fantasize about.

Labor scholars should not miss the point that the acquisition and experience of pleasure is a social force that shapes and guides labor market participation. Since capitalist production strips the joy from labor, people search for occupations where they can still be artists or masters of a craft, and through their artistry find pleasure in work. Contemporary workers are trying to reclaim the joys of craftsmanship by selling their homemade crafts on Etsy.[14] Women have fun at work by facilitating parties where they sell sex toys using their social networks.[15] People craft and sell their own beer.[16] Cam models are just one cohort of workers who are seeking freedom from alienated labor, and who are also seeking to reconcile pleasure with their labor.

5

"I Get Paid to Have Orgasms"

Pleasure, Danger, and the Development of Resiliency

Pleasure is not only a motivation for entering the camming industry, it may also be a prerequisite for monetary success. Cam models reported incredibly high rates of job satisfaction. In my survey sample, 86.6% of respondents reported that they were satisfied with their camming job—almost half of respondents answered they were highly satisfied. Only 3.9% of respondents said they were dissatisfied with camming. Drawing inspiration from feminist Carol Vance, I argue that models who experience high levels of pleasure can manage the dangers associated with sex work and thus will report high levels of job satisfaction. As Vance writes, "The tension between sexual danger and sexual pleasure is a powerful one."[1] Models can experience high levels of pleasure precisely because the online context provides a space where many models feel free to safely explore their sexuality in pleasurable ways, despite the risks involved. In Vance's words, "As feminists, we need to draw on women's experience of pleasure in imagining the textures and contours that would unfurl and proliferate in a safer space."[2] In the camming field, pleasure does "unfurl and proliferate" because the online context acts as a psychological barrier that allows cam models, for the most part, to manage the dangers of their work.

Those models who experience less pleasure than danger usually do not continue to work in the field, and may not be successful. If they do continue, they report being very dissatisfied with their work. Timothy was one of only four models who expressed dissatisfaction with their camming jobs. Timothy, a 20-year-old gay White cis man from the United States, began camming out of dire economic necessity; he left home at 18 because his mother was a drug addict. He said:

> I hate camming. I really do. My boyfriend does it with me sometimes. But I hate cam modeling. The compliments are nice, but it takes a drag on

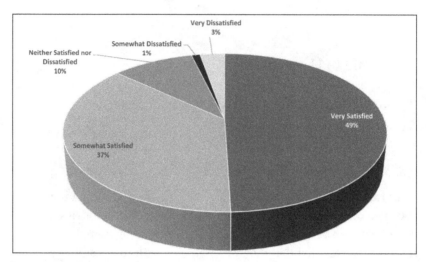

Figure 5.1. Job satisfaction in the camming field.

your sex life. Makes it feel like a chore and the fun goes away. It's fun the first few times. Then it just gets boring. . . . I've had family members see me, also I've been harassed while online. People who've found out about it have called me a whore, a slut, or immoral.

Timothy made clear that the dangers and drawbacks of the camming field far outweigh the pleasures for him. Crucially, because clients are purchasing embodied authenticity, performers who experience pleasure in their work will have an advantage over models like Timothy. While the previous chapter highlighted pleasure as a motivation for entry into the camming field, in this chapter, I explore the complex forms of pleasure cam models experience that not only keep them in them in the business, but which contribute to their monetary success.

"It's a Blast": The Joys of Camming

Cam models frequently said that camming was fun. The experiences they have at work produce positive affective states of pleasure. Mariam is a 23-year-old straight Middle Eastern trans woman originally from Tunisia now living in France. She said camming was "something fun that I do from the comfort of my own home." Naomi, a 38-year-old queer White trans woman who has both escorted and cammed, said:

I was literally thinking about that topic [pleasure] just the other day, when I was coming back home from some work and I was remembering that scene in *Pretty Woman* where's she's like, "And I did it the first time [escorting] and I cried the whole time." I was like, I just had a blast! . . . But, yeah, it's super fun. . . . What I like about camming is every person who does it has their own style. Like, the style that I kind of fashion after, that I latched onto and was like, oh, that's what I wanna do, is a girl who basically just talks the whole time; she just holds conversations with everybody and I'm like, that just looks fun! You're getting to know people; you're chatting, and it's a blast.

Evie, a 28-year-old bisexual White cis woman from Australia, said, "the work is fun and entertaining. I enjoy dressing up and chatting with people online." Evie's comment was similar to the perspective of many cam models who discussed pleasure on the web forums I examined. One model said, "I also like privates where they want me to try on all my clothes and panties. This is just pure fun. I love posing and being silly, trying to figure out cute outfits for them."

Customers often ask cam models to perform shows that the models find funny. In our interview, Amelia, a 29-year-old straight White cis woman from England, and I talked about one of her favorite private shows.

> AMELIA: I had a guy ask me to dress up like Mary Poppins once, and I gave that the "old college try" [laughs].
> AJ: Right [laughs]. That seems like fun; was that fun?
> AMELIA: I've obviously got the English accent, and he was like, oh, I would really like to fuck Mary Poppins. So, he's like, will you sing the Mary Poppins songs to me? So, I had to kind of look up Mary Poppins, and I'm not the best singer, but he liked it. . . . To be honest, it was probably one of the more fun days because it was, it was really hard not to laugh because I'm trying to be like, sexy, and I just found it so funny.

Unlike their experiences of vanilla employment, cam models reported regularly having fun at work. Research on the contemporary workplace emphasizes the importance of fun activities and job responsibilities—when work is pleasurable, workers are, unsurprisingly, more satisfied and produce better work outcomes for employers.[3]

Pleasure through Touching Encounters

For many, sex work is not merely a calculated economic exchange of services. Instead, the encounters between clients and workers are both physical and affectual.[4] Sociologist Kevin Walby astutely observes that

> the labor process of male-for-male Internet escorting differs greatly from the ill-treatment common among on-street sex trade and even bar hustling: Internet escorts deal with a clientele that more or less represents the transnational capitalist class, a clientele that often seeks camaraderie and temporary companionship.[5]

Internet-mediated exchanges provide better conditions of labor for escorts, which can help foster intimacy between sex workers and their clients. Walby calls these affectual exchanges "touching encounters." While his work focuses on the male-for-male escort market, my data suggests that these affectual exchanges and pleasures exist for webcam models as well.

Cam models emphasized the importance of touching encounters and highlighted these experiences as a benefit of their line of work. One model on a web forum said, "My favorite privates are ones where we just talk. I love talking and getting to know people better. These privates have lasted over an hour sometimes." Aarav, a 25-year-old straight Asian cis man from India, told me a pleasure of camming was "meeting new clients and customers around the globe." Human interaction can create touching encounters that are pleasurable not for the sexual climax they produce, but for the emotional intimacy they facilitate between people.[6]

The pleasures cam performers experience underscore the dynamic relationship between affective and corporeal pleasures. Matt, a 23-year-old straight White cis man from the United States who lives in Mexico, said:

> [Camming is] something I really enjoy doing. . . . I've had quite a bit of jobs in the past, but not one of them have been as fun and amazing as camming has been. . . . The money is good and I love earning money do-

ing what I'm doing, like being able to jerk off and make money—like who doesn't love that, who doesn't love that? But my favorite thing though is the interaction with the other people. Like, getting to know everybody, talking to everybody. . . . I've met so many amazing people doing this.

In many cases, the encounters between performers and clients are not purely sexual, and given the mutual perception of safety, friendships can often emerge. These intimate encounters contribute to a pleasurable affectual experience that is very similar to noncommercial relationships.[7] Crista, a 27-year-old White polyamorous cis woman from the United States, told me about her relationship with one of her regulars:

> This guy doesn't expect a whole lot of sexual things from me in our private conversations. So, when we're talking on Kik,[8] we're talking about stuff that's going on in the world or how our days are going—things like that, and I don't expect any money from that type of interaction. . . . If I'm feeling really badly about something or something big happens, there are times when he is the first person I tell. So, it is kind of like, I do want somebody to be proud of me and I do want someone to be happy for me in these certain situations and I feel like there's no one else I would want to say that to right when it happens. So, I mean, money is kind of how it starts, but I have really become attached to this one guy. . . . I'm attached to him in this weird way and I still don't know what to make of it quite yet. But, yeah, I mean, he makes me happy; he's a positive part of my life.

The intimate relationships cam performers develop with clients exist in a space of blurred boundaries. The client Crista described is still a customer, yet he has also become a close friend. She takes money from him on cam, but doesn't when they talk offline. Crista's story suggests the importance of a sociological analysis of pleasure—pleasure is often found by exploring social relationships that defy normative cultural scripts.

Sexual Pleasure

The experience related by Sherry,[9] a 50-year-old straight White cis woman from the United States, highlights the sociological nature of sexual pleasure in camming:

> One aspect that I would like to reiterate is how this has helped me keep sexu-
> ally interested, and active, even after menopause. I went through a period
> of time (pre-camming) where the newness of our marriage had worn off,
> and life circumstances kept us from playing with others for several years. I
> lost interest in sex pretty much hands-down. It just wasn't exciting anymore,
> and menopause caused a lot of changes that made sex even painful at times.
> When I started this adventure, I became aroused and quite interested again. I
> can say that I am probably more sexual today than I have been since my 20s!

Sherry's comments point to the importance of worker subjectivity and
using an intersectional framework to study pleasure. The acquisition of
pleasure in camming does not fulfill some set of universal human needs
as biological theories suggest. At age 50, Sherry has gone through meno-
pause, which decreased her sex drive and caused vaginal dryness. She and
her husband had been swingers but had stopped having encounters with
other people as a result of her decreased sex drive. For Sherry, her experience of pleasure while camming is a reflection of both her physiology and
her specific life experiences. Societies often tell 50-year-old women that
they are no longer sexy and beautiful. When camming, Sherry did not
derive pleasure solely from masturbating on cam or having an orgasm.
She also derived pleasure from being a 50-year-old post-menopausal
woman in a room full of people telling her she is sexy and paying to watch
her masturbate and perform sex acts.

Carl is a 31-year-old bisexual Black man from the United States who is
known for his anal shows. Figures 5.2–5.4 depict Carl performing what
he calls "extreme anal play," which he told me provides him with much
pleasure.

Carl's performances and thus his acquisition of sexual pleasure are
shaped by the regulations imposed by the websites on which he performs. On Streamate, for example, fisting is prohibited. As a result, Carl
makes videos of performances that he can't do live. Describing figures
5.2 and 5.3, he told me, "I recorded a custom video over a year ago. . . . I
wanted to make a 20-minute video which reflected the highest extremes
of what I could pull off at the time with no fear of Chaturbate flagging."
Carl is aware of the ways that cam sites cam limit his pleasure, and as
result, he finds ways to push back against these regulations by making
videos that satisfy his desires.

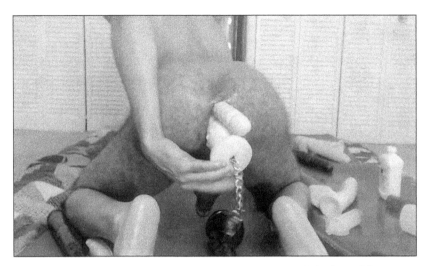

Figure 5.2. Carl recording an extreme anal show, which he would be flagged for on websites such as Chaturbate. In this picture, Carl has two dildos of different lengths and widths inserted in his anus.

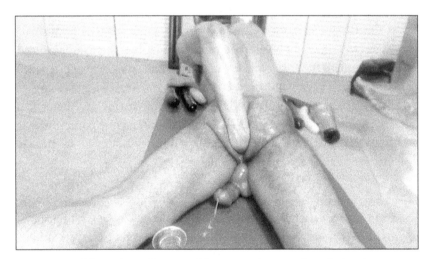

Figure 5.3. Carl fisting himself as part of the same video recording. Carl is also ejaculating.

Figure 5.4. Carl doing a show in his kitchen in 2015. At the end of this show, he took his biggest dildo, shoved it deep inside, and induced an anal orgasm. Carl does this to signal the end of a show.

Carl's performances on cam sites are subject to surveillance and policing. On Chaturbate, for example, "[o]verly large sex toys or animal-shaped sex toys may not be used on camera, and objects may not be used as sex toys unless they are typically marketed and sold for that purpose." This language is vague and what constitutes an "overly large sex toy" is left up to moderators to judge individually. Another rule on Chaturbate states, "Any action that may be deemed obscene in your community is prohibited." How obscenity is defined is subjective. Sites often include disclosures, such as this one from Chaturbate:

> The foregoing list is non-exclusive, and we may, at any time, prohibit any activity that we determine, in our sole and absolute discretion, to be inappropriate. We reserve the right to terminate or suspend your access to all or part of the service at any time, with or without notice, for engaging in any inappropriate activity.

Breaking rules can lead to a performer getting "flagged"—having their show suspended by site moderators. Multiple violations can lead to warnings or to immediate bans. Who gets flagged, how often, and for what is at the discretion of moderators. Carl talked about cam site regulations and punishments:

> It's vague and nondescript, basically their B-line, we'll know it when we see it, which is a problem because that means you could be flagged for basically anything if they're not very specific about it. And when it came to my shows because I have a tendency to use some really big sex toys, they started flagging me a lot for that.

While it is crucial that the cam industry provides a space for Carl to experience his pleasure publicly, this example also shows how pleasure is regulated and controlled by the field in which Carl and other performers operate. Cam sites often enforce rules and regulations in discriminatory ways. As a 31-year-old Black cis man performing extreme anal shows, primarily for other men, Carl's performances are monitored closely and scrutinized because race, gender, sexuality, and age shape how online sex shows are perceived, especially by website moderators. As Carl noted:

> I have seen some of these female cam workers get away with stuff that I haven't been able to; so, I suspect there's a bias because . . . I'm a male performer and I think maybe some of the administrators more than likely are male. So, if they are likely to be bothered or disgusted by looking at me rather than the female cammer that's doing [anal shows with large sex toys].

Black men's sexuality has long been policed and seen as the cause of various social problems.[10] For Carl, regulatory forces in the industry shape his experiences of pleasure. Importantly, in addition to regulating Carl's access to pleasure, overly aggressive website moderators can negatively affect his wages. Carl recalled a night when he almost lost out on a lot of money due to being flagged on Chaturbate: "[T]his happened last year, I think it was the Thursday after the Super Bowl, it was one of my best paid shows that I'd done in a long time, and it almost didn't happen because I got flagged right before." The regulatory regimes imposed on performers are an example of the ways that social context shape our access and experiences of pleasure. Carl's performances and experiences of pleasure are also affected by social forces beyond the regulations imposed upon his body by the field.

In *Extravagant Abjection*, Darieck Scott explores the relationship between Blackness and abjection. Scott argues that Black men's history of abjection creates an opportunity for Black power. Black power is not only found in organized political movements but is also realized in the experience of abject Blackness. Scott examines the ways Black men's bodies have been assaulted and raped within the overlapping systems of White supremacy and capitalism. Borrowing from Fanon, Scott argues that Black men, especially queer Black men, must always tense their muscles; they must always be on the defense, and on high alert, expecting their bodies to be policed and subjected to violence. The metaphor of tense muscles that both Fanon and Scott use relates to the images of Carl fucking the tense muscles in his pulsating anus. There is power in abjection, and while Scott often seems skeptical about the pleasure found in Black abjection, he no doubt recognizes the potential for that pleasure. Tensed muscles, Carl's fist, Carl's butt plug—all may become "a way in which the colonized knows and resists his historical subjugation."[11] Carl is bottoming, and through his bottom performances, he derives power and pleasure from sex acts that some people may see as humiliating and violent. In abject Blackness, performers like Carl can turn what can seem like violent and degrading performances into a complex form of pleasure that simultaneously disrupts discourses about appropriate Black male sexuality. Scott describes how bottoming

> becomes a metaphor and a model for one of the black powers we are seeking in abjection: among its many inflections of meaning, it evokes the willed enactment of powerlessness that encodes a power of its own, in which pain or discomfort are put to multifarious uses."[12]

Carl's bottoming performances give him pleasure, but not just because the hard thrusts of his hand cause him to ejaculate. His pleasure is situated in Black abjection, and the power of these performances also lies in their potential to crack various systems of oppression. When Carl and I were discussing trolls and online harassment, he noted that he was most disappointed by customers' attempts to regulate his sexuality. The judgment he receives from Black customers affects him far more than the moderators' flagging of his shows. Carl said:

> The most disappointing, but also the most fascinating responses, as far as the negative ones go is, from other Black people telling me that the stuff that I'm doing is too extreme for what they expect a Black person to do. And I think [they] offend me more than even just the straight racists, 'cause I mean, when you're Black [in] America, you're gonna always experience racism at some time; so it's just like you're used to it. But it kinda plays into the whole double consciousness type struggle that you're not Black enough, and the whole idea that, oh, I'm too freaky to be genuinely Black because . . . the really crazy stuff . . . to see me doing it, is I guess, for some of them, is a disappointment, which I've railed against. 'Cause it's like I'm not gonna put myself into a box because I know that I have some really strange desires. I know that I can be kinda out there, but there have been years that I've kinda just been in some low, dark places because I feel like my sexuality is gonna be a hindrance to me. But ultimately, I just decided to just say, screw it, 'cause I'm like, why am I gonna burden myself over all this? I like what I like. I'm gonna do it, and if you have any problems with it, you can find somethin' else. . . . I'm not gonna just burden myself if you think I'm less of a Black person because of the stuff that I do. I'm not.

Every time Carl publicly fucks himself, he fucks systems that regulate acceptable modes of Black male sexuality. He acquires pleasure through his penis and prostate, but his pleasure is complex and also experienced through the affective resonance of his Black detractors who make him feel disappointed and sad. As Vance writes:

> Sexuality activates a host of intra-psychic anxieties: fear of merging with another, the blurring of body boundaries and the sense of self that occurs in the tangle of parts and sensations, with attendant fears of dissolution and self-annihilation. In sex, people experience earlier substrates, irrational connections, infantile memories, and a range of rich sensations.[13]

A sociological theory of pleasure shows us how these physiological and affective responses are situated within complex social systems that control and attempt to deny pleasure to marginalized subjectivities. As Carl's case shows, acquiring pleasure in camming can also be a mechanism of resistance—a method of cracking various systems of oppression.

Performers negotiate and acquire pleasure differently based on their subjectivity. Crucially, the more pleasure performers experience in the field, the more likely they are to continue camming. As one model on a web forum put it, "If you can't find some sort of pleasure, other than the money, you will burn out. Fast. You will hate what you do and it will show and your income will likely burn out too." Pleasure is not only a motivation for camming, but, as I stated in the introduction, it is also often the reason why people continue in the industry. The pleasure they experience allows them to deliver embodied authenticity to clients, which increases wages. This case study suggests that employee satisfaction is directly tied to pleasure. Future lines of inquiry should explore the role of pleasure in work.

Caution: The Dangers of Camming

While the camming industry is far safer than other sex work industries because workers do not face the regular threat of physical harm, there are still many dangers. Cam models face the bodily tolls of sex work, stigma, capping, doxing, and harassment. The tolls of daily sex toy use, especially without proper maintenance, can also wear on the body. Given that sex workers face widespread social stigma, if an employer finds out that their employee is also a cam model, it could jeopardize their job status and cause the worker economic harm. If a cam model's family or friends find out about the model's source of income, the discovery can produce social harm. If a performer's show is capped or recorded without the performer's permission, it can cause multiple forms of harm. Not only can capped videos "out" a cam model, but sometimes people who cap cam shows also try to sell them, thus stealing potential profit from the model. If a performer is doxed and a customer finds their actual location, this breach of privacy could lead to physical, social, psychological, and economic harm. Finally, frequent harassment by trolls can cause psychological harm.

The Bodily Tolls of Sex Work

Performers explained that, like other forms of bodywork,[14] camming can have deleterious effects on the body. While cam models do not face risks of physical violence in the way many street-based sex workers do, the work they perform can still cause physical harm. Many incorporate sex toys into their performances. Frequently used sex toys must be cleaned regularly and properly stored. Performers explained that frequent use of sex toys can cause a range of health issues such as urinary tract infections, yeast infections, and bacterial vaginosis. Models said, for example, that a client may request to see a cam model perform anal insertion of a dildo and then immediately ask the model to use that same dildo in their vagina. Doing so without cleaning in between can cause yeast infections and bacterial vaginosis.

Andres, a 20-year-old pansexual cis man from Colombia, and I discussed anal prolapse— when the walls of the rectum become loose—as another example of bodily harm. A person can manipulate the anus so that part of the wall of the rectum slides out of the anus; this is colloquially called "rosebudding." Having a prolapsed anus can cause anal leakage, pain, itching, and bleeding.

> ANDRES: A lot of people expect to see things that may even be harmful to you. Like things that you shouldn't do even if you can. I don't know. People demand a lot of things like, can you do a prolapse? I don't know if you know what it is.
>
> AJ: I do.
>
> ANDRES: [enthusiastically jumping back in] Oh, my gosh, I won't do it! Like, that could really damage me.

While rosebudding is a hard no for Andres, it is possible that there are models who might elect to perform shows that can have harmful effects on their bodies because these shows are lucrative. As the market becomes more saturated with models, they are under greater pressure to diversify their brands, which can mean adding acts to their lists of services that make them uncomfortable. Some performers, like Andres, have the privilege of refusing to perform specific acts, whereas other, more marginalized performers, who are more economically vulnerable, might feel compelled to offer services that they don't enjoy and which could have harmful effects on their bodies.

Anal prolapse can also occur unintentionally due to prolonged extreme anal play, and thus could be a consequence of some performers' work. Interestingly, though, for cam models like Carl who feel tremendous pleasure in extreme anal play, the potential consequences of anal prolapse may not deter him from performing these acts. Some models do extreme anal shows despite the risks. The presence of risk creates a wide range of affectual states; whether the presence of risk makes an individual feel anxious or excited will vary based on the individual and the social context. The presence of risk and its accompanying affectual state condition the individual's experience of pleasure.

Stigma

Sex workers face enormous stigma in society, and, as a result, many performers take great care to protect their anonymity, often creating manufactured identities. As an example, Luiza—a 32-year-old straight White cis woman from Brazil whom we've met before—explained how important her privacy is to her because of how deeply stigmatized sex work is in her country.

> At work, it would be horrible if anyone found out. I am afraid of people from my husband's work to know, too, because [in] Brazil people are very conservative [about] sex things; so it would be really hard. And my father is a really religious man, my mother is the same way, [and] my friends are religious. I think he would accept [it], but I have no way to talk to him about it. How am I going to tell him about it? I don't know.

The stigma that sex workers face can cause many different forms of harm. In Luiza's case, if her employer found out, this could jeopardize her job as an accountant, and thus produce economic harm. If her father and friends find out, she could face social harm.

Capping: "Getting Recorded Is Pretty Much Inevitable"

There are other risks associated with camming, which partially result from cam models being independent contractors. One such risk is a practice colloquially known as "capping"—shorthand for "capturing": customers filming cam models shows and then posting that content on pornographic websites. Quantifying how often capping occurs is difficult; most models did not discuss capping in numerical terms but rather offered some version of "getting recorded is pretty much inevitable."

Many models said that capping merely is part of the reality of adult webcam modeling, and anybody who voluntarily cams must accept it. A model on a web forum posted:

> Once you get online to do camming that is just the reality. The only reason models don't have videos of themselves out there is just because of the sheer volume of models; the person that decides to record and post them just hasn't met them yet. It's one of the risks you'll have to come to terms with in this line of work.

The idea that capping is inevitable and unavoidable was a common theme in my interview data. Naomi said, "capping—I kinda just accepted that it's gonna happen. So I can't really get mad about it."

In my research I uncovered three basic strategies models use to grapple with capping. The first was to use the Digital Millennium Copyright Act (DMCA) to try to have the videos removed. The DMCA is a US federal law crafted to protect copyrighted digital material. Models can contact the website where the capped material appears and request that the content be removed. However, requesting a "takedown" require that the model fill out a form—if they use their real name and contact information, the person who posted the copyright-protected material can potentially find out their identity. Alternatively, a model can contact the website that they cam on and have the site file a DMCA complaint.

Given the limitlessness of the Internet and the sheer number of videos that could potentially exist of any model, they could spend hours searching the web for videos of themselves. Models said they often employed the help of friends, assistants, and customers to help them find videos. There are now law firms devoted to helping online pornographers protect their intellectual property. Cam models can pay a firm to monitor capped content and file DMCA complaints on their behalf. Employing a law firm or service to handle capping is expensive, and thus generally this strategy is used only by successful full-time models. If cam models were not independent contractors and worked for a traditional pornography company, the company, not the worker, would be responsible for handling DMCA takedowns. The consensus among the models was that searching for capped content and filing DMCA complaints was too time-consuming to do on their own, and in the end not worth the effort.

A second strategy was to be more selective about the cam sites one performs on and more thoughtful about setting prices—capping is more likely to occur with public shows and in low-priced private shows. Rebecca, a 34-year-old polyamorous White cis woman form the United States, told me that she would only perform exclusive shows because people who cap shows are most likely to record cheaper "gold" shows. She also said she would not work on cam sites such as Chaturbate where performers only do public shows. She said:

> I don't do gold shows [because] the buy-in is so low that guys will record it. Like, anybody can buy into that show and see whatever they want to. But my exclusive rates are like ten dollars a minute and most trolls that are looking to record my shows aren't gonna spend ten dollars a minute.

By being selective about cam sites and pricing, models can minimize capping, but there's no way to eliminate the issue.

A third strategy was to capitalize on capped videos posted on file-sharing websites. Some performers argued that they are in the sex business and that capping is free advertising to potentially drive more traffic to their cam room or other social media accounts. One model on a web forum stated, "Not every cam girl cares [if] she's posted on [tube] sites. It's free advertising, after all." Another said: "Yeah, most people who frequent cam sites are looking for live interaction more anyway . . . since a member will see the video, decide there's something they like and then 'Omg I can chat with her live?!'" In other words, many cam models saw capping as a mechanism that can drive traffic into their rooms and thus help them earn more profits.

Models can take a more proactive approach to capped content by searching for it and tagging themselves. A model may not have originally intended to pursue a career in traditional pornography; however, once content is posted on major pornographic Internet hubs, cam models may find themselves with an additional stream of income. In the end, cam models saw capping as a danger of camming, but, overall, not one that outweighed the pleasures.

Doxing: "Keep Your Info Locked Away"

Doxing refers to acquiring, through research or hacking, identifiable information about a person and then sharing it. Doxing is often used to harass models. Clients use the White Pages, reverse phone searches, and people-finder databases that compile public records to locate models. Models protect the computers they use to cam by maintaining up-to-date firewall and virus protection to reduce the chances of their being hacked and their personal information shared. It is vital that models create manufactured identities to protect their real ones.

Previously, I highlighted the pleasures found in touching encounters between cam models and their clients. The drawback of these affectual relationships is that if models get too close to their clients, they can and do reveal personal information about themselves. Models often develop relationships with their regular clients, and as a result must be extra careful about what they say online. I read one account on a web forum in which a model said she had mentioned that she was trying to sell her home, and, on another occasion, that she had cammed from her yard. She also named the car she drove. A stalker pieced this information together and used a multiple listing service and Google Earth to find her home. He then stalked her, which ultimately required law enforcement intervention.

Additionally, on some cam sites, clients can network on customer lounges or virtual spaces. Doxing can be facilitated through these networks with ease, given that many of the customers who frequent adult cam websites also network with each other. One client member on a forum said:

> The safety threats that models can face, if that is in question here, are (to name a few) identity, location, security/safety, family safety, etc. There are

a lot of fucking lunatics out there and you never know who's watching. An MFC member came to me last winter and showed me a screenshot they took of a model who was camming near their window paired with Google Streetview and Google Maps pins on the exact location of where that model was camming from due to the shape of the skyline behind her. He was proud that he had deduced the exact location, floor and side of the building the model lived in. This is terrifying. I went straight to the model, we both reported him to MFC support and I'm very glad they took immediate action.

Social media platforms can be used to find a model's offline identity. Models must be sure that their social media is linked solely to their manufactured cam model identity, or personal information can be gleaned from social networking websites. A client posting on a web forum said:

I was on Facebook trying to get in contact with someone who used to cam on MFC, and I imported my Skype contacts, and found a personal profile for a different model, even though her Skype was her model name and model email, she must of joined Facebook or Skype with the same email or something, of course I was quick to tell her about it.

In the case above, no harm came to the model because the client stumbled upon her information and, not wanting an ill-intentioned client to do the same, warned her.

Models often take pictures using smartphones, which presents another problem. Such photos are embedded with geotags that a crafty stalker can use to find the model's location. While users can turn geotags off, geotagging is the default setting on smartphones; a cam model must know to disable the feature. Models may also directly contact clients for many reasons, such as notifying them of performances off-cam (e.g., at a strip club), marketing products (e.g., pornographic videos), selling additional sexual services offline (e.g., escorting), or simply maintaining rapport. Models said that personal phones should never be used for such contacts, and that they keep separate work phones for safety.

Interestingly, again, the models in this study emphasized that doxing is expected. Much like capping, it is commonly perceived as a threat that comes with the job. One model on a web forum said:

As a cam model (or any type of sex worker) you are encouraged to keep your information as locked away as possible. You are told to expect that people might try to find out who you are and stalk you, you are made well aware that getting involved in sex work could possibly hurt your future and present employment and if you care about that, either be safe or don't get involved at all.

This model, like so many others, emphasized an individualistic logic that suggested that doxing is a danger inherent to camming, and if models want to experience the camming's pleasures, they must deal with such dangers appropriately.

Harassment: "Trolls Come with the Job"

Despite the ability of models (on most major cam sites) to ban customers who harass them, webcam models reported regular experiences with verbal harassment. Despite its prevalence, models were often dismissive of this harassment—saying, "Well, trolls come with the job." In Internet slang, a troll is a person who participates in online forums, chat rooms, message boards, and other forms of social media by posting inflammatory comments that are meant to cause conflict, disruption, and emotional responses. A troll may enter a model's room and posts menacing statements in the public chat space. In addition to public harassment, on popular cam sites, people can use internal messaging systems to contact models. Clients often send incessant and unwanted messages to models. In order to deal with trolls, cam models use what they call "the banhammer." If trolls harass them, they immediately block or ban them. Models can block customers for set periods of time or ban them indefinitely. Like a hammer, the ability to instantaneously ban customers is a powerful tool. One model on a web forum explained:

> I think the best thing is always: ignore. Don't egg them on. Don't try to make an example out of them publicly and just block and forget about it and not let it infect the rest of the Twitter fanbase and start a smear campaign. It's horrible but it honestly doesn't surprise me . . . camgirls are public figures and every public figure gets crazy people. With people hid-

ing behind keyboards, it brings out a lot of ugliness. It's easy to get emotional and caught up in it but I find that makes it far worse and gives the attacker more control and attention which is what they wanted. Most of these people are no physical threat at all and just kinda come with the job.

This is a typical perspective, suggesting that other models "ignore" trolls and avoid "egg[ing] them on." Cam models frame abusers as trolls. The connotation of identifying harassers as Internet trolls is that these are harmless people who are speaking the way they do only because they are online. Models believed that they cannot and will not act on their words. One model posted, "I've been on the internet long enough to know most of these guys have 'internet tough guy syndrome.' It's posturing; they talk a big game but most of them can't even muster the give-a-shit to go to the grocery store. They're self-entitled shut-ins." The assumption here was that trolls are recluses who pose no tangible harm.

In some cases, trolls on cam sites were even seen as comical—or as potential comic relief for a public chat room. Another performer posted, "How you deal with them: Ignore and ban. Don't even bother to answer them, unless you want to entertain your customers with it. Life is too short to spend time on their bullshit or let them ruin your fun." Notice, this model said, that if you use the banhammer and ignore the trolls, you can still enjoy and find pleasure in your work.

Models maintained that any connection between trolls' verbal harassment and physical harm was spurious. Their logic seemed to suggest that the trolls' behavior did not constitute "real" harassment, "real" harm, or "real" danger because there was no threat of physical harm. What the models consistently described was harassment. Yet they were just as consistently dismissive of it. A model said:

> The most they can do is doxx you, and if you've ensured you[r] info is safe that won't be a problem. Even if it does get leaked, these guys have no idea what your living situation is and for all they know you could be living with a swarthy mountain man with a huge firearm collection willing to wreck them the moment the front lawn starts rustling. The likelihood of them coming after you is extremely low. There are women who have a massive internet hate brigade after them and the worst they get is still just empty death/rape threats.

This model's comment again adopted an individualistic point of view, positing that as long as a model has taken care to protect their information, they are safe. Moreover, it reifies the problematic idea that the absence of physical harm means the absence of any harm. This model asserted that even models who have "massive internet hate brigades" who regularly harass them are facing *only* empty "death/rape threats." Nonetheless, subjection to death or rape threats is harassment. These comments highlight how the computer becomes a psychological barrier. Threats are perceived as harmless because they occur in cyberspace. Yet how does persistent harassment by trolls affect models psychologically?

In many of my interviews with cam models, we discussed harassment by trolls and the toll it takes. Carl and I discussed how trolls made him feel:

> CARL: Sometimes I get racist remarks; so that's always a bummer. It's not as a bad [or as] often as an occurrence as I feared, which is good, but occasionally I would just hear, like, some dumb remarks like, oh, Martin Luther King didn't die for you to do this, and I'm like, fuck you, and I just kick 'em out [chuckle)].
>
> AJ: Ban!
>
> CARL: Yeah, and some people will troll in other ways, like one guy threw in a lot of really gory and nasty images in my show and I couldn't quite stop him for a while and I ended up having to mute the entire chat for people who aren't paying customers, even though I normally allow it, and I don't normally mind, but I had to just for that one show, all of them just to stop this one guy. And I apologized to everybody else that I had to do that, so, there's that.
>
> AJ: Can I ask, What was he posting?
>
> CARL: It was just some really grotesque imagery, like stuff . . . like some really diseased people, like warts and gashes and infected looking imagery.
>
> AJ: Nobody wants to see that.
>
> CARL: I left that show really pissed off. Like, I kept a brave face, but as soon as I logged off, I almost like just punched a wall, just how upset I was [scoffs].

Carl shared with me that he generally bans trolls and moves on, but on occasion he must deal with trolls that really make him angry and very upset. The psychological tolls of dealing with trolls minimize the pleasures of camming.

Take, as another example, my conversations with Adeline, a 25-year-old polyamorous White trans woman from the United States.

> ADELINE: Sometimes it really is [bad]. Not that often does it get too bad, but I've had sometimes where, like, this one guy was creating a million accounts. He had like, thousands and thousands of accounts, and every time I'd block him, he would come right back and it was impossible. And I just had to log off for the night, and that was the worst harassment that I've gotten.
>
> AJ: Can I ask what type of things he would say?
>
> ADELINE: Yea, he would try to make me, like, trigger [me] in any way he could about trans issues and stuff. Like, he would say I'm balding or something. He would just come up with a bunch of mean things to say.
>
> AJ: And no matter how many times you banned him, he'd find his way back?
>
> ADELINE: Yes.
>
> AJ: Did you try to seek any assistance from the website?
>
> ADELINE: I did not. . . . Well, he never came back. I logged off for the night and I never saw him again. If he would've came back, I would've, probably.
>
> AJ: Right, do you find that customers like that are frequent? Is that something that you have to put up with on a regular basis?
>
> ADELINE: I think the more frequent harassment would be, like, just one or two things said and then I can block them. And this is pretty constant, but then it's not an issue. They're gone.
>
> AJ: And is that something that affects you a lot? . . . Does it ever take a toll on you or does it not really bother you very much?
>
> ADELINE: It definitely has. I think I remember a few times, like, ya know, putting the cam down a little bit just to, like, calm my face. But, it's like mostly probably just trolls being trolls.

My conversation with Adeline was very telling. She gets harassed by transphobic trolls, and while she can ban them, their torment still takes an emotional toll on her. Adeline also noted that a determined troll could keep creating new free accounts to avoid her bans and continue to harass her. If she had to log off and stop working as a result of a troll's harassment that harmed her economically. Moreover, as she said, trolls do impact her affective states, and thus can harm her psychologically. Notice, though, that despite Adeline's acknowledgment of this harm, she still said it's "just trolls being trolls." Just like the experience of pleasure, all social experiences are shaped by context. The online context shapes cam models' dismissive attitudes about the abusive behavior of trolls.

The pleasures of online sex work create an environment in which models feel mostly safe and, as a result, may become desensitized to harassment. On the one hand, the computer becomes an effective psychological barrier, meaning models can experience more pleasure because the absence of physical contact makes them more comfortable. However, despite the overall effectiveness of their emotional management strategies, there do seem to be psychological and economic costs of being subjected to regular harassment by trolls. More empirical research is needed to explore the effects of harassment on online sex workers.

Conclusion

According to the logic of neoliberalism, the cam models in this book are empowered independent contractors. They are autonomous entrepreneurs who "get paid to have orgasms" and "have a blast," and the dangers of camming force these sex workers to develop an ethos of resiliency. Like many other subaltern groups, since they are constantly forced to advocate for themselves, they develop agency. They also gain autonomy because the cam site owners, who function largely as absentee landlords, "allow them" the privacy to control their pages. This ethos of resiliency allows cam models to cope with the dangers of camming while still experiencing high levels of pleasure.

The resiliency developed by cam models can also have positive effects on their lives offline. As Carl's and Adeline's stories demonstrate, dealing with trolls can be emotionally taxing; however, cam performers also told me that their interactions with trolls online actually help them deal with harassment offline. Crista and I also discussed how dealing with trolls has been a source of empowerment for her.

I don't think that camming is, like, intrinsically sexist. I feel like I notice sexism a lot more in the rest of the world now and I try to interpret it in a different way when I'm not on cam. So I go on cam to be sexualized and it's okay there, but when it happens to me in my personal life, in the real world, it is so much less okay than I think it was before. So before, you know, like, you experience sexism all the time and it kind of washes over you, like, that's just part of life, but now, I feel like I'm a little bit more even empowered to say, that's not allowed here. . . . I'd be more likely to confront them now than I would before I started camming. Because I kind of do feel, like, more independent sexually and, like, more protective of my sexuality now that I don't feel like anyone really has the right to objectify me in these ways out in the world.

Dealing with harassment online has prepared Crista for dealing with people who sexually harass her in her everyday life. Later in our interview, she also stated that the rise of public sexual harassment cases in the United States has made her even more aware of how crucial it is that she can defend herself from men who sexually harass her.

While this new form of digital sex work creates an opportunity to develop resiliency, sexual empowerment, and sexual pleasure, we can also see how the neoliberal ideas adopted by models could thwart progressive political goals. I found widespread use of individualistic logic to explain the dangers of camming, mirroring neoliberal responses to many social ills, such as poverty. Remedying online harassment is an individual model's problem. Models overwhelmingly emphasized that those who get upset about capping, doxing, and harassment are just not cut out for this line of work. In the end, this logic does not help to alleviate the problem of harassment for cam models as a group. In other words, the problem with neoliberal politics generally is reflected here— when individuals come to rely too heavily on the logic of self-help, it simultaneously unburdens larger social structures from their responsibility to apply laws equally and in just ways.

As feminist scholar Brooke Meredith Beloso argues, "we stand to realize that the exploitation endemic to some sex workers is not just something that happens to prostitutes; rather, it is part and parcel of everything that happens under the sign of capitalism."[15] People face myriad forms of discrimination in the capitalist workplace. Harassment is not unique to webcam models. One could argue that as long as any laborer working under capitalism adopts a neoliberal perspective, it will thwart their ability to confront and remedy workplace discrimination through political mobilization aimed at challenging the failures of capitalism. I caution, though, against a flippant dismissal of these workers as neoliberal capitalists void of progressive political imagination. These cam models may not be fighting the tyranny of capitalism, but they are on the frontlines of the battle for sexual freedom. Yes, cam models could be more critical of their employers and the larger capitalist system that structures their exploitation; they could organize around these issues. But in the conclusion of this book, I raise the question, What would come of such activism? What type of interventions would help protect cam models from privacy violations, trolls, and online harassment? Who would police and punish the trolls? Perhaps more regulation and more oversight are not what cam models or any sex workers need.

6

We Are Camily

Community, Social Capital, and the Problem of Exclusion

A vibrant community of webcam performers has developed in tandem with the camming industry. The camily, as many performers refer to it, is a loosely tied network of performers who provide one another with various forms of support and friendship. As urban sociologist Al Hunter has described, scholars have conceptualized communities as either ecological/physical (spatial and temporal), social structural (social networks and institutions), or cultural/symbolic (shared identity and symbols). The community that performers described to me is in line with both the social structural conceptualization of community and the cultural definition.[1] Cam models use web forums, social media, and conferences and events to interact with one another in a loosely structured social network that has been designed by cam performers for cam performers. In addition, cam models share an identity as sex workers; the stigma they face as a result of this marginalized identity is what motivates them to form and sustain the camily.

The creation of communities by sex workers is nothing new. Sex workers are driven to form collectivities that allow them to survive and fight the legal persecution, stigma, and regular violence they face. Carl, a 31-year-old bisexual Black cis man from the United States known for his anal shows, observed:

> Polite society . . . completely shuns us; we're on our own. So, in that sense, it's like we need each other 'cause when it comes to the popular perception, we're gonna lose, nine times out of ten, because everyone else believes that we're like a bunch of whores that don't want to do an honest day's work, which, again, kinda bugs me because I'm like, but I do an honest day's work!

Urban sociologists have documented the ways people from marginalized social locations build communities for survival in the face of persecution.[2] As Carl said, the collective experience of stigma that sex workers face makes them dependent on one another—they need each other to survive in societies that pathologize and criminalize them. The motivations for joining a community can still vary widely—that is, what motivates sex workers to find support and community varies based on the form of sex work they perform, the conditions of labor, and their own subjectivity. Carol Leigh, longtime sex-worker activist and co-founder of BAYSWAN (Bay Area Sex Workers Advocacy Network), once said, "Prostitution is not a monolith. The newspapers use the plight of the most vulnerable women to symbolize the entire field, ignoring the diversity of the sex-worker community."[3] Street-based sex workers, online escorts, strippers, pro-dommes, phone sex operators, sensual masseurs, pornographers, and webcam performers all have different experiences of labor. In addition, race, nationality, gender, sexuality, ability, and age also shape sex workers' experiences and, thus, their motivations to find and form communities. Webcam performers have been motivated to form a community based on their *similar* experiences of stigma.

Defining the Camily

Though dominated by performers in the United Kingdom, Canada, and the United States, camming is an international industry—one that contributes to the evolving definition of what constitutes a community. Cam performers depict the camily as a space for people to find friendship and support as a group of marginalized workers. Performers frequently described themselves to me as introverts who throughout their lives have had trouble making friends. Moreover, many models said their sex worker identity further complicated their ability to make friendships and participate in other communities. Candice, a 23-year-old biracial cis woman from the United States (who doesn't label her sexual identity), told me:

> I'm very introverted. It's hard for me to make friends in person, let alone find anyone who isn't in some way against sex work. Even before I was a sex worker and just a model, it was very hard finding people

who were accepting and didn't just want something. I never even knew webcamming was a thing until June of 2015. In August of 2015, I gave it a try because I knew some people who made lifelong friends from it, and I didn't want to be lonely anymore. The money is an upside, of course; I can make $500 in four hours just sitting in my bedroom, not even masturbating or doing anything sexual. It's not always like that, but for the most part, I'm just grateful I have friends who genuinely care about me and vice versa. It's not only about sex; it's about finding other people who are similar to you.

Candice's comments underscore the importance of friendships in forging and sustaining community, and researchers in various disciplines have already highlighted the crucial role of friendship in community development.[4] In Candice's description, the camming industry is not just about work; she also has the opportunity to interact with people "who are similar" to her. As sociologists McPherson, Smith-Lovin, and Cook note, "By interacting only with others who are like ourselves, anything that we experience as a result of our position gets reinforced. It comes to typify 'people like us.'"[5] In the camily, cam workers' identities as sex workers bring people from very different social locations together; these digital sex workers see themselves as like-minded people who are open-minded about sex and not ashamed of their sexuality.

When I asked specifically about the benefits of camming, Candice continued to stress the importance of friendship and community. She said:

You can make your own special place where people want to come hang out and support you. I've made way more friends with women from SuicideGirls and MFC than I ever did in high school, college, or at any normie job. A lot of the women who do this sort of work always have a story, and, often times, it's so related to something you've been through; so you don't feel so alone or misunderstood anymore.

Candice made clear that she has made more friends with other women camming than she has at any other point in her life. It was common for performers I interviewed to discuss the importance of making friends with other cam models who can understand them in a way that others cannot. There is pleasure in social belonging. In addition to the value of friendship in forging a distinct camming community, these friendships and the interaction that sustains them have both immediate psychological and economic benefits.

Web Forums

Online web forums are the primary mechanism for the development of social capital in the webcam community. A MyFreeCams (MFC) model created AmberCutie's Forum (ACF), one of the first and longest-running web forums exclusively for cam models. The founder and moderator wrote on the website, "ACF was created in 2010 to provide a helpful community for cam models to interact with one another, as well as discuss anything and everything with their members. We also created CamGirlWiki.com for aspiring cam models to learn the basics." ACF allows clients to participate, but models-only sections are restricted to those verified as models by the moderator. Participation in the models-only section builds social capital. ACF is one of the most active web forums for cam models; in 2018, it had 40,250 members, almost 30,000 discussions, and nearly 1 million messages.

Another active web forum is Stripper Web (SW). SW is larger than ACF, but it is not exclusive to cam models. The site features a section called Camming Connection that is popular among performers. SW has been around since 2002. In 2018, the entire site had over 122,000 members, more than 171,000 threads, and almost 2.7 million posts. Like ACF, it is model run and moderated. On SW, veteran members are nominated and voted on to become moderators.

Some web forums were not founded and run by cam models. For example, two sex entrepreneurs, Tristan and Rutger, founded WeCamGirls (WCG) in 2012. Tristan told me that they have great experience building communities and review sites, mainly in the Netherlands. Their site, which is not available to clients, features extensive reviews of cam sites and studios. As of 2018, WCG had over 14,400 members, 90,000 forum posts, and 10,000 forum topics. It also had over 3,300 reviews. The content is created and driven by performers, making it a useful resource for models. WCG won the award for Best Live Cam Online Community at the 2018 Live Cam Awards.

These web forums are all in English and appeal most to performers in the United States, United Kingdom, and Canada. Alternatively, there is Adult Video Chat (AVC), a vibrant web forum based in Romania. As of 2018, it had over 13,800 members, 93, 900 posts, and 11,200 topics. As I discuss throughout this book, language is an essential factor in conditioning models' experiences and success. It is thus important to recognize how language and nationality affect access to the camily, the development of social capital, and the ability of performers to mobilize their social capital.

Conventions, Summits, and Awards

In addition to virtual spaces, performers also interact and develop social capital at events such as CamCon. Launched in 2014, the event brings performers, fans, and sex entrepreneurs to Florida, USA, for fun and socializing in the sun. Its website says, "CamCon set out to create a Model Experience like no other show in the world. Our show has created an environment where models leave every year creating lifelong relationships, with likeminded people." CamCon is focused on providing models a fun space to network, whereas other events, such as the Bucharest Summit, focus primarily on sex entrepreneurs, such as camsite owners, studios, and third-party billing companies. The May 2018 Summit program agenda featured presentations by companies and professional development seminars for performers and industry. There was a seminar for models on performing fetish shows and a seminar on legal issues in the industry for studio owners. The Summit features business booths where industries can promote services. There are also awards for both performers and sex entrepreneurs. While the Summit focuses on the capitalist production side of camming, CamCon focuses more on social networking and social support.

In addition to conferences and summits, the cam industry now even has awards ceremonies. I spoke with Alex, founder of the Live Cam Awards (LCA), which are modeled after the Adult Video News (AVN) awards. I asked her why she created the awards. She explained:

> The answer is very simple: at that point, in 2014 when I started promoting it, there was no awards show dedicated to the live cam industry; of

course, AVN had a category for Best Live Cam Site and one for Favorite Cam Model of the Year, but there was no other awards show rewarding all the cam models categories, all the cam sites, and all the other aspects of the industry. Being a cam model myself for 11 years, on a small niche, fetish [website], I have seen the rise of the industry and the amazing changes that took place in the last decade. The first edition took place in March 2015, during the European Summit in Barcelona, where we held our first three edition[s]. In 2018, we will move to a new venue and a lot of changes. Last year, I won [the] Businesswoman of the Year title during the Bucharest Summit, and it's the first time a cam model g[ot] this kind of award from the industry. I wanna use it to empower cam models even more, and this year . . . I decided to invite cam models to host the award show with me. We always had a connected community in Romania, thanks to one of the biggest forums of the industry, adultvid-eochat.ro, and now there's so many events and finally models are getting the recognition they deserve, are getting out of their comfort zone, and start[ing] to attend events to educate themselves.

LCA gives awards in three divisions: model and talent (e.g., performers), studios, and industry categories (e.g., cam sites). Crucially, for models, LCA gives awards in a diverse range of categories, recognizing not only youthful, thin, cis camgirls, but also trans, male, mature, and BBW cam models, to name a few. Receiving recognition for their work does not just create incentives for cam models to work hard; it also creates opportunities for cam performers to provide support to their peers.

Social Capital

"Social capital" refers to the shared values, trust, and social bonds that help sustain vital social networks and facilitate cooperative social action. Social institutions such as the economy, family, education, and politics all function at high levels of efficiency when high levels of social capital are present. According to social capital theorists, a lack of social capital can have deleterious effects on society. As famously observed by public policy scholar Robert D. Putnam in *Bowling Alone*, since the 1970s, the US has witnessed an unprecedented and dangerous decline in social capital. As the title of Putnam's classic suggests, Americans used to participate in bowling leagues, and now they bowl alone. Economic growth made the United States a wealthier nation, and, as a result, more White, cis, straight[6] people gained more options and buying power. Many baby boomers moved their families to suburbs, with more shopping malls and color televisions, but they were also working more to have these options.

Most importantly, for Putnam, our economic growth also led to a decline in social capital. People became more isolated—both physically and socially. As a result of people working more, and some living in suburban areas, there is less voluntary participation in organizations and community groups. Putnam and others have argued that we should all be very concerned about this drastic loss of the "third spaces" that used to support community.[7]

Addressing the limitations of Putnam's classic, I argue that, as opposed to focusing only on the decline of social capital, it is crucial to think about how digital technologies may also be helping to revive and reformulate social capital. Adult webcam performers create new forms of social capital that help sustain the new online sex industry, creating a community of workers who provide one another with various forms of support—emotional, instrumental, informational, and appraisal. Through their interactions both on- and offline, they build social capital and a strong camily.

Social Capital and Camming

Sociological research on social capital shows that an individual's social networks can facilitate productive and often successful business relationships; in short, social capital has economic benefits for individuals.[8] Success in camming is not merely a reflection of individual personality, the right lighting, or performance quality. To some extent, cam models' success is also a reflection of their social capital within the camming community. Cam performers build social capital by sharing information and supporting other performers. Drawing from sociologists such as Mario Small, the point that should not be glossed over is this: social capital is developed through social engagement. Yes, by just searching web forums (or even Google), cam models may get specific information about what equipment most models prefer or other strategies for earning good money. However, these actions do not build social capital. It is the reciprocal sharing of information and mutual support that create social capital.

Community engagement is quantifiable. How many times a person has posted is visible on a web forum. The number of posts conditions one's status on the forum, which is visible to other users; for example, a new member is assigned "newbie" status and, as they post and interact more, over time, they become a "veteran" member. Models that do not post are even labeled "inactive," while others who actively post are marked as "VIP" cam models. On the SW forum, long-time members get voted into positions as moderators. Importantly, only those active on web forums get to become moderators—that is, gatekeepers in the camily. The more performers interact with one another and support one another on web forums or on social media platforms such as Twitter, the more social capital they develop within the community.

Sharing information on web forums, engaging on Twitter, or sharing drinks poolside at CamCon builds social trust between performers. Performers share secrets of the trade, which is of crucial importance. Good capitalists would keep this information all to themselves. However, as sex workers, who are marginalized and stigmatized by society at large, performers are willing to defy normative capitalist logic and put the camily before their individual economic concerns. Performers said sharing information and supporting others help everyone do better. Collective support, not competition, helps models become successful. Amelia, a 29-year-old straight cis White woman from England, has cammed sporadically for six years. We discussed the blog she created to help new cam performers. She noted that while sharing tricks of the trade can benefit individual performers, doing so offers additional benefits:

It also benefits the industry. . . . [I]f guys aren't happy with a girl, they'll start saying things like, oh, all camgirls care about is blah, blah, blah, and then they'll be very generalizing. If one girl has like pissed them off or written them off or whatever, then it sort of turns into camgirls in general, and then, they'll be very vocal about it. They might not come back to the site. Whereas if we keep the customers on the site, they will definitely spend on other girls. It's very rare that they will stay only with one girl . . .

because men, in porn, generally like variety. . . . So even my most valuable regulars will go to other girls from time to time, and I don't have a problem with that because I know they'll be girls who have regulars and their regulars will come to me. And as long as we all give them a good service, they'll continue to stay on the site. So I definitely want other girls to do well so that we can all do well.

Far from purely altruistic, Amelia explained that performers benefit from supporting one another.

I spoke with Cat, a former cam model, who started a website, O Camgirl, to help new cam models. We discussed the webcam community and what role sites such as O Camgirl play in it. Cat told me:

There is absolutely a webcam community, which is supported by such forums as WeCamGirls, Webcam Startup, and, yes, O Camgirl. There was very little unbiased information available when I first set out into this industry. That was my initial reason for starting up a blog that aimed to provide a voice of reason in an industry that's so overrun by people trying to get ahead, no matter the cost to others. It's rather disgusting, really. Through running O Camgirl, I've come into contact with so many like-minded people, and I've been really blessed to get to see another side of the industry, and to get to connect with all these models and insiders. We're all in this together, and it's awesome to get to help and connect people in some way.

As Cat noted, many cam performers see themselves not just as individuals making a living, but also as part of a community. In her words, "We're all in this together."

A cam model's position in the camming industry network shapes their connections and social capital within the camily. As Kwon, Heflin, and Ruef write:

[W]hile one can assume community social capital is accessible to everyone, community members' ability to mobilize it for entrepreneurial activities may be contingent on two factors: their degree of embeddedness in the local community and differential mobilization of social resources across racial or ethnic group.[9]

Models' degrees of embeddedness in the camily influence their ability to mobilize social capital within the camming industry. The more models are involved in the camily, the more likely they will be able to apply cultural capital learned from other performers and capitalize on friendships while camming. Drawing from Kwon, Heflin, and Ruef, I argue performers' subjectivity also shapes their access to the camily and ability to capitalize on social capital.   ·

Social Support and Social Capital

For many performers, what makes camming a community is the support they provide for one another, which is why, for many performers, they are camily. Francisco, a 21-year-old queer Hispanic cis man from Mexico, told me, "I made a lot of friends through camming and found lots of supporting people." Social scientists have noted the importance of four types of social support: emotional, instrumental, informational, and appraisal. As emotional support, models encourage each other. They help each other drive traffic into one another's rooms, which is an example of instrumental support. They provide information about the best webcams, lighting, and software and share strategies for everything from branding and marketing to dealing with trolls. In these ways, performers provide one another informational support. On web forums, performers complain about bad days where they made very little money, and other performers provide constructive feedback that the performer can use reflexively to evaluate their shows to see what adjustments they can make, which is appraisal support.

Performers' comments often highlighted the importance of multiple forms of support and showed how these forms of support frequently overlap. Luiza, the 32-year-old straight White Brazilian cis woman we've met in previous chapters, created a group on Skype for independent cam models that she told me they all use to help one another and provide informational support. She said, "[We] help each other. We say, oh, go to this site; don't go to this one because it's a scam, and we help each other." Luiza also talked about how members of this group and another group of performers on Snapchat do what they call "takeovers." They go on social media and share pictures of other performers with their existing fan bases. This practice encourages their followers also to follow other performers. Instead of thinking, well, if I share their photos, it might compromise my business, Luiza said, "It's pretty cool, because guys follow your [cam] friends, besides you." Takeovers, a form of instrumental support, exemplify the benefits of social capital. Members of Luiza's group all help drive traffic to each other's rooms, which can have a positive effect on their wages. If performers share, not compete over, clients, they can also share in each other's success.

Cam performers' support of one another can have positive effects on their income. Robin, a 40-year-old straight White cis woman from Canada (introduced in chapter 3), said:

> Stripper Web is the first [forum] that I had found, and if I ever have a question or I'm having an issue or whatever, you can always write it in there and people will help you. Like, I got the newest, the Windows 10, update for my laptop, [and] after I got it, none of [my] cams would work. I was like, what in the hell? I'm, like, I don't know what to do. So, I went on there, and there's work arounds and all that; and it was a day of no camming, and I was fixed instead of an oh-my-God [moment].

The informational support Robin received saved her time and money.

Andres, a 20-year-old pansexual Hispanic cis man from Colombia, spoke to me about community on Chaturbate:

> First of all, and mostly, I like the sense of community. They're like a big family, and when I started camming there, people would come to my room, other models and tell me like, hey, you can do this; you can try this. If you need any help [just ask].

Andres went on to detail the way that community members provide crucial instrumental support. Beyond just encouraging words, he said, "because of a great sense of community, other models will tip you, I don't know, even $1 maybe, just to activate your room, to break the ice. So it is, like, really cool." Andres explained that sometimes if his room was slow, other performers came into his room, which helped drive new traffic to it. In addition, by tipping him, other performers provided both emotional and instrumental support that also had positive economic outcomes. Despite the support that many cam models provide one another, cam models experience unequal access to the camily and, as a result, they have unequal access to social capital, which can affect their success.

We Are Not All in the Camily

Many cam performers do not attend CamCon, summits, or the Cam Awards because these venues can be exclusionary. Some models believe these venues, especially conferences and summits, are only for successful full-time performers with large followings. Crista, a 27-year-old polyamorous White cis woman from the United States, like several other models I interviewed perceived industry conferences as exclusionary. As a result, she said she'd never go to a convention or summit but does participate in web forums. Crista said:

> I don't think I would go [to a conference] . . . because . . . I don't think I would fit in there . . . it's something that I do [camming]; it's how I make a living; but I don't put myself on the same level as the ones that you see that are on every day, and they're making like $10,000 every couple of weeks. . . . I feel like, that's when they go.

There are also economic and political barriers to participation in in-person community events, which are generally held in Romania, Columbia, or the United States. Full-time performers with large followings have clients willing to fund their travel or the money to cover the costs of registration, lodging, and transportation. Part-time workers in the field, who are disproportionately low-wage cam performers, will generally not be able to fund this travel. Economics can create an insider/outsider dynamic, where cam models see conferences and summits as catering to successful cam insiders. Political barriers and immigration policies around the world often impede, not encourage, global travel and have the most constraining effects on people from the global South.

The ACF Verification Policy

Cam models also reported exclusionary practices on web forums. To further probe exclusionary practices that reject some performers from the camily, I examine the verification policy to access the models-only section on ACF that existed from 2010 to 2017. In order to build social capital, performers regularly interact in the models-only section of web forums such as ACF. It is crucial that performers have a free safe space in which to discuss their work experiences and support other models. As one model explained, ACF is a "safe space to talk about things with other females. That's why we love models-only. It is safe space, for females." ACF allows customers to join the forum, and so models-only was created to secure a female-only space for camgirls. To protect this space for female models, like many other womyn-only feminist spaces, men are not allowed access. To gain access to the models-only section, one's identity as a female model must be verified by the moderator.

To verify that a person is an active cam model, the moderator uses a verification system. Initially, in 2010–2017, the system the ACF moderator designed required that a model seeking verification send her a direct message from their MFC account. MFC accepts only cis women as models. As a result, by using MFC to screen models on ACF, the models-only section denied access to trans women and cis men who are not allowed to work on MFC, as well as performers who work independently (e.g., on Skype). ACF policy stated:

> Please accept my apologies, but only female models who can verify their accounts are accepted at this time. You're still very welcomed to post in the public sections of this forum, and I guarantee there is still a LOT of great info to be found without having access to the private section. If ACF changes this policy, or creates a section for Male and Transgender models, I will update this section with information on how to verify. Thank you for understanding.

The moderator diplomatically apologized for not allowing trans women or men in models-only and encouraged the use of open sections on the website. While the moderator acknowledged that a more inclusive policy would be ideal, this policy was not changed until early in 2017. That April 13, the moderator posted the following update: "We are beyond just cam girls . . . ACF is now also verifying accounts for transgender models, couples, and male models!" The moderator then posted instructions for verification that do not require an MFC direct message. While the ACF policy is now more inclusive, verification still requires proof of the cam site you use. The implication is that independent cam models cannot be verified. The ACF policy also rules out retired or inactive models. Moreover, it is still important to now also think about the implications and legacy of the former policy. By examining the ACF verification policy, I show how the exclusion of some cam performers from the camming community is not arbitrary or coincidental. Performers can reify existing systems of oppression and the negative consequences those systems have on already marginalized people.

"Transgender Models Can't Get Verified Here?"

In 2014, a trans woman wanting to get verified to use the models-only forum on ACF started a thread, "Transgender Models Can't Get Verified Here?"[10] In her first post, she said, "I was looking to get verified here to take a look at model only section for useful tips and advice, but I came across this." Below the text, the poster pasted the forum's policy on transgender and male models. Then she continued:

> This is kind of disappointing. I'm a cam girl, I'm female (legally too), and I happen to be transgender (mtf). I don't understand why trans women can't have access to [the] models [only] section. I mean, I'm used to discrimination, but I wasn't expecting it on a community forum for cam girls. It seems unnecessary.

Conversation among models ensued. One responded:

> Trans women are women. They face the same (if not more/worse) dangers as cis women do, by getting naked and putting themselves out there on the sexual part of the Internet. I would love to see trans women included in the models only section.

Another model agreed, saying, "I love this forum, but I would especially love to see the discrimination against trans women end." A few other women also spoke out against the policy, but most stood by the moderator.

Those who defended the policy emphasized restricting males' access to the models-only section. Another model responded:

I understand that there's an issue with some knowing what camgirls post mainly since some personal stuff has been brought out . . . but I feel like with the slight boom in male cam models, perhaps we could make a separate section for them that the female models could help with. I get how they won't want to post in the members section for fear of being mocked, since that's already happened a few times. I just feel bad for these models. I feel they want the help, but they feel they can't ask for it.

In the past, according to models, male customers tried to create fake MFC accounts, just so that they could be verified on ACF and have access to the models-only section. Many of the models who defended the policy did so because of their fear that male customers would enter the space to gain access to private information about models. Another model chimed in:

I think this rule is only in place because it would be really easy for a determined individual with unsavory intentions to create a transgender account on [other websites] for the sole purpose of getting verified here and accessing the sensitive information in models only. Crazier things have happened.

Many posters seemed to understand that trans women are excluded, but did not frame the implementation of this policy as discrimination. Instead, they saw it as a necessary evil to protect themselves from the nefarious intentions of some male customers, which is an all-too-familiar argument offered by trans-exclusionary radical feminists (TERFs) in feminist womyn's-only spaces when trying to defend their exclusion of trans women.

The original poster responded to this line of argumentation by emphasizing the consequences of this policy for trans women who cam:

I appreciate the response, but I'm not sure if we're on the same page here. I'm not advocating for a men's section or men's inclusion on this forum. I'm only trying to understand why trans women are being excluded from the cam resources here and being lumped in with men. I understand the importance of protecting the privacy of camgirls on the site from men. But that doesn't apply here. I think there is something that needs to be clarified: I am a woman. I am a camgirl. I am not a man. I am not a camguy. There is a very large difference between crossdressers/sissies/dragqueens/camguys, and trans women. Trans women are women. The others are men. Does that make sense? I am a woman, legally, visibly, and fully. I do not want, nor do I need a separate but equal solution. There are large amounts of guides, tips, and tricks such as for lighting that I am unable to access because I am not seen as a woman, even though I am. I am a camgirl just like any other.

As the OP's comments made clear, she is a woman. She is not practicing deception or trying to do anything duplicitous—an offensive claim that trans people are forced to fight against incessantly.

In her own defense, the moderator rearticulated the argument made previously by the other models. First, she argued that while she understood the effect of the policy on trans women, this policy was justified because the policy protected the anonymity of the models-only section. Second, she added that her time is limited, and her motives for creating and moderating the forum were benevolent. Given that her motivations were well intentioned, and that a more inclusive policy would be incredibly time-consuming to manage and threaten the perceived bureaucratic efficiency of the current system, the policy would remain as it was.

Members of the web forum also expressed concern over the perceived difficulty in implementing a more inclusive policy. In response to the OP, one model said, "Believe me, many would love for you to have access; It's just too difficult of an undertaking at this point." Another model declared:

> I wish the amount of shitty liars wasn't such a large percentage over honest trans camgirls, so that [the moderator] didn't have to make this really difficult decision in the first place in order to do her best to protect the women in the models only section. It's a huge forum but a small community run by a single camgirl and her husband going through some big elaborate process to verify that a trans woman is in fact a trans woman and not just a very clever dude, I imagine, would take a crazy amount of man hours that are likely already stretched pretty thin for our gracious host and her fella.

The conversations here highlighted that many workers in this industry do not question the binary logic of Western gender, and, in turn, did not question the discriminatory gender policy under discussion—in fact, most supported it.

Lessons from the Exclusionary ACF Policy

My analysis of the ACF gender policy shows that while the moderator implemented the policy, some camgirls legitimized it. Performers themselves adopted this gendered policy from MFC and used it to structure their interactions with other webcam models. In doing so, the moderator of the webcam forum and the supporters of the discriminatory policy were engaging in online disciplinary practices. Here, the moderator—a cam model herself—served as a gatekeeper in the policing and confirmation of female embodiment, and she did so in a way that reinforced the binary construction of gender. The participants on the forum who overwhelmingly defended the policy also indirectly worked to enforce and manage it. The policing of normative embodiment happens not only under the directives of capitalist managers, but also at the hands of the workers themselves. The discursive boundaries drawn and managed by camgirls exclude people who are not cis women from the camily. The exclusionary rules of participation on web forums and the high costs and exclusionary design of some conventions and events restrict trans women's, male models', and low-wage-earning models' access to social capital. A lack of social capital can have real effects on the livelihoods of cam performers excluded from the camily.

Additionally, the responses of cis women on this board reinforced the binary construction of the sex/gender system. Many of the models here still relied on sex/gender system based on a binary logic, whereby sex shares a mimetic relation with gender—this binary construction of the sex/gender system is discursively produced, and thus socially, culturally, and historically constructed. The binary sex/gender system serves the interests of heteronormative and patriarchal social systems while marginalizing those individuals whose identities do not neatly fit within these rigidly defined boxes.[11] The dialogue on this board is evidence of the pervasiveness of the gender binary and has implications for thinking about its adverse effects on trans women in the camming industry.

Conclusion

The exclusion of trans women from the feminist space created on ACF sits squarely within a much longer history of discrimination against trans women in feminism.[12] The exchanges on this forum reenacted previous schisms between feminists about the inclusion of trans women in female-only spaces, exemplified by the infamous Michigan Womyn's Music Festival.[13] As another example of the legacy of cissexism and transmisogyny in feminism, in her controversial book *The Transsexual Empire*, Janice Raymond argues that trans women are surgically constructed women, who may now be anatomically female, but lack experiences with patriarchy that, like scars, mark women for life. She contends that when trans women participate in feminist politics, it is as though they are raping women. According to Raymond, trans women are really men, who have so much privilege that they can even colonize women's bodies and social and political circles.

On this web forum, we see arguments such as Raymond's die hard. As part of the discussion over the ACF verification policy, one model added the following long but telling comment to the ongoing dialogue:

> I have absolutely nothing against being transgender, when it comes to stuff like this I cannot stand it when people can't accept it so please don't jump down my throat, I'm just trying to explain another point of view. I'm guessing a reason might be that even if you get all sorts of operations and you feel like a woman and obviously naturally had a personality that felt female, you are still the same person as you were when you were male. What you look like doesn't matter on a forum, it's about what's going on inside, and though there are hormones etc you cannot have surgery on what's on the inside. It's like if a man put on a woman's body I still wouldn't be comfortable with him in the changing room because it's not to do with how he/she looks. I am not comfortable changing in front of my gay friends either while I'll happily change in front of lesbian friends. I'm not entirely sure why, it's not any discrimination against men, it's just how I feel. . . . It's such a tough situation, though. I imagine it'd be very difficult for [the moderator] to be able to monitor who are the genuine transgender models and who are just the dudes who like to dress up as women and try and dirty talk models for free in their rooms (it happens

a lot). It's easier to have a clear cut rule than pick and choose. . . . The dynamic of the models only section is nothing like the public section, and a large reason behind that is that it's all women. I do think it'd be good to have some more of the helpful threads available, and some of the support threads too for male and transgender models, but a large amount of what goes on in the models only section are really girly stuff, like need a womb girly. It's nice being able to talk about these things just with others who understand. I think it'd be great if the world were more accepting. But I think this goes all ways. It's good to accept new people into your world and accept different dynamics, but it's also good to accept when people like to do something a way that doesn't necessarily suit you. Yes it sucks, but yes that is life. It's absolutely nothing personal. . . . The forum works as it is, I don't think it's fair to come onto a forum and practically accuse the site creator of discrimination in your first/second post because you haven't been instantly let into the private section. I don't think it has anything to do with discrimination.

There is a long history of exclusion, cissexism, and transphobia in feminism and feminist spaces; I have just documented yet another example, here in the camily. Crucially, what I have added to this history is documentation that the policing of boundaries occurs in virtual communities just as it does in physical communities. Feminist spaces are important. However, as history has already shown us, exclusionary feminist spaces harm some of the very people that those spaces purport to help.

Performing in a Sexual Field

Display Work, Manufactured Identities, and Gender Performance

In display industries, women have more sexual capital than men, and earn higher wages than men as a result. This is not because they *are* women; they make more money because they *perform* femininity in valuable ways. Discourses of masculinity shape sexual scripts, and while women usually perform emotional labor for and talk with clients along with performing sex acts, men are often expected by customers to meet what Michael Johnson has called the "ejaculation imperative," and drop, pop, and roll (drop their pants, get erect, and masturbate). Cam shows that feature more extensive conversation between client and cam model will be longer. If men are expected to rub one out quickly, that makes for a shorter show. The gendered sexual scripts in camming make women more likely to earn more money because their shows tend to last longer. The structure of desire in the camming field privileges women—albeit in uneven ways—because even though both trans women and cis women outpace men in earnings, their bodies are valued differently.

Erotic webcam performers engage in what sociologists Ashley Mears and Catherine Connell call "display work." Mears and Connell have studied display-work industries such as fashion modeling, stripping, and pornographic film acting. These are all industries where people make money by selling performances in which they show off their bodies to paying customers. Display industries are the only capitalist markets in which the pay gap between women and men is inverted. In regard to the inverted wage gap, Mears and Connell write:

> This theory is a proposal in need of more original and comparative data on these and other types of display work. For now, we raise the proposition that women's sexualized bodily capital will be more highly valued

than men's sexualized bodily capital given certain organizational features of the workplace, namely freelance and winner-take-all labor markets.[1]

There is still a lot to be learned about display industries, and I have taken up Mears and Connell's call for more original and comparative data on display work. I also consider how the online context shapes display work, the economic outcomes of display work, and the experiences of display workers. My findings, like Mears and Connell's, show that, in camming, female cam models do outearn their male counterparts. I expand upon Mears and Connell's inaugural work by using an intersectional framework and exploring how various facets of worker identity shape both experiences and economic outcomes in a new display industry.

The Sexual Fields Framework

Performing sex is not just about masturbation, erotic dance, fucking on cam, anal shows, and so on; normative discourses about gender, race, age, and ability shape performances of sex. When a client logs into a cam model's room, they are not just there to purchase a cum show—a glimpse of a human stimulating their genitals to orgasm. Rather, who performs the cum show and how they perform it are crucial. Customers are purchasing a particular type of embodiment that delivers a performance of masturbation. Performers earn money by designing performances and manufacturing identities that draw on cultural and sexual scripts in their cam shows. External cultural and sexual scripts guide their performances, but so does the more localized sexual field in which they perform.

Sociologist Adam Isiah Green has adopted Pierre Bourdieu's work on field theory to explore the social organization of desire and the complex ways that individual desire reflects common ideals—not just the desires of the individual.[2] Our erotic habitus, the sexual capital we have, and the sexual field in which we operate shape our desires and sexual behaviors. Every sexual field has its own structure of desire that guides people's behaviors and thus creates a system of stratification. Green writes:

> *sexual capital* situates actors differently in the status order, conferring advantage on those who possess it, including rights of sexual choice, social

significance, and group membership, and conversely, invisibility, marginality, and in some cases stigma on those who do not.[3]

The camming industry has created a structure of desire that combines normative cultural scripts with consumer desire for embodied authenticity. Cam models perform in ways that adhere to hegemonic discourses about attractiveness, but they must also construct an online cam persona that customers perceive as authentic or real. Taken together, dominant cultural scripts and embodied authenticity guide behavior in this sexual field. Importantly, as Green states, "it is impossible to understand sexual social life, including interaction, partnership choice, and sexual practice, without an analysis of field properties that socialize the very things we want, do, and desire."[4]

In order to make money, performers must deliver performances of sex that are valued by participants within this sexual field. As a result, many performers construct what scholars of sex work have called "manufactured identities."[5] Given that some cam models' subjectivities and bodies already represent normative idealized cultural scripts, they do not have to manufacture identities; they can be their authentic selves. Cam performers with normative bodies get to be themselves and profit both because their performances fall in line with normative cultural scripts and clients see these performances as authentic. In addition, because these performers are being themselves, they report more pleasurable and fun experiences camming. Now, cam models with non-normative bodies and identities must manufacture identities and perform sex in ways that are not in line with their actual identities. While performers with non-normative identities can earn high wages and can still enjoy their work, their work will involve more strategic labor and more acting, which can negatively affect their experience of pleasure in camming. I highlight the ways the specific structure of desire within the camming field affects the experiences and workplace outcomes of cam models. My analysis of this sexual field also uses an intersectional framework and recognizes that gender, race, class, nationality, sexual identity, age, and ability shape the structure of desire in any sexual field.

Manufactured Identities

Creating a manufactured identity is a central component of all sex work. Sex work scholar Teela Sanders writes that sex workers create manufactured identities as an emotional management strategy. Sex workers in various segments of the erotic labor market also craft manufactured identities for protection and as business strategies. Webcam performers craft manufactured identities that can protect them from doxing and potential cyber stalkers. In addition, some performers also manufacture identities as a form of stigma management. In addition to changing her age, Lily, a 31-year-old bisexual White cis woman from the United Kingdom, said, "I also wear wigs and makeup in an attempt to not look fully like me as I have a lot of friends who go on the site I am on."

What is interesting is that webcam models are also selling embodied authenticity. To clients, webcam models are real people broadcasting themselves on the Internet. It is interesting to examine how performers manage performing authenticity and realness while also manufacturing identities that they believe have high market value in the camming field. Emma, a 29-year-old straight White cis woman from Canada, explained to me:

> I have tried to remain as genuine as is possible in this industry. There are times when I feel I would benefit from lying about my age. At 29 without children, I don't quite fit into any of the major categories customers tend to seek out. I would likely gain additional traffic if I advertised myself as under 25. When I started out, I felt the need to identify as single even though I was married at the time. Presently living with my boyfriend, I often do lie about the fact that he lives with me. I try to allow for the fantasy of my being somewhat available, for those who would seek out my services to assuage their loneliness.

Performers like Emma often highlighted that they want to be as genuine as possible. However, most models recognize that there are also benefits to manufacturing their identities in ways that satisfy customers' fantasies. They understand the monetary benefits of adhering to the field's structure of desire.

Crucially, those performers whose bodies already conform to normative US-centric beauty ideals do not have to manufacture or craft an alternative identity. People with privileged embodiments frequently said they did not manufacture identity. Andres, a 20-year-old pansexual Hispanic cis man from Colombia, said, "I don't change any part of [my identity] as I consider my users as friends and like to be honest with them." Candice, a 23-year-old biracial cis woman from the United States who doesn't use labels for her sexual identity, told me that she never changes any information about herself and does not manufacture a cam identity:

> I tell my cam family how old I am [and] what country I live in; because of my modeling, people know what state I live in. I tell them I have a Daddy (boyfriend) who I live with. They know I swing either way; I don't really care for labels. Without ever giving away my real name, I'm pretty open and honest about my life.

Similar to Candice, Vicki, a 20-year-old bisexual White cis woman from the United States, simply told me that she changes nothing: "I come as I am." Performers like Andres, Candice, and Vicki can come as they are because they have privileged embodiments. They are capitalizing on existing privileges that mark their bodies as hot and, thus, already sexually valuable. Young performers and those who are White were the least likely to actively manufacture a cam identity that is different from their offline identity. Andres and Candice are both people of color, but both are in their early 20s and are privileged by colorism within the system of White supremacy.[6] They are both cisgender and able-bodied. The crucial point is, people with the most privileged embodiments do not have to craft manufactured identities and, most often, do not have to perform sex in ways that are inauthentic or not in line with their real desires. People whose bodies have the most sexual capital in this field are also able to earn decent wages, feel empowered and agentic, and derive pleasures from their work. Pleasure is derived from the successful accomplishment of normative embodiment.

Manufactured identities and all these performances shift over time. The identities performers craft are not static, but in flux. Performers who have been camming for long periods may no longer manufacture identities once they have acquired a loyal following. Mihela is a 29-year-old straight White cis woman from Romania who has been camming for four years. When I asked about her manufacturing a cam identity, she responded, "I did this at the beginning, but now, I show myself as I am, years, heterosexuality, relationship." Identities offline and online are malleable and shift over time, especially as we move in and out of different social contexts and fields.

Manufacturing Invisible Identities: Age, Sexual Identity, and Relationship Status

While many performers are hesitant to be dishonest about their identities because they know authenticity and realness are critical in camming, many also change aspects of their identities on their profiles to enhance their marketability through the normative performance of sex. When manufacturing an identity, it was most common for performers to alter their ages, sexual identities, and relationship status. Interestingly, performing sex online in socially valuable ways means performing youthfulness, bisexuality, and singleness, and each of these areas shares an important relationship with gender performativity. These identities and performances are examples of what I call *manufactured invisible identities*. Performers have the easiest time manufacturing aspects of their identities that are not necessarily visible to clients. An individual's age, for example, is not necessarily as readable on the body as race is. Certain aspects of performer identity can be easily manipulated and performed in ways that produce sexual capital within the hierarchy of desire present in this online sex market.

Performing Youthfulness

Performing youthfulness is an essential aspect of how cam models perform sex online. Scholars have written about the ways society values youthful appearance and demonizes aging bodies.[7] It is critical that future scholarship pay more attention to youth privilege and theorize around the relationship between gender and age.[8] Gender scholars have studied the aging double standard, or the ways women in various cultures globally are punished for aging, while men are rewarded for it. In camming, like other display industries, however, youthfulness is valued for all bodies, especially for men. While youthfulness is the ideal, many female performers can find work in Mom I'd Like to Fuck (MILF) and

Mature categories, and men who are not youthful can generally not find work at all or must lie about their ages to be marketable. In camming, what I call the *gendered age tax* exists more for men than it does for women. In this display industry, both the wage gap and gendered age tax are inverted.

I asked all survey respondents if and how they manufacture their cam identities. Specifically, I asked them if they altered any part of their identity on their profiles. By far the most common answer was that they lowered their age. Performers who said they make themselves younger insisted that there is a market demand for young bodies—that in the camming field, clients believe that younger bodies are the most attractive. Jimena, a 33-year-old gay Hispanic trans woman from Colombia, said, "I put less age because clients [are] attract[ed] more to young girls." Performers said standards of beauty are directly correlated with age. Rachel, a 36-year-old straight White trans woman from the United States, told me, "I change my cam age from 36 to 28, because, due to societal standards on age and beauty, you have to fit into the young nubile category as long as you can." Cata, a 34-year-old bisexual cis woman from Costa Rica who did not identify using racial categories, said, "My stage age is 28 [because] when I started working, I thought it would be beneficial for the job." Interestingly, the emphasis on performing youthfulness was a significant concern not only for female performers.

Cis male performers frequently noted the importance of youthfulness in performing sex. Arvav, a 25-year-old straight Asian cis man from India, told me, "I have changed my age from 25 to 22. This is simply [because] many older people prefer younger guys." In sex markets, youth is a valuable attribute, especially for male performers. The cis men in my sample who were over 40 shaved at least 10 years off their age. Steve, a 43-year-old straight White cis man from the United States, said:

> When possible, I identify as 30 years old. . . . I look much younger than 43 and seem to attract more clients that way. . . . A few MILF cam women have labelled me as in my 20s for the purpose of their shows when I have appeared as guest cock.

For male cam models, being over 30 comes with a penalty that these men don't want to pay.

Many performers rationalized altering their ages and performing youthfulness by saying that they look young anyway. This is significant because, again, performers are selling embodied authenticity. If someone who is 50 tells people they are 20, clients will likely know they are being dishonest and not purchase their services. How much age can be manipulated is limited, but performers can generally manufacture an identity as much as 10 years younger than they really are. This was especially true for cam models who told me they "look young anyway." Many of the performers I spoke with explained their behavior in this way:

> I'm in my 30s, and I advertise that I'm in my 20s because no one believes me when I tell them I'm in my 30s.
> —Halona, a 32-year-old queer Native American woman from the United States

> I say I'm 25 years old. I lie because my webcam persona is a dream girl. She is the product of men's fantasy. So I say I'm younger because I look younger, and being 25, I'm appealing to the young guys (18–20) but also to the older ones.
> —Luiza, a 32-year-old straight White cis woman from Brazil

> I advertise online that I am still 23. I look younger than I am, and since there seems to be a cultural ideology that, after a certain age, women are either no longer sexy/appealing or less so, it's a career longevity thing.
> —Jen, a 25-year-old bisexual White cis woman from the United States

> I say that I am 19 on cam because I've found that many men gravitate towards teens when they are looking for someone to masturbate to. There's probably some sense of taboo involved [with] older guy/younger girl [scenes].
> —Allison, a 20-year-old bisexual White cis woman from the United States

Halona, Luiza, and Jen asserted that they look young anyway, so they implied that they might as well capitalize on cultural scripts in ways that benefit them. Moreover, as Allison suggested, there is a market for teenage performers that models can capitalize on. Given the prevalence of taboos against intergenerational sex, the camming market, like other sex industries, provides a space for its exploration. However, no matter how performers manufacture age—they must all be 18 or older—this exploration is conducted in a way that is legal, consensual, and not exploitative.

In sum, women, unlike male performers, have more agency in their decisions to perform youthfulness. Men are more constricted by cultural scripts of age and gender than women in this particular sexual field. In other areas of social life and employment fields, women are penalized for aging. In camming, female performers can capitalize on it. Rochelle, a 55-year-old bisexual White cis woman from the United States, averages $2–4,000 a month camming. She explained that while she initially tried camming on MFC, which didn't work out, she found she could excel on CB as a performer by branding herself in the MILF category:

> I worked on MFC for a very short time. There was no room for a performer of my age. A majority of the clients watched the Juiceboxes (girls under 30). I moved over to Chaturbate 2 months later and never looked back. There is a large audience for MILFS/GILFS [grandmas I'd like to fuck]. . . . I'm now reaching 100,000 followers.

The camming field has room for mature women, who are often fetishized by younger men. In this sexual field, the hierarchy of desire means that the gendered age tax disproportionately affects male models. Moreover, by performing in MILF, GILF, and Mature categories, women can contest and subvert overlapping discourses of age and gender in ways that make them money and make performers feel empowered.[9] Again, the theoretically valuable point is that it was only women in my sample who could market themselves in this way and capitalize off of being older, which is important because, generally, it is older women—and not older men—who are erased from the cultural view.[10] Women in the camming industry still prioritize youthfulness because the field does highly value youth. However, women's sexual capital does not entirely disappear as they age. As shown in this section, actual age is invisible and requires that performers disclose their age to clients; thus, performers can manufacture age and perform youthfulness to meet the field's demands.

Performing Bisexuality

In addition to performing age, performing bisexuality is also an essential part of webcam performers' manufactured identities. Adopting a bisexual identity allows performers to seem available to all clients. In this field, straight cis men are the most likely to manufacture and perform bisexuality, although many other performers also alter their sexual identity as a form of strategic branding.

In my sample, 13% of respondents identified as queer offline. Despite the fluidity of the term "queer," there were performers who changed their identity from queer to bisexual. Naomi, a 38-year-old queer White trans woman from the United States, explained:

> I pretend that I'm more interested in men than I actually am. I do this because my fans want to imagine that they could be with me, and if I tell them I'm only romantically interested in women and femme enbies [non-binary people], they get discouraged and often leave. So, I pretend, which lets them pretend.

Like Naomi, Mike also found it helpful to perform bisexuality. Mike, a 32-year-old queer White cis man from the United States, said, "I identify as queer in real life, but sometimes I just say bisexual online, as it makes things simple." For queer performers like Mike, identifying as bisexual is more intelligible to clients than identifying as queer.

Lesbian and straight women often identify as bisexual because they believe male clients will find this categorization desirable. Tiffany, a 23-year-old lesbian Black cis woman from the United States, said:

> Well, I tell people on here that I have a girlfriend of three years; so, I do tell people that. I've told them I've been with lesbians, pretty much all my life, since I was 14 years old. I have only dated women, and I have never been in a relationship with men but I do let them know that I have sex with men. But I don't identify as bisexual. But like, for them I do.

Sexual scripts and perceptions of audience desire shape these decisions. Lesbians are designing performances for cis male clients, and the guiding assumption is that these men find bisexuality attractive in women.

Straight cis women who perform bisexuality also adopted sexual scripts related to the desires of straight cis men. Kaya, a 23-year-old straight Black cis woman from England, said, "The only thing I change is my orientation; this is because I think my customers find it more of a turn-on if I can talk about experiences with other women and what we could do together, for example a threesome scenario."

For straight male performers, it is vital to their success to perform bisexuality. Straight male performers must incessantly demonstrate through their performances that they are not gay-for-pay (even if they are). In relation to the porn industry, there has been a discussion in both the mainstream media and the academic press about men in the sex industry who are "gay-for-pay," or straight men who perform in gay porn for money.[11] While not straight, Carl, a 31-year-old bisexual Black cis man from the United States, explained how the "gay-for-pay" phenomena could adversely affect male cam performers:

I know that [there are] some people that, they had the perception of me being involved in gay-for-pay. . . . [O]ne guy got super upset with me one time because when I admitted that I, well, have been with my girlfriend, he was like, man, I'm sick of all you guys who are like, just pretending to be gay, and all of this; and then he left in like huffin' and puffin', and I was just kinda stunned. I'm like, but I never said I was gay, at any point. I mean, I'm sorry that's what you thought, but you never asked. And I never actually said, I'm gay; I'm not. I'm attracted to women quite much. So, I'm into guys and trans women [too].

Carl identifies as bisexual, but when a client thought he was straight and being deceptive, he lost the client.

Customers will immediately read unconvincing performances as deceitful, and the performer will lose that customer. For this reason, straight cis men from all over the world manufacture a bisexual identity that they then perform on cam, which is part of their performance of sex in the camming field. The following examples illustrate this point:

I consider myself to be heterosexual, but on my cam persona, I define myself as bisexual. I'm sexually open-minded and, as a male cam model,

I think I can target more gay and bisexual male clients than women. For this reason, I define myself as bisexual on cam.
—Alvaro, a 32-year-old straight White cis man from Spain

I change my sexual orientation from heterosexual to bisexual as I can target male clients, which are a majority.
—Daniel, a 32-year-old straight White cis man from Spain currently living in Poland

I identify myself as a bisexual on webcam while I'm heterosexual in real life.
—Artem, a 21-year-old straight White cis man from Russia

Alvaro, Daniel, and Artem all brand themselves as bisexual because their target audience members are men, and their manufactured identities, as well as their performances of sex, are guided by US-centric sexual scripts adopted by this particular field. Hence, whatever their actual location in the world, performers all operate according to this culturally specific logic. These particular straight male cam performers make decisions based on assumptions about the preferences of their audience whom they perceive to be gay men.[12]

While it was generally the case that straight cis men performed bisexuality, some cis men took a different approach based on a logic that some gay male clients like the challenge of turning straight men gay. Lenny, a 34-year-old polyamorous Black cis man from the United Kingdom, exemplified this alternative perspective:

I advertise as a year younger, advertise as heterosexual but offer a wide range of bisexual services in privacy. Open bisexuality deters some customers, and they prefer it to be some form of discovery that they can make a straight guy turn bi, heighten[ing] their intrigue thus creating more dialogue to prolong the session and the idea that they are interacting with a willing open-minded individual.

These cases suggest the relevance of both performativity theory and sexual fields theory to understanding cam models' choices. Performers do not perform based solely on their desires. While people may interpret sexual scripts differently, as exemplified by the different approaches adopted by performers like Alvaro, Daniel, Artem, and Lenny, the theoretically valuable point is that performances of sex are shaped by sexual scripts that are dictated by the camming field.

In addition, in a society that too often erases bisexuality, this industry values it and performers consciously work to make bisexuality visible in the field. Additionally, the ability of performers to move in and out of sexual identity categories and enjoy sexual encounters with people of genders with whom they typically wouldn't engage attests to the fluidity of human sexuality.

Performing Singleness

Performing singleness is another essential way in which models manufacture identities and perform sex. Building sexual capital in online sex work requires appearing romantically available to clients, which means that performing sex in this field requires performing singleness. Researchers have neglected this area. How does an individual's status as a single, coupled, or married person affect sexual capital? I spoke with performers about their relationship status and how it affected their work and marketability. In general, performers said that performing singleness helped them appear more available, even though they are working and uninterested in forming romantic relationships with their clients. Erica is a 28-year-old polyamorous White cis woman from the United States:

> I change my relationship status since being married definitely decreases traffic and interest. A lot of men want to believe they have a chance to date or pursue me and are loyal customers because that fantasy is part of their experience. I am upfront with everyone that I am not looking to date; and I don't lead anyone on, but sometimes, knowing that possibility is there is enough for a lot of people.

Sadie, a 33-year-old bisexual White cis woman from Canada, expressed a similar sentiment. She said, "I do identify as single or in an open relationship online. Members in the past have been jealous and unhappy about my being married. I don't wear my rings on cam or in photos."

Illustrating the way cam performers consciously perform being single, Sadie removes all cultural markers that symbolically identify her as unavailable. Performers repeatedly told me that having sexual capital in the camming field requires that they perform being single and that doing so has economic rewards. Melissa, a 25-year-old bisexual White cis woman from the United States, said, "I advertise as two years younger and single when I'm not actually single. Both of these things help raise earning levels, especially the single one. Girls who are public about their boyfriends make significantly less money." Audrey, a 24-year-old straight White cis woman from the United States, underscored this point:

> I have been in a long-term relationship while camming and am now in a more casual on-again-off-again relationship with someone new, but I consistently say I am single on cam. In my experience, I feel that members pay more if they are led to believe they could possibly have a chance with you. I find it profitable to keep up the fantasy of being a lonely, horny, single girl.

No doubt, the cultural script of being a "lonely, horny, single girl" creates enormous sexual capital for models. Performers who were married or in a relationship realized their relationship status was a hindrance to their success in this sex market.

The importance of being single and available was a factor highlighted primarily by women. Hegemonic masculinity requires that men feel in control, and they often gain a sense of manhood from dominating and controlling women.[13] By performing availability or singleness, women are doing the labor of bolstering their male clients' masculinity. Male models usually do not perform this form of gendered emotional labor for their male clients. Their interpretation of gay sexual scripts guides male performers' shows. Male performers may believe that for their ostensibly gay male clients, single status is not as important. Two gay men in my research sample, Jose (a 24-year-old White cis man from Canada) and Timothy (a 20-year-old White cis man from the United States), are in relationships, and neither felt it was necessary as gay men to change their relationship status. When I asked if they manufactured their identity, Jose said:

I usually answer questions about a boyfriend with, yes, a few or several [boyfriends], which is partially true. I have been in an open relationship for most of the years I have been online. This is also to be flirtatious, to encourage viewers to fantasize about my personal life.

Jose said that being gay and polyamorous allows him to be honest about his relationship status because he is still ostensibly available. This idea is supported by research that shows that the practice of non-monogamy is common among gay men.[14] Importantly, while the idea that consensual non-monogamies are most popular among gay men is a culturally pervasive script, it is crucial to note that people of various genders, sexualities, races, and so on practice and enjoy consensual non-monogamies.[15]

Strategically Navigating Visible Identities: Gender, Race, and Ability

Given that the client traffic in the adult webcam industry is driven heavily by the United States, US-centric discourses of femininity and masculinity shape performances of sex in the camming field. Moreover, these gendered discourses also overlap with other social factors such as race, nationality, age, and ability. In what follows, I explore how performers navigate aspects of their identity they see as visible to clients, such as gender, race, and ability, and how their performances strategically capitalize on discourses surrounding their embodiment.

Performing Femininity

All humans reside within a physical body, yet our bodies are also social bodies. Our bodies are reflections of the social order—of society. Social anthropologist Mary Douglas famously pointed to the ways social meanings or symbols are inscribed onto bodies and how, as a result, our bodies become a mechanism for the maintenance of systems of inequality.[16] Discourses of femininity are inscribed on bodies, and cultural scripts tell us what bodies are socially desirable. Different social contexts or fields then shape how those cultural scripts are deployed and interpreted.

Cam models' performances of femininity directly influence how they perform sex in the camming field. US-centric discourses of femininity also shape how models' performances are perceived and valued by clients. On mainstream websites, the successful accomplishment of normative gender produces profits and pleasure. People with non-normative embodiments do make money in this industry, but precisely because customers fetishize them and perceive their bodies as non-normative. Take, for example, my conversations with Gia, a 27-year-old queer White trans woman from the United States who has been camming for over two years, very successfully. Gia told me:

> In terms of me doing sex work, there's some glimpses of hope that people look past me being a woman with a penis, but for the most part, it's like people don't want to pay you as much as cis women. And ya know, [customers] just mostly want me to top them, which is a thing that I'm like not into, like at all! It's like kind of hard to like to even pretend. So, I feel like that's the biggest thing I get is older men, wanting to experience a chick with a dick—to top them, usually, which if you're not looking to me as a person, as a woman, you're fetishizing [me].

The sex/gender binary is pervasive, and many people still hold tight to the socially constructed idea that assigned sex must dictate gender. As social psychologists Suzanne Kessler and Wendy McKenna argue, one's genitals, specifically the absence or presence of a penis, are the defining feature of the process of attributing gender.[17] Performing femininity under these culturally defined conditions means that trans women such as Gia will often make less money than cis women because many cis men read her embodiment as other—not female—even though Gia is a woman.

Moreover, in our interview, Gia told me, "[I must] embellish how attracted I am to cis men." In performing femininity, she is often asked to perform sex acts that she finds fetishizing and undesirable, and she must feign interest in men who fetishize her. Gia's story gives us insight into how bodies reveal social hierarchies and inequalities, and the ways that in the camming industry, gender and embodiment shape access to wages and pleasure in unequal ways. Put another way, when comparing trans women and cis women's experiences of display work, it is crucial to understand that even if trans and cis women earn similar wages, cultural scripts in the camming field ensure they have vastly different and unequal work experiences.[18] Race further complicates these inequalities within the cam industry.

Tiffany and I discussed the complex relationships among race, gender, and embodiment in performing sex online:

> I can say in this business, the adult industry, being a Black girl, you can be super successful because of weird fetishes. And, we have so many looks to us; we all look different. One girl can look like this; Black girls can look like that. We have so many ways. So, I can tell by my customers. I get White guys. I get Black guys. I get Asians. I get all types of customers [that] have that fetish for a Black girl, and would never go for a Black girl in real life—that's why they're on here. So, I think that's really cool [chuckles]. I noticed that me being 21, they love the young girls . . . I can say when it comes to my body type, being petite, that really helps; they like that I'm petite and I have a butt. I have really small boobs [, and] some guys just have that fetish. So that definitely helps. But I can say, girls with more curves, they do get a lot more attention. Girls with big ol' boobs, girls that have a big ass, like, if you have both [laughter], you're perfect, so it does help in some way.

In performances of sex, many performers use sexual scripts that are both highly racialized and gendered. Race and gender are identities that are usually visible to clients, and cam models cannot as easily manipulate them in the same ways they manipulate age, sexuality, and relationship status. However, performers can exploit cultural scripts for profit. In our conversations, Tiffany often attributed her success to her body. She capitalizes on fetishes for Black girls by branding herself in the Ebony performer category. Notice, though, that Tiffany's experiences of fetishization were positive. She thinks that it's cool that men who don't typically date Black women have space to interact with them sexually. Tiffany also recognized that her youthfulness, along with her petite body and large butt, helped her make money. In figure 7.1, Tiffany has blonde hair and red lipstick. She capitalizes on and performs sex in ways that adhere to whitewashed cultural scripts. Interestingly, Tiffany also suggested that her small breasts appeal only to men with small boob fetishes

Figure 7.1. Tiffany in her studio room looking into her webcam. She is wearing a pink-and-white polka-dot bathing suit.

and that having "big ol' boobs and a big ass" is perfection. Tiffany is correct; despite the structure of desire in the camming field, how customers interpret cultural scripts about beauty and sexiness will vary based on race, nationality, age, and so on.

I spoke with a performer named Crista whose comments helped me to unpack further how racialized femininities influence performances of sex in the cam industry. Crista, a 27-year-old polyamorous White cis woman from the United States, explained:

> I have a relatively thin athletic build. I think that I do have a sort of body type that looks younger than I am. I'm 27. But I think people see me, and

they think I might look a little bit younger; but I know men definitely are looking for young girls, teenagers, [and] that type of thing really plays a huge role in how well girls do. And I think, definitely personality . . . I think having some level of, I dunno, insight or understanding about the world, having deeper conversations than just, talking about sexual things does play a role. I mean, there is definitely a lot of sexual stuff going on, but when that isn't happening, a lot of the conversations are really interesting. And I think like part of that is what gets people kind of interested in staying in the room.

Like Crista, many women throughout this book talk about the importance of personality. It is crucial that we appreciate the gendered connotation of the word "personality." Part of performing sex requires performing femininity by doing emotional labor and often having deep conversations with male clients. Crista also got uncomfortable when she started telling me about how she performs racialized femininity:

Two nights ago, I was online, and there was this guy who was [pause] there's a big, like, White supremacy scare going on right now, and somebody was sending me a lot of tokens during a cum show while he was saying, like, a lot of [comments] like, breeding your White pussy type of thing; and it made me really uncomfortable. He would ask me to say certain things about, like having a pure baby . . . a lot of guys have pregnancy fetishes, and he wanted me to say something along those lines. And I was just like, no. Like, I could never say that; I wouldn't want to be associated with that. . . . It makes you feel conflicted because they're giving you money and . . . either I have to kick this guy out, even though he just gave me $50, but I can't let him stay here because he's saying some, like, really messed-up things. So, I think they're doing it on purpose; like, they want you to have to feel like you should go along with it because they're paying you for it, and, so, I think that they are trying to manipulate you a little bit by giving you a lot of money and thinking they can do that because they're giving you money for it.

Race is a visible identity, and performers must often consciously make choices about performing racialized femininities and masculinities. Crista's story suggests that clients often expect that she perform White femininity. Even when Crista refused to say things such as "I wanna have your pure Aryan baby," this exchange still underscores the crucial relationships among performing sex, gender, race, and embodiment. Sexual racism shapes performances in the field and performers must choose how and when to exploit racist tropes for economic gain.

Amelia, a 29-year-old straight White woman from England who has cammed sporadically for six years, also discussed how gender, race, ability, and embodiment shape her performances of sex:

> I am a U.K. size 10. I'm not sure what size that is in America, but it's slim. I've got a 34 DD natural bust. So I'm blessed with quite decent proportions. I'm an hourglass shape. The Crohn's [disease] keeps me very thin. So I've never had an issue with weight other than being underweight. So when I'm at a healthy weight and I am curvy, I know that I am naturally what a lot of men would like to see. The only thing I think that I could benefit from now is that my ass isn't particularly big. And we're now in more of a culture where people like the Kardashian kind of ass. . . . I get those [clients], like, can you ass-clap? No! I'm a White girl. I have a flat ass. I can't ass-clap, like, I'm sorry [laughs]. . . . I've noticed that over the last couple of years, like more and more requests are like ass stuff, particularly things that's like ass-clapping, booty shaking, and if I was to get any sort of cosmetic procedure, which I'm not planning on doing, it would probably be like butt injections just because that's what I get requests for. Um, but yeah, I definitely think being White, like the White slim woman, benefits me and is why I've been able to have some success. Because I've had girls contact me through my site before. And they're like, I'm doing everything you said, but I'm still not really seeing the money. And so, they'll ask me to like be in one of their shows; and then I'll see that, oh, you're a Black woman, and I don't wanna be like, oh, you'll never make money because you're Black, because that's not true. But you're probably not going to making as much just because, unfortunately, on those sites, race tends to be a fetish thing . . . it jades you, when you think about things like this. Like, you would never talk about, in polite company; you don't talk about race, but the way guys will talk to you in cams about fetishes and race and things, like, the way they speak in public chat, the way they speak to other cam models based on my experiences talking to other cam models, like, they're so racist and horrible. In all honesty, if I

was an Asian camgirl or a Black camgirl, I don't know how I would deal with it? It's just, ugh. I would hate to be like, oh, you need to embrace this like, Asian fetish thing. 'Cause in the street I'd be like, if a guy treats you like that, that's disgusting.

First, Amelia is very clear that her normative feminine embodiment is what makes her performances of sex valuable. As she noted, she is slim, has large breasts, and is White. She also said that her Crohn's disease had played a role in why she has remained thin. Chronic illness and disability are not always visible and very often do require disclosure. Amelia's story should remind us of the importance of being able-bodied in performing normative femininity. Amelia told me about how her Crohn's disease often negatively affected her ability to work. She can often hide her pain from clients, or not cam during flare-ups, but either choice can adversely affect her income. Her story is a reminder that being able-bodied is essential for understanding the structure of desire in this field.

Second, Amelia also highlighted that both cultural and historical context shape beauty ideals. She joked that, over time, clients have come to want to see large asses and that performances involving ass-play are increasingly more valuable. Amelia coyly linked this shift to race when she noted that she cannot ass-clap because she is White. While she made this statement in jest, her comment speaks to the importance of analyzing the ways sexual scripts shift over time, and are shaped by race and culture. Third, as Amelia continued to reflect on her racial privilege in the industry, she reinforced that it is White femininity that is most highly valued, and she can capitalize on these discourses by performing White femininity.

Performing Masculinity

Discourses of masculinity are also mapped onto bodies and enacted under other normative regimes such as race, age, nationality, and sexuality. Male performers use their bodies as symbols of masculine power. Professor of Gender and Women's Studies Susan Bordo writes, "Of course, muscles have chiefly symbolized and continue to symbolize masculine power as physical strength frequently operating as a means of coding the 'naturalness of sexual difference.'"[19] In camming, the most valued male bodies are fit, well-toned, and muscular. Given the under-representation of trans men in this field, it is critical to note that it's the bodies of toned, fit cis men that have sexual capital. While Bordo and others have recognized the relationship between masculinity and the body, sexual scripts also map onto these culturally defined understandings of masculinity. Performing masculinity is not only about oiling up a six-pack before a show; it is also about performing in ways that adhere to sexual scripts that are valued in the camming field. Jason, a 24-year-old bisexual White cis man from the United States, said, "I change my age down to 21 instead of 24 because most LGBT men tend to like guys that are 18–23. . . . I'm five-foot-eight, but I tell people I'm six feet because the community likes tall guys." Importantly, Jason performs masculinity in ways that he believes adhere to gay sexual scripts.

Perceptions of sexual scripts in gay communities often shape the way male performers design their performances. These scripts stifle the agency of male performers. Aron, a 31-year-old bi-curious White Hungarian cis man, said:

> The male community, I think, it's not so diverse, because gay guys usually look, nowadays, actually online, almost the same. Most of them are like, somewhat muscular, maybe a few extra pounds, tattoos or not, but they're really similar; and you don't really see fat guys broadcasting and earning a huge amount of money or, I don't know, building a huge fan base. . . . I would say that [gay men] like athletic people who seem healthy, who look like they're taking care of their bodies, and they're shaped nicely and they seem to be eating healthy, not like pizza and junk food all the time. And I think this is a huge factor. And on heterosexual people, it's much more diverse because they seem to have a lot more fetishes, or their interests are way more branching out into different body types and whatever. So, I would say that as a guy, you don't really have the possibility to just eat whatever you want [and not] take care about your body and then be crazy successful because not that many people are going to go into the room.

Aron underscored Bordo's point—for male cam models, there is an expectation that their bodies be lean, healthy, and muscular. Aron and I discussed his tattoos and the ways that his tattoos helped him market

Figure 7.2. Aron is looking down. He is wearing a grey sleeveless hoodie that shows off his tattoos.

himself to clients who are very focused on young and muscular male bodies. Large tattoos, often referred to as "pieces" or (especially if they cover a major portion of an arm or leg) "sleeves," are seen as masculine symbols in this field. Aron's comments also highlighted the importance of examining how sexual identity and gender shape sexual scripts. Aron articulated pervasive stereotypes about gay men, which suggest that gay men are superficial and seek out only men who are fit, athletic, and muscular. While there are fields, such as bars and events catering to bears, where gay men with more massive physiques have enormous sexual capital, in the camming field, like most sex industries, gay, fat, hairy men have low sexual capital.[20] While there is a thriving niche market of big beautiful women (BBW) and supersized big beautiful women (SSBBW), there is no market for fat men in camming.[21]

Aron also noted that the cam industry places greater scrutiny on male bodies and shows more appreciation for diversity among female models. I asked Aron to tell me more about this particular point.

> I think it is [harder for men], yes, regarding the body type; it's definitely harder. . . . [Also] with gay people in my room, they usually just wanna see my dick or my ass, or they wanna see me cum or jerk it or whatever. And that basically, that's it. Yeah, that's it. Not really extreme, and then you don't have too much fantasy there. But with the girl performers, you have, I don't know you could write a whole book just with the names of the fetishes and then the kinds of requests people are asking. And there are, of course, the viewers who are female. I didn't really have too many of them, but . . . you can [tell they are women] even without them telling you they are female; you can tell because . . . [of] how they are communicating and what they are saying. If a guy's coming into the room, even if he says he's a 19-year-old girl, if he starts with show me your dick or show me your ass or something, that's a guy. That's a guy. No girl ever starts with show me your dick.

According to Aron, gay sexual scripts often mean that male clients request a limited repertoire of sex acts and often focus on immediate gratification—as in the client who enters his room and immediately demands to see his dick. These scripts can adversely affect the earnings of male cam models.

Jose, a 24-year-old gay White cis man from Canada, also told me about his performances of sex online:

> I have not yet changed my age, but I do feel a certain pressure to be or appear younger online. I may change my advertised age in the future. I maintained that I am male online. I maintain that I am gay online. Some commenters are surprised by this . . . I am white/white-passing and do not comment on my race online. Online, I state that I am based in [Northeastern US city], but do not make mention or answer questions about my nationality. My online name XXXXXXXX Jose,[22] somewhat intentionally gives mixed signals about my origins. I think this name is why people often ask questions about where I come from.

Jose noted the ways that sexual scripts are gendered, raced, and aged and how these factors influenced his performance online. He mentioned that clients are often surprised that he identifies as gay, which is because most male performers identify as bisexual, and, again, gay-for-pay discourse shapes clients' perceptions of performers. Interestingly, Jose intentionally ambiguously performs both race and nationality. While Jose is White, he uses this cam name to exploit racialized discourses of the hot Latino, and the ability to do so is a privilege of his Whiteness.

Unlike Jose, for performers who do not identify as gay, straight cis male performers often devise and create strategies to perform sex that allow them to navigate their encounters with what they perceive to be all gay male clients, and, in doing so, they bolster their masculinity. A primary strategy to maintain their masculinity is to use heteronormative sexual scripts to design their shows. Specifically, one way straight men can maintain their masculinity is to perform on cam as a member of a couple with a cis female performer—a topic that I discussed with Ronnie.

Ronnie is 35-year-old White straight and polyamorous cis man from the United States. He started doing porn when he was 19. He has attended college and is still trying to break into the porn industry. Ronnie said he began camming because he's an exhibitionist and because it's fun and gives him access to money. Ronnie will not cam alone; he cams only with women. He has performed with at least ten different women, none of whom were his girlfriends. Finding women to cam with is an example of a strategy employed by straight cis men unwilling to service male clients alone. Ronnie said he cammed with open-minded female friends from school, and he used career websites catering to the sex industry such as SexyJobs to find women with whom to cam. Ronnie and I talked about why he cams only with women and not as a solo cam performer:

> Well, ya know a lot of times, it gets annoying because it's like, so many guys that are trying to hit on me. And that's, I mean, most of the demographic, ya know, porn watchers are men.

Ronnie said he does not like to perform alone because men always hit on him, which he finds annoying. He said that even when he performs with women, however, men still hit on him:

Figure 7.3. Ronnie working with a female cam model. A woman is lying on her back on a bed with Ronnie's penis in her mouth.

> A lot of times, there's like guys that are literally just like talking about me, and kind of hitting on me during [the show], ya know, me with the girl doing what we're doing and stuff.

Ronnie's understanding of his own manhood shapes his performances of sex. Unlike many other cis male performers, he has no desire to perform bisexuality. Performers like Ronnie find strategies to navigate the structure of desire in the camming field without compromising their masculinity. In order to feel comfortable, Ronnie goes out of his way to perform straight White masculinity.

Matt, a 23-year-old straight White cis man from the United States living in Mexico, also actively stylized his performances in ways that helped him maintain his sense of masculinity.

> There are things I don't do as like a straight male. I don't do any like anal insertion. I don't do anything like that. I don't have any like dildos or toys for that, but other than that, pretty much anything goes. Like, if you tip me . . . I'll go—you want to see me dance, I'll dance. You want to see me

jerk off with a bottle of mustard? Like, I'll do that [laughter]. It's whatever you want. . . . So, like when I first started like doing it, I definitely thought I was going to get like a lot—I was hoping for girls. But, like me as a person, I've always been like really comfortable with my sexuality. Like, I know who I am; like, I'm not like a homophobe or anything. I have a lot of good friends who are gay. So, it's not something—it never really like bothered me, but it was, it wasn't like what I expected going into it. I definitely was hoping it would be a bunch of girls. . . . So, at first it was kind of like, I was sitting there like, man a lot of guys are watching me; that's kind of weird, but like I said, I'm always really open—I'm still open-minded, but as an open-minded person, it never bothered me. It was just not what I expected. But I definitely enjoy it though. I think it's mainly the fact that there is like a screen between me and them. Like, I can't see them, so I think that's like one of the biggest things that helps. . . . 'Cause I do know if I was like in a club with all the people in my room, like, I would definitely not want that. . . . I mean, some of 'em are amazing, amazing people; and I know they would never try anything, but like a lot of the people they are, they're very demanding. They want it, and they want it now.

The scripts that guide Matt's performances of sex are highly gendered. Like Ronnie, Matt created boundaries in the sex acts he will perform that allow him to maintain his masculinity, which is also bound to his sexuality. He admitted several times that when he started camming, he hoped he'd have more female clients. First, performers want to enjoy their work and find pleasure in their work. If performers have to perform acts that they do not find enjoyable, and like Ronnie even make them feel annoyed or disgusted, then quite simply, they cannot enjoy one of the benefits of camming—personal pleasure.

Matt also worked very hard to explain that he is not a homophobic person, but at the end of our conversation, it was telling that he also admitted he would not ever perform a form of sex work where other men physically touched him. Interestingly, again, we see that the online context is essential. The Internet becomes a way for straight cis men to perform sex work in ways that do not comprise their masculinity. The online context allows men like Matt to enjoy their work, which he said he really does. A sociological analysis of pleasure, in this case, is revealing. Matt may not be attracted to men offline, but he acquires pleasure from what sociologist Kevin Walby calls "touching encounters"—their affectual exchanges, and performing in the online context allows him to enjoy sex acts performed for other men.[23] He performs sex acts for other men and retains his straight identity. Matt's story and on-cam performances make clear that human sexuality and desire are far more fluid than the rigid identity categories we draw on to signal community membership suggest.

At the end of this section of the interview, Matt also stated that his male clients could also be demanding. The other straight and bi-curious cis men I interviewed, such as Aron, mirrored this sentiment. Matt and Aron both remarked that their male clients are demanding. Men often expressed to me that they felt pressured by clients to drop, pop, and roll. While many clients want to talk and develop intimate bonds with performers, many of the men with whom I spoke suggested that masculinity shaped their performances of sex in different ways from how femininity was shaping the performances of their female peers. Male performers face what Michael Johnson calls the "ejaculation imperative."

> I offer the notion of the "ejaculation imperative" to describe and explain how the anatomical function of ejaculation embodies and perpetuates dominant masculine identity. I argue that ejaculation symbolically represents "maleness" within the United States, where males are taught from a young age to produce an erection that results in ejaculation, thereby learning to inextricably link their identity with their physiological performance. . . . The social meaning attributed to ejaculation is powerfully equated with the dominant masculine identity. . . . I start from a position that notes within our dominant culture how ejaculation and the mechanisms of time and performance define "success," which[,] in turn[,] cause this imperative to become the embodiment of men's masculinity.[24]

In the sexual field of camming, US-centric discourses of masculinity shape the imperative to drop, pop, and roll. Aggression characterizes hypermasculine sexual scripts. The performance of sex is not a slow or romantic encounter. Matt explained this well and how it affects the performer. Matt said:

I'm not going to say it bothers me when people like just come in my room and like, show me your dick! Like, 'cause you know, I am on a porn website—that is my job, so it doesn't bother me. But it's like, you want to say hi first? Or like, hey what's up how you doin'?

Matt's tone suggested to me that while it doesn't bother him enough to refuse a demanding client's money, he ideally would enjoy more intimacy with his clients. However, the gendered nature of sexual scripts often prevents this experience. The ejaculation imperative is a vehicle for masculine validation in camming. Customers can bolster their manhood by demanding to see Matt's dick and that he jerk off immediately and cum. Performing masculinity diminishes the pleasure that many male cam performers experience while performing sex. Moreover, hypermasculine gendered scripts can have an adverse effect on wages.

Conclusion

One explanation for the inversion of the traditional gendered wage gap is that there is simply a higher market demand for sexual services performed by women than men in this field. However, what I have also shown here is that this wage gap is also a reflection of the gendered and racialized sexual scripts that performers draw on in creating manufactured identities and performing sex in this field. In performing masculinity, and adhering to gay sexual scripts, male cam models are at a disadvantage. If a performer does a private show at $3.99 per minute, a male performer who is instructed to only jerk off to climax will make less than the female performer who has a lengthy conversation and a striptease, long before she even touches her genitals.

The camming field values embodied authenticity, and customers are skeptical about male performers being gay-for-pay. From the start, male performers' embodied authenticity is often questioned. In this field, if cis men are most likely to perform bisexuality, this reality also helps to explain why women earn higher wages. Clients want to believe that attraction is mutual. Women's performances are more likely to be read as authentic, unlike those of cis men, who are often caught up in the gay-for-pay stigma and seen as deceitful performers only out to make a buck. While sexuality is a seemingly invisible identity category that is easily manipulated for marketing purposes and profit, gender and the gay-for-pay discourse make performing bisexuality more difficult for men. This finding is in line with popular cultural imagery that fetishizes female bisexuality and, at the same time, mistrusts and demonizes male bisexuality.

It is a crucial finding that display industries are currently the only markets where women outearn men. What does it suggest if the only industries in which women have advantages over men are industries in which women must display their bodies? On the one hand, this situation reifies the idea that women's most significant and only assets are their bodies and beauty, which is sexist. However, the performances women provide clients are not just the source of decent wages; these shows, in many cases, also empower women and provide them with pleasure. Thus, there is absolutely nothing wrong with women using sexual capital just as they would use economic, social, symbolic, or cultural capital.[25]

8

For Black Models Scroll Down

Sexual Racism and the Camming Field

On August 1, 2015, a popular performer named Sunny Olivia started a wave of controversy when she performed for approximately 3,300 viewers in a Nazi officer's uniform, in front of a giant Nazi flag. While many customers questioned the performance, some people posted racist and anti-Semitic comments. Vocativ, an online news service, reported that Olivia made approximately $30,000 in tips before MyFreeCams shut down the performance.[1] Immediately, customers and other cam performers began protesting the performance and calling out Olivia for her use of racist imagery. Many performers and customers took to Twitter using hashtags such as #shamemfc and #suspendOlivia. While debates over free speech dominated the August 2015 Twitter war, to learn more about this particular incident I also turned to various web forums, specifically to hear what other performers thought of Olivia's performance.

The Twitter debate revolved around those defending Olivia's artistic choices and supporting free speech even when the content was in poor taste, versus those rebutting the free speech argument by calling her a racist promoting hate speech. The web forums, however, revealed something different. While there was some degree of free-speech debate, the performers posting on the web forums were familiar with Olivia's brand, which she had built around shock value and not performing traditionally erotic or sex-focused shows. One poster brilliantly summed up the controversy and the sociological significance of the moment:

> I think there's probably a lot of undue extrapolation going on from both sides of the argument. . . . Olivia's supporters will look at her wearing Nazi garb and reciting Nazi speeches before playing a pop song and dancing and laughing and say, it's art! She's clearly making a nuanced comment on Nazism! The plight of the Jews! The futility of war! The human condi-

tion and how we process atrocities! Our responses to authority and our willingness to follow orders! How society has trained us to react with Pavlovian fervor to scant iconography! Olivia's detractors meanwhile will look at the same thing and say, she's racist! She's a Nazi! She's exploiting human tragedy! She hates Jews! She's encouraging hate speech! None of which is really the case on a fundamental level. Without knowing Olivia's intent, all we have is a video/live feed of her wearing a Nazi uniform. There's no real way to ascribe meaning to her performance without undue extrapolation.

For what it's worth, I don't think she's racist, but nor do I think her "art" has any substance or intellectual weight behind it. Nothing about anything I've ever seen her do suggests to me that she's a satirist. I think she just enjoys dressing up and through her years as a cam girl has learnt that the more controversial the character she dresses up as, the more attention it will get. She knows that there will be as much negative attention shone on it as positive and she knows that her fans will blindly support anything she does and defend her "artistry" and she knows that the more vocal her detractors are, the more her fans will step up and support (read tip) her. In short, I think she's a poor artist but an incredibly smart business woman. She knows how to manufacture a shitstorm in which dollar bills get blown directly in to her bank account.

I think I decided long ago that Olivia's brand of entertainment isn't for me. I can't really fathom what her regulars get out of tipping what they do for what she does on cam, the artistic merit of which eludes me. But I can't help but respect her as a business woman. She carved out a strange, strange niche for herself, hooked big tippers, and now courts controversy for monetary gain. And it works for her.

This cam model made clear her belief that Olivia's performance was not a nefarious plot to promote a neo-Nazi platform. Olivia was making money. As other performers stated on the board, "Olivia is [just] a troll," and taking to Twitter and wasting energy calling her a racist and campaigning to have her suspended (which did not work) may have missed the more significant point here.

Let's return to the Vocativ report that Olivia made $30,000 for this short performance and that 3,300 people logged in to see it. While I was not able to substantiate these claims, let's assume she profited well

Figure 8.1. MFC cam performer Sunny Olivia performing in front of a Nazi flag.

from the performance, and not just from that day's tips. This incident generated much publicity for Olivia's already unconventional brand. We should also ask ourselves, What does it suggest that a performer on an erotic website could profit so much from a Nazi-inspired performance—that so many people were not only interested in watching but that she'd be rewarded handsomely for it? This was not just a story about a racist performer named Olivia. It was a microcosm of a much broader story about the entanglements of neoliberal capitalism and White supremacy.

The Olivia controversy is an interesting springboard for analysis of how the system of White supremacy shapes sex markets. In the camming field, White supremacy is institutionalized. White supremacy does not just dictate the behaviors of consumers such as those who tipped Olivia, global White supremacy structures the entire market; this is how Olivia knew she could exploit and use Nazi imagery to make a profit. As the aforementioned poster said, "I think she's a poor artist but an incredibly smart business woman." Olivia was undoubtedly not the first capitalist to exploit racism for profit, and she indeed won't be the last. What also came up in the web forums was that some performers questioned to what extent participants in the camming field, including cam site owners, moderators, and performers, exploit racist discourses in service of profit. The answer is—to whatever extent they can under the law. If a behavior or action is legal, and there is a market for it, capitalists love it—even if it's racist. White Supremacy and capitalism are bedfellows.

Sexual Racism

Sexual racism shapes the structure of desire in the camming field— the structure of cam sites, the cultural scripts deployed in the field, and interactions between performers and customers. As political scientist Sonu Bedi puts it, sexual racism is "prioritizing an individual as a possible romantic, intimate partner on account of their race in a way that reinforces extant racial hierarchy or stereotypes."[2] When customers select performers based solely on nationality or race, they are motivated by sexual racism. As urban sociologist and sexualities scholar Jason Orne describes, sexual racism is not only about the individual choices people make when using racial factors to select sexual partners. Sexual racism is established by larger structural and cultural forces. According to Orne, "sexual racism is a system of racial oppression, shaping an individual's partner choices to privilege whites and harm people of color. It manifests itself on three levels: structural, cultural, and interactional."[3] As Orne argues, sexual racism takes three interdependent forms; I analyze how each form operates in the camming field.

First, structural sexual racism occurs at the level of the sexual field. In this chapter, I analyze how the camming industry and cam sites structure interactions between cam models and customers in ways that sustain sexual racism. Second, in my analysis of cultural sexual racism, I examine how cam models' performances and customers' desires draw upon highly racialized sexual scripts created within cultures, which under global White supremacy privilege Whiteness. Further, I show how the bodies of people of color are often exoticized and consumed for their otherness. Third, I also analyze the ways sexual racism operates at the interactional level in the camming field, and I argue that when individuals draw on racist cultural scripts in their sexual interactions, they reproduce the system of White supremacy. Sexual racism in the camming field is best understood as a complex interplay between structural, cultural, and interactional forms of sexual racism. It is the dynamic nature of sexual racism that buttresses its power and permanence.

My focus on sexual racism and how it disadvantages cam models of color fills a gap in the growing body of scholarship about sexual racism online. Contemporary research on sexual racism online has tended to focus on gay communities and sexual and romantic interactions between men.[4] The focus of this existing research has been on how people who are seeking partners on the Internet use website filters to select only people who are their "type"; people use the language of personal preference to legitimate their racist cleansing of eligible matches.[5] On cam sites, just like on dating apps and websites, customers can use such filters. These filtering mechanisms allow customers to search only for certain nationalities or races of models, which is a form of sexual racism. In applying the framework of sexual racism to my case study of the camming industry, I contribute to the burgeoning research on racism online and in sex work.

Sexual racism is a factor that thwarts the success of Black women in the camming field. I empirically show how the financial outcomes of Black performers are affected by the institutionalization of sexual racism in the camming industry. Drawing from statistical analyses of models' success as measured by a website-generated "camscore" with the independent variables of race and nation of origin and qualitative data from the study, I demonstrate the intricate ways that one popular webcam site, MyFreeCams, perpetuates race-, class-, and gender-based inequities. This line of inquiry is crucial because the analytical framework of sexual racism has not been applied in the sex work literature. Even in the best of the literature on sex workers, race is usually a footnote in a larger narrative about class and power dynamics between sex workers and customers. Placing race at the center of analysis addresses a longstanding oversight in the sex work literature.[6]

MFC Is Not a Black Girl Site

Marginalization of Black women on MFC was the subject of many threads on popular web forums and thus my selection of the site for this case study was informed by reports of racism made directly by models. One model on a webcam forum said:

I do not see Black women banking on MFC. And I see a lot of great personable Black women! I don't think it's because they don't have the drive or the motive to do MFC, I think it's because MFC caters to men who like tiny White women.

In my study, cam models generally acknowledged that, overall, Black models did not do well on MFC. A typical comment on various web forums was that "MFC is not a Black girl site." One performer stated, "I agree with MFC seeming to be mostly in favor of petite White women, though I do see a few Black girls earning on there. Compared to the amount of White women who bank, the 3–4 Black women I've ever seen in the top half of the first page really isn't a lot." Interestingly, many of the models in this study, including Black models, adhered to neoliberal ideas about success on MFC (and other websites). Many argued that it was not racism, but Black models' failure to craft entertaining shows that explained their lack of success on sites such as MFC. Put another way, despite the recognition that Black women were not among the top earners on MFC, the explanation for this most often fell back on neoliberal ideas about the importance of rugged individualism. A Black cam model posted:

I think that it helps if people stop pigeonholing themselves. I am *so* much more than my skin colour. I think that Black women will make it to the top when they stop thinking of themselves as Black and start thinking of themselves as business people like any other business person. I was super shitty on MFC up until now. Was it because I was Black and didn't stand a chance? No, it was because I was absolute shit at the MFC system. I didn't understand it. I hated free chat and didn't like the environment. Then yesterday I had another $200 day when before I was going days with making nothing or $2 max on MFC. My skin colour didn't suddenly change my attitude did. . . . I am not my skin colour. I am not my hair. I am not my weight. I will make top dollar because of my mind and my abilities. I am Black and I am sure I made more money yesterday than some of the White girls on this site did. I have gained a ton of weight, but I'm sure I made more money than some of the little pixie girls did yesterday. There will *always* be something that we are told will hold us back or hold us down but that's bullshit sweety; so, pay it no mind. What *will* hold you back *every* time is your mind. Your outlook on life. You are not your skin.

Many performers said that success hinges upon having a positive attitude and being skilled at your craft. Neoliberal capitalism teaches workers that lack of success is the result of individual pathology. This rhetoric blames the poor for poverty—not the economic system designed to ensure poverty through the exploitation of alienated labor. In the camming field, a cam model's lack of success on MFC or elsewhere is often blamed on laziness or poorly designed shows. According to this logic, it is not that MFC is not a Black girl site; if Black women on MFC do not do well, it is because they are doing something wrong. I explore models' assertions that MFC is not a Black girl site. Specifically, I answer the following questions cam models posed: (1) Are Black models less likely to succeed on MFC financially? (2) If Black models do not earn high wages on MFC, how do we explain their poor outcomes on the website?

Measuring Success on MFC

Success on MFC is measured using a "camscore." A model's camscore is listed publicly on their profile. The camscore is a number generated by the site that reflects the money made by the model based on the ratio of number of hours spent online to the amount of money made in tips—models that spend the least amount of time online but generate the most money in tips have the highest camscores. The camscore is a number that is used to quantify success on the website. Unfortunately, there is no publicly available information about the actual algorithm site moderators use to generate this score.

In addition to the camscore, all of the models on the site create public profiles for themselves. On their personal profiles, models provide basic information: their name on the website, gender, body type, ethnicity, hair color, eye color, weight, age, city, country, sexual preference, and so on. I used data provided by the models about their identities to test for statistical correlations between cam models' identities and camscores. Independent variables included race, nationality, age, education background, and sexual orientation. To examine sexual racism in the camming field, I focus only on my analyses of the variables race and nation of origin, and the dependent variable—camscore. Given that cam models create manufactured identities, a limitation of my quantitative data is that data on cam profiles can be falsified. To address this issue, I excluded data from the sample that I knew was falsified (e.g., a top-grossing model reported her age as 109) and I later use qualitative data to probe the trends I found using the statistical analyses. Collectively, I use this data to answer whether Black models are generally not successful on MFC.[7]

Who's Successful on MFC?

MFC and other cam sites advertise and report that models can and do earn high wages. As demonstrated in chapter 3, webcam performers' wages are likely far lower on average than webcam sites report. In my sample, the mean camscore was 5,691. Most of the camscores fell below the mean value, and extremely high camscores were less common. Only 27 models had camscores above 20,000 and the lowest camscore in the sample was a 34.8. While the cam-site owners and studios advertise and tell models that they can earn over $10,000 a month, this data also suggests that high incomes can occur but are not typical. The Horatio Alger myth dies hard on MFC, and this story becomes even more telling when we control for race and nationality.

I examined the frequencies for the categorical variables of race and country of origin. Models in this sample were from an extensive list of places: the Bahamas, Bermuda, Brazil, Bulgaria, Canada, Colombia, Costa Rica, the Czech Republic, Denmark, France, French Polynesia, Germany, Greece, Hungary, Italy, Iraq, Japan, Kazakhstan, Latvia, Lebanon, Lithuania, Mexico, New Zealand, Panama, Philippines, Poland, Romania, the Russian Federation, Slovakia, Slovenia, South Africa, Spain, Ukraine, and the United Kingdom. However, the modal category for race was Caucasian, and the modal category for nation of origin was the United States. Descriptive statistics showed the mean age of models was 25.91. This data suggested that despite the diversity that exists in the industry, MFC was dominated by relatively young White women, mainly from the United States.

Among models that had high camscores,[8] White women were over-represented. There was only one Black model among those in the high camscore range, and no Hispanic models. There were, however, 11 models who identified as Other or Various Ethnicities, as well as four

Asian models in the high camscore range. Among models with low camscores, a disproportionate number were women of color. For example, all the models from Colombia in the data set had low camscores. Models from the United States, followed by models from Canada and the United Kingdom, were overrepresented among the models with high camscores. Crucially, my statistical analyses showed that race had a significant impact on camscore, when controlling for nationality, such that, while models from the United States tended to have the highest camscores, for Black models race mitigated any potential advantage they might have gained from their US nationality.

This data empirically showed that models' perceptions of MFC were correct. Black cam models were significantly less likely to be successful on the site. While I initially set out to explore the claim that Black models were not successful on MFC, the data showed even more than this. Not just Black women, Latina women, as well as women outside of the United States, Canada, and the United Kingdom, also had lower camscores. Now we must turn to an explanation of why these disparities exist. The explanation is not that White women from the United Kingdom, Canada, and the United States are just better cam models. It is also not that Black women and other women of color just do not work hard on MFC. A critical analysis of sexual racism in the camming field does explain these disparities.

Sexual Racism in the Camming Industry

Sociologist Eduardo Bonilla-Silva has discussed what he calls "color-blind racism"—when racial inequities are perceived, mainly by Whites, to no longer be a problem: "Instead, whites rationalize minorities' contemporary status as the product of market dynamics, naturally occurring phenomena, and Blacks' imputed cultural limitations . . . and the beauty of this new ideology is that it aids in the maintenance of White privilege."[9] Racial inequalities are ostensibly explained away by individual choice and preference, not by structural forces. Here, one could argue that models of color, particularly Black models, are less successful because consumers, particularly in the United States (where traffic is disproportionately driven from), prefer White models. Feminist scholar Siobhan Brooks argues:

Racism against Black women in this industry [stripping] is usually viewed as normal because, like other appearance-based industries (such as modeling or acting), the sex industry is based on ideas of customer taste and preference. Thus, if Black women are not desirable, it is the objective result of consumer taste within a free market—not structural anti-Black racism operating within the psyche of the customer or club management.[10]

Like Brooks, my experiences in the stripping industry provide me with an inside perspective from which to better understand the ways that structural racism shapes sex markets. Consider this vignette:

> Like most of the dancers I worked with, I hated mandatory meetings. The managers would drone on about lateness and calling out on weekdays (when most dancers didn't want to work but were required to), but this one meeting was different. The manager informed us that the owner had taken over another club on Long Island (a suburb about 40 miles outside of New York City). The room was filled with excitement as the manager explained that selected dancers would be chauffeured from Queens by limousine to the club. The managers presented this as a unique opportunity to make "real money." We were told that this was an upscale gentlemen's club and that we'd need long gowns and that this club would not tolerate any "ghetto dancers." They explained their use of this all-too-familiar racist euphemism as indicating that you couldn't dance to rap music, or that you couldn't throw up pole tricks and do floor work. Dancers of color knew exactly what this really meant. Due to de facto racial quotas, a limited number of Black girls were to be selected. Given that I was told that I looked "ethnic" and not Black, I was told I could go. When I got there, the club was patronized almost exclusively by affluent White men. I only worked there for a few nights because I did not make good money there. I realized that in this industry, as a woman of color, if you worked in a White gentleman's club, you were tokenized and if you weren't interested in playing the token/fetish card, you'd be ghettoized to either clubs catering solely to Black men or to racially diverse working-class clubs. I did well outside of upscale White gentleman's clubs, and I loved the diverse middle/working-class club where I worked. However, I also acknowledged that institutionalized White supremacy meant that I also didn't really have much of a choice.

While Brooks and I are writing about exotic dancing, our insights apply here as well. Through the lens of colorblind racism, Black women are less successful on MFC and as webcam models in general because Black bodies do not have high exchange values in the market. As sociologist Ashely Mears explains, "An invisible hand of racism guides the market, which producers understand as a rational, efficient force against which they have no power. Within our contemporary laissez-faire racial ethos, the seemingly natural force of the market ensures the invisibility of racism."[11] From the perspective of neoliberal capitalism, the lack of success Black women and women from outside of the United States experience on MFC is not the result of structural racism, but of capitalist market forces and individual consumer preference.

Despite these neoliberal explanations, the reason I did not do well in the affluent White strip club was not because I didn't perform well. Cam models of color and models not from the US do not have lower camscores solely because of poor choices or not having outgoing personalities—nor is this solely a reflection of consumer preferences. Instead, another way to read this data is that cultural, structural, and interactional sexual racism shape experiences on MFC, in the camming industry, and in sex markets more broadly.

Cultural Sexual Racism

Race and nationality play a role in the monetary success of webcam models. In camming, bodies of color have lower sexual capital. Cultural sexual racism affects perceived attractiveness, which shapes a performer's overall sexual capital in the field. Orne writes:

> There are cultural components as well [to sexual racism]. . . . What images are around? What understandings of race construct our definitions of what is happening? What kinds of beauty are favored? How do we determine who the hottest people in the room are?[12]

The institutionalized system of White supremacy affects what "looks" are valued in the marketplace. Mears's ethnography of fashion modeling and analysis of racial discrimination against Black fashion models is instructive for the analysis here: "Beauty is desired because it is idealized and unattainable, two criteria that are fundamentally incompatible with historical representations of non-white women."[13] For Black women modeling clothing or performing erotic sex acts, their bodies will generally be held to a normative standard of beauty that idealizes White aesthetics such as fair skin color; straight hair texture, color (often blonde), and length (long); eye color (blue, green, hazel, etc.); and body shape (thin).

Participant observation on MFC also suggested that Black models with higher camscores seemed to adopt what Mears calls a "look" that adhered to a US-centric feminine White aesthetic—that is, as it was coded here, Black women *appeared* to have achieved longer hairstyles through the use of chemical straighteners and weaves, wore colored contact lenses, and had thin physiques. Among cam models with high camscores, I observed no Black women who had natural hair—that is, not chemically treated or with weaves/extensions. The only Black model in the top-earning camscore range was very light-skinned, thin, had incredibly long hair, and green eyes. I observed Black women with short hair and larger physiques only in the low range of camscores.

White women have more sexual capital because they have a look that is culturally idealized, whereas Black women's bodies and aesthetics (not that these factors are monolithic) are devalued. Brooks has analyzed "racialized erotic capital" in sex work, a term she coined "to suggest that erotic capital is affected by variables such as weight, skin color, speech patterns, gender presentation, and hair texture."[14] Race conditions a cam model's sexual capital; having lower sexual capital decreases earning potential. Koken et al., who conducted a comparative analysis of male and female escorts, write that among their sample

> [t]here was general agreement among the women that a racial hierarchy stratified the sex industry, placing white women on top and women of color—particularly African-American women—at the bottom. . . . [W]hile white women's fees ranged up to $1000 an hour, no woman of color in the sample charged more than $500. . . . Thus it appears that the value of being white translates into a real business advantage.[15]

Here, in their sample of escorts, we see how the prostitution market is racialized and adversely impacts the wages of women of color. In camming, too, lower sexual capital is conditioned by racist cultural discourses about "look," and the lower a model's sexual capital the less they make in tips.

Structural Sexual Racism

The website owners and moderators have played a role in structuring racial inequalities that then propagate class-based inequalities on MFC. As Orne writes, "structural sexual racism has to do with the availability of partners within the environment. How segregated is the community, city, or space? . . . Are the circuits segregated?"[16] The structure of the website and the creation of the camscore embed sexual racism into the cam site. The camscore is the default category used to sort models' profiles on the homepage (figure 8.2).

Customers can elect to change this filter, but doing so would require navigating from the main page and that the customer be aware that they even have this option, which may not be widely known. It is likely that the website founders and moderators created this scoring system to publicly rank models because once a public ranking system is employed, it creates a competitive climate in which, in theory, models are motivated to work harder and invest more time in preparing entertaining shows—as models also receive monetary bonuses for high camscores. The camscore creates a status system among models and could in theory help motivate models to make more money, legitimately benefiting both them and the website owners. However, it is crucial to take seriously the consequences of making the scoring system public and using it to sort profiles; why aren't profiles displayed at random? By creating this ranking system and making it public, the website operators also reinforce racial inequalities on the website—again, customers must scroll down to find Black models. As one model on a web forum declared, "I would love to see more Black models on the first couple of rows on MFC; it seems like if you are not skinny and White you won't make it very far." The camscore system on MFC institutionalizes a structure of desire that privileges White women, placing them on the top of the homepage. As a Black model on a popular web forum said:

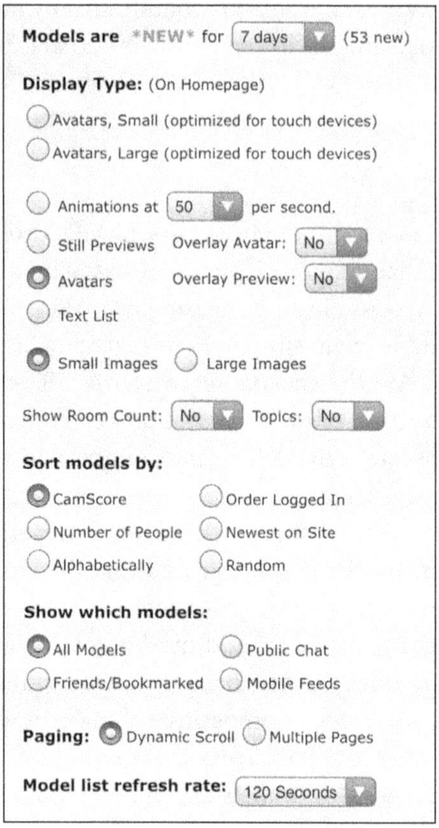

Figure 8.2. Default customer settings on MFC.

MFC can be quite discouraging . . . maybe there's not that many Black models because of the cam score thing? It's one reason why I left! Yeah, this just makes me not want to cam anymore, but I have to, it is my only source of income. I want Streamate to hurry up and approve my profile so that way I don't have to deal with too many rude freeloaders.

Importantly, the sexual racism that this model experienced was compelling her to leave the site and move to another site with no camscore system. The issue with the camscore system is that a model's score dictates their placement on the website and Black models have lower camscores than their White co-workers because of cultural sexual racism.

A lower camscore means a lower position on the website—and a lower position on the website means decreased visibility. With 1,200 models online, and over 80 rows of avatar pictures on the homepage, a model with a high camscore who thus appears on the top of the page has a great visibility advantage. In addition, we must not forget—the camscore is a reflection of earnings. This means having a lower camscore has consequences not just on the website; it means the model is earning a lower wage and thus the camscore has real-world consequences. A low camscore literally places the model on the bottom of the status hierarchy. Once in this lower position on the website, a vicious circle develops. We know that rising tides do not actually lift all boats; those with the highest camscores remain on top, and so those with the lowest camscores remain on the bottom. The imagery here should be striking—as being on the bottom of the page both symbolically and structurally reproduces racial and class-based inequalities. The camscore system has a ghettoizing effect. Feminist porn studies scholar Mireille Miller-Young has discussed the ghettoization of Black women in hip-hop pornography; Black women here, too, are ghettoized on MFC. The causal mechanism for the ghettoization of Black women on this website is not individual—but structural. This *is* structural sexual racism.

Interactional Sexual Racism

Sexual racism is also interactional. It is crucial to examine how individuals draw on racist cultural scripts in their interactions with other people. Individuals do not cause sexual racism, but sexual racism does shape people's interactions on a micro-level. Sexual racism shapes customers perceptions of the personalities of cam models, and thus the types of shows the client will experience. The assumptions customers make are not theirs; they are learned in and produced within culture, and they no doubt disadvantage Black women. Consider the words of one Black cam model who posted on a discussion board:

> So, it's pretty obvious that almost at any given time out of the 1000+ girls on cam (mfc), only about 30 or so are Black. And of those 30, there are about 15 of us who are American and Black. . . . I like to focus on my room and not worry about who's better or worse and that works for me,

but I can't lie, it is a little discouraging that I rarely ever see more than 2 Black girls in the entire contest. . . . I also am a natural submissive, but I notice people associate Black women with domin[ance] and aggressi[on]; so, oftentimes, I find myself femdomming more which is ok, but its not what comes natural for me. Being a fetish can be fun and it can stand you apart from others, but it can also be frustrating sometimes when you get constant N words and you're pretty for a Black girl quotes. . . . *Australian and UK Whites love black girls!

In the United States, Black women have long been stereotyped in popular media with the Sapphire trope,[17] which portrays them as aggressive, loud, rude, and overbearing. As this model explained, she has a submissive personality but must often perform in ways that enact this racist cultural trope. Moreover, even though she is submissive, there are customers who likely assume she is not and as a result do not click on her avatar/room. At the interactional level, sexual racism shapes how customers talk to cam models; this model, for instance, must put up with clients calling her "N words" or telling her she is "pretty for a Black girl." Her statement that "Australian and UK Whites love Black girls!" illuminates how sexual racism is always contextual and shaped by different cultural scripts globally. While models did not use the language of sexual racism, their comments animate the theory.

Having designed a platform on which cam models and clients interact, MFC established the camscore system and set up filtering options for its customers (see figure 8.3). Those who run the site have created an environment that nurtures sexual racism, even if they did not themselves create racist cultural scripts.

This filtering system on MFC allows clients to eliminate from their view models from particular regions. This function would allow, for example, a customer the ability to filter many bodies of color from their view by electing to hide Africa, Asia/Pacific Islands, and Central/South America. Alternatively, the filter could allow customers who are seeking only bodies of color to filter out countries dominated by White folks. Given widespread migration and globalization, the idea that any filter can cleanse all Black, Latinx, Asian, White, or other bodies from view is as naïve as it is disturbing.

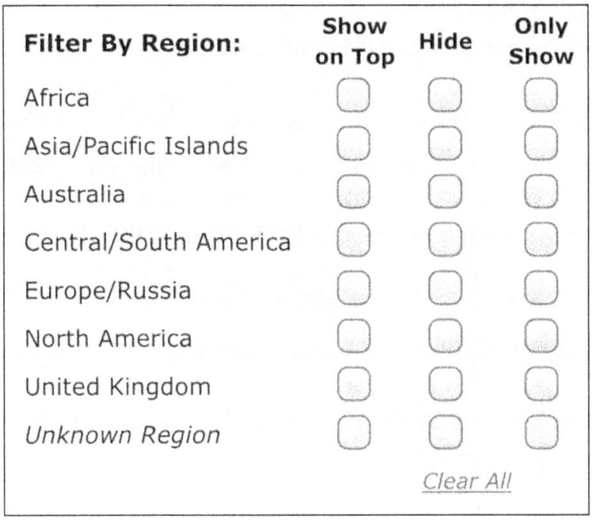

Filter By Region:	Show on Top	Hide	Only Show
Africa	◯	◯	◯
Asia/Pacific Islands	◯	◯	◯
Australia	◯	◯	◯
Central/South America	◯	◯	◯
Europe/Russia	◯	◯	◯
North America	◯	◯	◯
United Kingdom	◯	◯	◯
Unknown Region	◯	◯	◯
			Clear All

Figure 8.3. Filtering options on MFC.

Customers participating on an open section of a webcam forum talked openly about their use of MFC filters. One customer, who identified himself as a person of color, was talking about the difficulty he had finding Black women on MFC. Another poster made a recommendation: "Not sure if you're looking specifically for models in the U.S., but I have noticed that quite a few beautiful women of a darker complexion are in Colombia, and can be easily found by filtering by region to show Central/South America." The original poster stated that he found some brown-skinned women from Central/South America very attractive, but then went on to say:

> My only complaint is the language barrier. I actually recently filtered out *all* non-native English speaking countries because although I find a lot of models from all over the world pretty and even interesting, if the level of communication isn't there I find the interaction boring.

Here we can see how sexual racism shapes customer behavior at the micro-level. Clients do use these filters to cleanse from their view entire nations based on ethnocentric and racist stereotypes. This customer filtered out *all* non-native-English-speaking countries. The idea that models in Central and South America cannot speak English well or at all guided his behavior. This customer was making an evaluation of entire populations of people based on limited experiences with cam models who did not speak English well enough to meet his standards. As I noted earlier, it was not just Black women who did not perform well on MFC. Models from outside the United Kingdom, Canada, and the United States also had low camscores. Models from Central/South America had exceptionally low camscores and sexual racism can help explain why. When some customers assume that all models from predominately Spanish-speaking countries cannot speak English "well enough," and filter these models out as a result—that is sexual racism. This example is also a reminder that White supremacy functions globally, and harms people of color throughout the world. Examining sexual racism requires that scholars and activists think transnationally.

Sexual Racism and Strategic Branding

Cam models are aware of the sexual racism that permeates their field, especially Black performers on cam sites like MFC. Cam models frequently remarked that they must market themselves in ways that take sexual racism into account. A Black model on a popular web forum said:

> Being a minority means that I can't really follow the same formulas that work for a lot of girls on cam. I have to first convince users to come into a Black room in general, which can be a task in itself when a lot of them are not used to looking for us as an attraction. Then from there I can start.

Cam models of color must develop strategies to counteract both structural and cultural sexual racism. Performers said they sometimes change their location and race on cam sites. If a model who resides in Colombia lists that she is from the United States, she is much less likely to get filtered out. As examined in the previous chapter, models discussed strategically manufacturing identities. Here we see that models of color, as a form of strategic branding, must often manufacture identities that allow them to manage sexual racism. A performer who posted on a web forum underscored this point:

There are probably a lot of members who remove the Black checkbox from their list of models showing. Personally, I've experimented with this a little. . . . I'm a bit of a lot of things; so I could technically say a lot of those checkboxes. I wouldn't say I'm White . . . but I have had my ethnicity set as various, Black, Asian, and not specified. I got the most traffic when I had it set to Asian—that's another kind of fetish that's also pretty gross but plays out differently to the Black fetish. I didn't get as much when I had it set to Black, and what I did get was mostly the Black fetish types who wanted a stereotype. I keep it at various now because that's the true one anyway, but that's why I don't blame the other models for changing it. I have seen a lot of Black models listing themselves as Asian and I feel like it's sad but this is exactly why.

Being multiracial allowed this model to manufacture her cam identity in a way that would not compromise her embodied authenticity but that gave her a unique vantage point, what sociologist Patricia Hill Collins has called the "outsider within" perspective from which to observe sexual racism in camming.[18] As she said, it is no surprise that some Black models might often use various strategies, including changing their racial marker to a non-Black identity, in order to navigate sexual racism in the camming field.

Conclusion

This case study of one popular cam site—MyFreeCams—identified a problem that occurs across the camming field. While other websites may not use camscores, they do have filters and thus also provide a structure for sexual racism. As digital media scholar Safiya Umoja Noble discusses in *Algorithms of Oppression: How Search Engines Reinforce Racism*, too often people see digital platforms as neutral technologies, incapable of discrimination. Noble's research has shown that, in fact, algorithmic oppression is widespread across the Internet.[19] The camscore on MFC is further evidence of algorithmic oppression online.

The presence of sexual racism in the camming field means that bodies of color have lower exchange values and that women of color earn less than White women for performing the same labor. The benefits of camming presented in this book are thus highly racialized and, for some models subjected to sexual racism, not even felt. Sexual racism ensures different experiences and different financial outcomes for cam models based on race and nationality. Sexual racism ensures that White women, who overwhelmingly attribute their success to their talent, are most likely to be figuratively and literally on top.

Color-blind racism maintains racism in general—it operates at a very subtle level and often is buttressed by the invisibility of its existence to those who benefit from it. White privilege is also at work in the camming field. This privilege is invisible to those who have it—many of the highest-grossing models on MFC and in the field more broadly (almost all White) may not realize that the women of color at the bottom of the page buttress their position at the top of the page. The success of many White models is not just about their successful accomplishment of embodied authenticity—it is also a reflection of the privileges of Whiteness under global White supremacy.

9

Getting Kinky Online

The Diffuse Life and BDSM Play

"Kink" is an umbrella term used to describe a range of non-normative sexual practices. Performing kink and catering to taboo sexual desires can be quite lucrative. Cam models who specialize in kink can charge anywhere from $10 to $15 per minute for performing kink work. Rebecca, a 34-year-old polyamorous White cis woman, has been a sex worker for 16 years and has been camming for over seven years. She specializes in kink, makes $7,000 per month camming, and has earned as much as $12,000 in one month. Many performers stated that they could charge a high premium for kink work. Halona, a 32-year-old queer Native American woman from the United States, said:

> I'll do any type of show as long as my shows can fit within the budget of the individuals paying for my show. On a personal level, age play and race play really bother me, but if my client is paying me enough to be uncomfortable . . . I do charge a premium price for anything I'm not comfortable with; then I don't mind doing whatever.

A woman on a popular web forum, talking about performing race play, posted, "I do it in exclusive. It's 14.99 per min for that [and] they pay it." The high premiums performers can charge for fetish work help attract models to perform in this segment of the cam market. Performers not trained in providing safe, sane, and consensual[1] BDSM shows to clients generally do not find pleasure in this particular work, and, more importantly, can cause harm to themselves and clients. Despite these limitations, exploring kink play in the camming field is one way people can find ephemeral moments of freedom and pleasure.

The restrictions that culture places on people's desires force them to often seek out sexual gratification in secrecy, where they feel safe from surveillance, judgment, and sanctions. People carve out alternative spaces for the exploration of sexual desires. BDSM subcultures are a clear example of one such space.[2] Engaging in BDSM play allows people to escape the intense sexual and gender regulation that they face in their daily lives. Studies have also shown how people seek out the services of professional dominatrices, also called pro-dommes, to explore their desires for BDSM play in privacy and secrecy.[3] The Internet also provides an alternative space for the exploration of kinky sexual desires.

Performers highlighted that performing for clients provides them an opportunity to explore and enjoy kinky sex. Alexandra, a 28-year-old polyamorous White cis woman from the United States, told me about the benefits of camming for her sexual and romantic life. She said it "provides an avenue to experience BDSM without putting the strain on my partner who is not as into BDSM as I am. It helps me feel better about being polyamorous while being in a monogamous relationship." For Alexandra, her cam work allows her to experience satisfaction in her relationship. It is not just that her BDSM shows are sexually pleasurable for her; her cam performances also have a lasting, beneficial effect on her relationship. She identifies as polyamorous, and her cam work satisfies her desire to have sexual encounters outside of her primary relationship.

This data highlights the importance of a sociological theory of pleasure. Alexandra's pleasure is not only sexual; it is affectual, and the pleasure she acquires online reverberates through and affects her offline life. Our offline and online experiences share a symbiotic relationship—our lives are diffuse. Put another way, we must trouble the binary offline/online—the encounters people have online affect their lives offline, and our offline lives affect the interactions we have online. The pleasures we experience in either context can stay with us, even as we move in and out of different contexts.

Kink Work in the Camming Industry

In the camming industry, performing kink involves enacting specific BDSM practices and role plays, which involve exchanges of power within various forms of play, such as bondage and discipline, D/s (dominance and submission), and SM (sadism and masochism). BDSM "scenes" or "play" are interactions through which consenting individuals explore and transgress sociocultural boundaries. BDSM practitioners experiment with and explore their own subjectivities and desires in relationship to power and, in doing so, produce pleasurable experiences. Cam performers are often asked to engage in role-playing scenes (e.g., race play, age play) and other acts such as foot worship. I spoke with performers about popular kink requests from clients.

Role Play: Incest/Family Play, Age Play, and Foot Worship

Cam performers told me role-playing was popular among their clients. Amelia and I discussed a few of her most popular requests: incest/family play, age play, and foot worship. Amelia is a 29-year-old straight White cis woman from England who has cammed sporadically for six years. Like many youthful-looking models, Amelia often gets requests for incest and age play.

> AMELIA: I get a lot more incest requests because I look quite young. So I get a lot of daddy-daughter requests or brother-sister requests.
> AJ: Will you take those?
> AMELIA: I've taken them before, when I've been slow, on a slow night. They're not my favorite, and I say to them, again, they're not really prohibited. So I do have to say at the start of these incest requests that we have to say the character is over 18. I was like, I'm not going to pretend to be your nine-year-old stepdaughter because that's against the rules of camming. So yeah, it all has to be 18-plus, but yeah, I mean, I'm not really too bothered about incest fetish if it's a fantasy. It's a fantasy—as long as it's not involving children; like children is a hard no, and it is against the law anyway.

Incest- or family-play requests often involve role-playing intimate relationships between family members. Among young performers, popular requests include daddy-daughter and father-son, and among performers who market themselves as mature or MILF, mother-son is also popular. These fantasies and scenes allow people to push social boundaries around incest taboos, without actually breaking the incest taboo and, thus, facing the possibility of criminal and social sanctions.

Amelia also talked about how unlike incest- and age-play requests, she enjoys requests for foot worship:

> I enjoy foot fetish shows because, like I always find the foot fetish guys are the most polite. And one, it's so easy. They are always the nicest, and they're always very generous. . . . So, you just like point the camera at your feet, you fiddle, like you touch your feet, sometimes they ask me to like put lotion on my feet. And they tip really well, and they're always really polite, like, oh, thank you so much, that was great! Amazing!

Many models like Amelia enjoy foot fetish shows because they are easy and generally involve the performer following the client's instructions to display and pamper their feet. Foot worship is a kink service that cam models with little training can perform with ease, and for which they can charge a premium. In order to learn more about kink services online, I spoke with Elizabeth, another performer who has also intermittently been in the sex industry for a long period.

Cuckolding, Blasphemy, and Small Penis Humiliation

Elizabeth, a 38-year-old bisexual White cis woman from the United States, has worked in and out of the sex industry since the late 1990s. She has been an exotic dancer and dominatrix and returned to camming in 2014. Given that she specializes in kink work, we talked about the identities of her clients and what she sees as the most popular services she provides to them. In my conversations with Elizabeth, we discussed cuckolding, blasphemy, and small penis humiliation (SPH).

> I can honestly say that most of my regulars are mediocre White dudes. Just totally mediocre, middle-aged White dudes who are traveling on business and bored, but I have been getting a lot of Black dudes lately, too, because they enjoy being the stud to these White guys, the whole big Black cock, cuckold scenario. So I've actually set up White guys with Black guys before in my private chat, and put the camera on them to use them to humiliate the White cucks begging for it. That's huge. That is honestly, that is the biggest fetish—the whole, big Black cock and cuckold thing. There are many old White guys that wanna hear about their wives

or other girls being banged by a big Black man, who's far more superior in prowess than they are, and it's really fascinating to me; but that seems to be the biggest fetish right now.

Elizabeth said that cuckolding is one of the most popular fetishes she is asked to facilitate. In the kink context, a "cuckold" is a man who encourages his wife or girlfriend to have sex with other people. Watching his partner have sex with other men pleases him. Elizabeth suggested that, most often, she gets cuckolds who also want to be humiliated during the process. Some of her cuckolding clients want to add aspects of race play to these scenarios, as well. As she noted, these "mediocre White dudes" not only want to be humiliated by watching their wives get fucked by other men; they want those men to be Black. The racialized component is part of the humiliation fetish.

Black men have an inferior social position under White supremacy. Moreover, hegemonic masculinity requires that men feel in control and dominant.[4] In their relentless quest for masculine validation, men often assert themselves over other men and demean women. Therefore, watching his wife or girlfriend get fucked by a Black man, by societal standards, is a source of humiliation and an assault to a client's manhood. In a world that places unrealistic pressures on men to be the manliest among their peers, this role play can feel freeing for the client, and for Elizabeth, it is fascinating and lucrative.

Elizabeth doesn't only find her work fascinating; because of her own religious identity, she also finds great pleasure in performing role plays that push religious social boundaries.

ELIZABETH: Blasphemy is something that I always advertise. Blasphemy is a huge fetish, and I always love doing it; it must be so freeing, for some of these suppressed people. I am a nontheistic Satanist, and I enjoy the opportunity to release people from the shackles of religious convention even if it is only for a moment, because I feel that religion is a big part of what is wrong with this world. Also, I have the wardrobe and an endless imagination for the blasphemous to play this role easily and with little effort.

AJ: Can you tell me more about that? Like, so what would that show look like?

> ELIZABETH: Oh, my goodness, it depends. I do a succubus show, and
> I pretend and act out a lot of the stuff that I do. It can be bizarre, like
> really perverse mime and spoken improvisation. But some more
> direct examples I can think of are desecrating Bibles through various
> means or crucifix strap-ons. Just saying really horrible things about
> God, describing blasphemous scenes, like bending over priests and
> fucking them on the altar. Speaking of really unholy descriptive
> scenes, insisting guys condemn God and worship Satan.

For people who have had complicated relationships with religious institutions, especially those who have felt controlled by religion, engaging
in blasphemy play can feel freeing. Engaging in these sexual encounters, as Elizabeth observed, can be pleasurable for the performers and
freeing for the client. Kink is about pushing both personal and social
boundaries.

Elizabeth and I also discussed small penis humiliation, which is another popular request that performers get from cis men.

> SPH is huge. Guys like to be told how small their dick is, and that just
> seems to be the thing culturally that White dudes with small dicks are
> nervous about or something . . . or it's cause it's a humiliation thing, and I
> find it really interesting that it is seriously like one of the biggest fetishes
> right now. I think that like a lot of these dudes, they went to college right
> out of high school, married their high school sweetheart, had 2.5 kids,
> started to work jobs that made them miserable, and they do it; and they're
> unsatisfied. It's just like the typical American-dream-gone-complacent
> kind of thing. So, but inside they're, like, ahhhhhhh! And the only way
> that it can come out is through their sexuality because I don't think you
> can entirely ignore that. . . . And then, like some people just like kinky
> shit, and like it for that reason alone, not because of any like deep-seated
> meaning.

Given the emphasis some cultures place on penis size, the unrealistic
pressures of manhood, and the inability of many men to even talk about
their feelings of inadequacy, it can feel freeing for men to be chastised
for literally not measuring up. The example above also again highlights
the importance of examining how race affects people's sexual desires.

Race Play

Performers said that race play is another highly requested practice, but it was also the one that made performers the most uncomfortable, especially among models from the United States. A webcam model on a popular web forum who self-identified as Afro-Caribbean said, "I get less race play and nazi play requests since I stop[ped] camming on American sites as often." Context and culture are both crucial to understanding the social significance of sexuality and race and how both shape the requests for kink performances in camming.

Race play is a role-playing scenario that often involves using racial slurs during sex acts and in many cases specific role-playing scripts, such as reenacting a master/slave relationship on a United States plantation. For example, a Black man wants a White person to play the role of a slave owner and then degrade him as a slave. In a script where the Black man is in a dominant role, the role play could involve him either consensually fucking or raping the plantation owner's White wife. In both scenarios, the fantasy is used to reconcile the historical trauma of slavery and the legacy of White supremacy that still marginalizes and oppresses Black men. Ariane Cruz writes, "Like other BDSM practices, race play relies on the simultaneous observance and violation of conventional sociocultural taboos. In race play, the taboos of racism and interracial intimacy fuel the transgressive pleasure practitioners' experience."[5] Like Cruz, I refuse to pathologize or judge models who do race play or their clients for having these desires. Instead, I also draw from Christine Nash's *The Black Body in Ecstasy: Reading Race, Reading Pornography* and the concept of "racial iconography" to center my analysis of visual pornography on pleasure, not pain. There is pleasure in these highly charged racial imageries—not just trauma and oppression.

Like Cruz, in her brilliant account of Black women's experiences in BDSM, I found Black performers' attitudes toward and experience with race play to be widely different. Many Black women refuse to perform any race play. A Black female performer posted on a web forum:

> The fact that people think that I want them to racially humiliate me or pretend to have any sexual power over me because of race, excuse me, but what the fuck? White people have the power to oppress me for free—

every day—all day, so no! I get race play requests daily, and it says on my profile and show topic, no taboo fetishes/race play, race players will be blocked. So, not only are these men racist, but they can't read either. I'm sorry. I just really loathe race play.

As this comment attests, some Black female cam performers respond to requests for race play with disgust and anger. Some other Black women said they were initially opposed to race play, but over time, and with more experience in the sex industry, came to see it differently. A performer described this sort of shift on a web forum:

I have also decided to use it to my advantage, this race play thing, and recently added it to things I'll do list. The first time I got a user who had a racial fantasy, I was so offended. But as I've come to realize, fantasies are the forbidden things no one can ever do. Since saying the N word is seen as so bad, of course, it arouses some to say it. I'm just about to charge 100 tokens per N word!

Some Black women said that, over time, they came to understand the psychology behind race play and slowly became willing to capitalize on racial fantasy. For many Black women in this study, race play is not something they enjoy or find pleasure in, but they will do it, like any service, for the money. There were also Black women who said that the actual script mattered to whether race play was experienced as offensive and degrading or empowering and pleasurable. Another Black female cam model posted on a web forum:

Race play is a moral choice. If you are ok with it, then offer the fetish, but like someone else said, ask yourself if you'd be ok with a video getting out. I did a few shows similar to that, but it was in reverse (White guys wanted to call me the "n-word"). I stopped after a very short time. I could tolerate them calling me it in private via typing but some customers wanted me to call myself the "n-word," and I wasn't comfortable with that. I also wasn't ok with the thought of videos getting out, so I stopped doing them. I still do race play, but it's in reverse (Ebony Goddess, SPH, dick comparison, BBC [big Black cock]/strap-on, big booty). If you're fine with it, then I'd charge a shit ton of gold or require block sessions [guaranteed length of time booked] in order to do those shows. . . . I'd rake in as much money as possible.

All role play is about power, and for the Black women in this study, race play only became an option or empowering when they were the dom in the scene. As a sub, they felt degraded. For the performer above, you can call her an ebony goddess while she enacts fucking a White man anally or humiliates that same man for having a small cock, but White men may not under any circumstances call her a nigger. Tiffany and I talked about this point in our interview.

Tiffany is a 23-year-old lesbian Black cis woman from the United States. During our discussion of race and sex work, and race play specifically, she said:

> If you ever see those men—those big politicians are mostly White. When they get caught with a prostitute or escort, she's a person of color. She's Black [or] Mexican; she's not a White girl, ya know what I mean? Like, it's weird, but it's what they really want, deep down inside. . . . It's kind of like racism, 'cause you know, guys ask me to do race play. . . . It's a role-playing fetish that they basically want you to either, sometimes it's reverse, sometimes they want to you to say things like . . . I fucking hate you, White guy. This blah, blah, blah, just talk shit to him as a White man. And then sometimes they want to talk shit to you as a Black woman. . . . And call you a nigger, a slave, all types of stuff. . . . I do race play, but I have my boundaries. I will not call myself a nigger . . . you can't call me nigger. The most I will do is like, oh, you like this Black pussy? You like this Black girl and this White dick? It's still race play, but I'm not going to demean myself!

Many Black performers will perform race play but often do so strategically. Tiffany will act in a dom role and engage in humiliation and degradation of White men, but she will not allow these same men to degrade her. By managing such encounters in this way, she can find empowerment by either dominating these White men or in having the power to deny them the power to do the same to her.

The reluctance to do race play as a sub was not something I heard about exclusively from Black women. Carl, a 31-year-old bisexual Black cis man, said he's agreed to perform only a couple of race-play shows:

> I think I had one or two with the race play . . . on the milder side of it, it doesn't bother me too, too much, but some people use it as an excuse to like, I don't know, wanna get away with calling me a nigger or something. And I'm like, if it's that type thing . . . I'm probably not gonna do it because . . . it just makes me a little too uncomfortable. And I'm like, I mean, I get that in some sense, sexuality, like, particularly, with porn, people use it to explore taboos and whatnot; and I get that, and I understand that. . . . I mean, if maybe you're just doing kinda milder kinda teasing maybe, just or maybe just using it to kind of champion me in some weird ways, then hey, I'll roll with it. I'll do that. But, uh, if it's anything like, very derogatory, just towards just me being Black, I'm not gonna do it. . . . I sometimes kind of have that side of me too, having a fantasy of just being like, ravaged by a bunch of guys, and they say some kind of demeaning language, but then I get kind of turned on by it. I totally get that 'cause I have that submissive element to myself, so if they do it in that framework, I'm totally cool with it and not offended by it at any point. But once they really go towards the racial element and they go too far with that, that's usually when I'm just like, uh, back up, back up.

Similar to Tiffany's arguments, Carl agreed that if a client wants to use a race-play request only to degrade him for being Black, he's not interested. However, if the scenario includes racial language as part of gang-bang scene, for instance, this situation would turn him on. Carl also highlighted that kink is often used to push social and political boundaries, and while he understands that, he will not perform race play that is demeaning for money.

Importantly, unlike Black BDSM practitioners in a club or private party, cam models are not initiating the encounter. While cam performers consent to race play, for most models, the race-play scene is not their fantasy but rather the fantasy of their client. As Mireille Miller-Young writes, "If black prostitution offered white clientele the ability to enact racial sexual fantasy and black people an economy in which to exploit these fantasies for their own economic and personal needs, illicit pornographic film production provided another arena for these conflicting desires to operate."[6] Race play in the camming industry is just another part of a much longer history of spaces that cater to a White clientele's desire to explore racial fantasies, which also creates economic opportunity for Black performers willing to exploit that desire.

While many Black performers felt personally offended by race play, many White performers frequently said race play with Black clients made them uncomfortable. Language was often the deciding factor in how and whether White performers would do race play with Black men. Specifically, for performers of all races, the use of the word "nigger" was a point of contention. However, cam models saw racialized SPH, for example, with White men as harmless and, to some, downright pleasurable. A White woman on a discussion board commented:

> Race play has always been a difficult one. I will only do it in exclusive. So far it's mostly been cuckolding stuff, White guys into SPH vs BBC and the like. It's racist, but at least a BBC is a good thing to those guys. They never ask me to use the n-word, so it's been fine.

This performer will humiliate White guys for having small cocks and embarrass them for ostensibly not being well hung like a Black man. Notice that she argued that while it is racist to say all Black men have big cocks, she still framed it as positive, unlike using the word "nigger," which was seen by most performers as always negative. Many White female cam models also pointed out that White men seemed obsessed with Black men's cocks. In the words of one poster:

> I do race play. Fuck, I do cuck. I do SPH, [and] that shit [race play] is a *huge* portion of my fetish shows. If I left that out, I wouldn't think I was being honest to the role. I think it's less icky than just plain stupid. I tell my audience all the time that White men are more obsessed with Black cock than White women could ever be.

Another White woman commented:

> It's definitely a comfortabl[ity] level. I don't ever use the n word in my real life. But in [the] cam world, if it's [consensual] and in exclusive, I'm

alright with that. It's a fetish, simple as that. I've done race play with more than just Black men, but [the] majority of my race play is with them. I'm aware of my demographic . . . I also do a lot of cucking with that word. A lot of White men fantasize about Black cock. I mean no harm saying the n word if its consenting fetish play. . . . If you don't want to, you don't have to. That's the beauty of being a cam model. Saying no is important and sets boundaries. . . . Also I had an ex who would go nuts when I would say, "fuck me harder, n[igger]." . . . If I wanted him to cum quickly or get really turned on. He fucking loved it. I only did it because he asked me if I would. It was fun because it excited my ex, and I like a little spice in my vanilla sex.

There was a range in performers' level of comfort using the word "nigger" in race play. For some, it is a hard no, while for others, as long as they have consent, they see using this word as just another part of doing fantasy work. Another White cam model said:

When I started camming—hell, up until a year ago—I wouldn't touch the barest hint to racial play with a 30 foot pole in private. That said, it's a money maker, and I do so hate turning down money. I'll play the BBC/cuckold fantasy like a fiddle. I enjoy the hell out of SPH, and worked my way to either insulting the size of their dick based on race (Asian guys love it) or by comparing it to a bigger dick (White guys and BBC)—[other performers are][7] right about th[at] obsession. So, I've loosened up on my race play limits a lot, obviously. . . . That said, I still won't use racial slurs, and I still won't use historically loaded metaphors/role plays. I get that it's between consenting adults and the guy on the other end is clearly alright with it, but I personally can't find my comfort level. It feels too much—again, to me—like I'm propagating stereotypes, fetish related or not.

As this poster noted, race play, for a White person, can feel like reifying racism even though it is consensual fantasy. Again, many performers noted that White men seemed obsessed with Black men's cocks. In many regions and countries throughout the world, the Caribbean, Germany, and the United States, for example, hypersexuality has been central to the racist discourses that define Blackness.[8] The Mandingo trope—the image of large Black men with huge cocks preying on White women—has been central to definitions of Black masculinity globally, and kink work online is not the first sexual market to exploit it. The Mandingo trope is often used in race play and shapes the fascination White men have Black men's penises.

In the United States, for example, since slavery, White men have been obsessed with Black men's bodies. Whether embodied in the White man's 19th-century minstrel show or in the 21st-century social performances by affluent White boys who love Black music, but not actual Black people, White men reveal their internalized jealousy of Black men.[9] Centuries of successful cultural appropriation of Black culture by White men evidence the privileges of White supremacy, but also helps us understand White men's obsession with big, Black cock. Cis White men are trapped in bodies and lives that many do not want, but they need these bodies in order to live well under capitalism, White supremacy, and patriarchy.

Within the context of race play, many performers were not only willing to perform small penis humiliation with White men, but, as the posts above suggested, many enjoyed it. Perhaps, when women perform SPH with White men, it is a fuck-you to patriarchy and White male privilege. Women also described doing race play and SPH with other men of color. Unlike SPH with White men, these role plays with men of color were uncomfortable. One woman said:

The other day I got a guy into Asian race play and SPH. I was a little lost at what to say, so I made up some shit like, all you're good for is building railroads and go do my math homework, bitch[,] and my personal favorite, how did you unite a giant country with such little dicks?

Exploiting stereotypes about Asian men, this performer combined race play and SPH with an Asian client. In her post, she went on to clarify her interaction with this client by saying:

I actually have a great reverence for East Asian culture. The Chinese ability to unite all those people and places and become Chinese was phenomenal, from a historical perspective, and they created a written language without outside influence. I think that's amazing. My best friend in childhood was Korean; I love to eat and cook Asian food. I really want to visit

Thailand. I love Samurai movies. I have no hatred or dislike for Asian people. The thought doesn't even cross my mind. Anyway, it made me uncomfortable; and if I re-watched it, I'd think I was a bitch, but he loved it. And he stayed in my free chat for a while afterwards, and in a way, it lessened the sting for me. We were two consenting adults, so it didn't break any of my rules, but it was still very, very uncomfortable.

This cam model defensively argued that she is not racist and that while she performed the show, it was very uncomfortable. Performers get prompted to do race play by clients of many different races, although the most popular, especially among clients from the United States, is Black-White race play.

There are two issues I would like to raise regarding White women's responses to race-play requests from clients of color, especially requests initiated by Black men. First, many performers highlighted that they are unwilling to perform what they saw as the most degrading requests, shows involving the word "nigger" and slave role plays, but do race play shows if it involves making such statements as "you going to fuck this White pussy with that big Black cock." Some White female performers believe that the latter empowers Black men and that the former is racist play that demeans Black men. I wonder, though, Isn't it also demeaning to deny these men their fantasies? If some White women tell Black men they will not perform these services because it is degrading for the Black man, they are exerting racial privilege and engaging in the same racist behavior they seemingly want to avoid.

In addition, it was typical for White women to say that a significant reason why they reject race play featuring racial degradation and humiliation is because of the fear that these shows might get recorded and released on the Internet. The release of this content could potentially tarnish their brand and personal reputation if shown out of context, and they'd be labeled racists as a result. Elizabeth discussed this fear with me:

The first time that somebody asked me to do it [race play], it was a Black man. He was, like, call me nigger, and I just felt, like, I couldn't do it very good. It just felt weird for me, and I told him, I'm sorry, I'm trying. He's, like, well, in a way I think it's a good thing that it's hard. . . . [B]ut especially nowadays, I get so fucking scared. Like, if I was doing race play with someone and I got recorded, and then somebody, like, put it up, [and said] oh, she's racist and, like, took it out of context. So you have to worry about that, too.

Race play involving putting men of color on pedestals was more comfortable for White women. However, racial degradation and humiliation were harder for them, and as Elizabeth said, it should be. Her comments were really crucial in unpacking these performances. In our interview, her tone was sincere. She genuinely wanted to try to deliver this fantasy to her clients by being nonjudgmental, even though these shows made her uncomfortable. And she explained how it is also scary that she could deliver such a fantasy and then be called out as a racist for doing so.

Amelia, whom we met earlier, also described a race-play show that made her very uncomfortable:

> He wanted to do a slave scenario where I was the White woman who owned him. And he was, like, I want you to say the N-word, and I was, like, I can't, I just can't say it. I was, like, I know, even if you're Black and even if it is your fetish and you're giving me permission, I just, I can't. Because the other thing that I have concerns about, I was, like, you could be recording this, and then you could put a clip on the Internet of me just saying the N-word, ya know? It's not, it's not something I would ever want to do or want on the Internet. So, I'm afraid I'm gonna have to turn you down.

Amelia also underscored the two issues I just raised. First, Amelia and other White cam models often deny race-play requests because they are concerned about client's capping and publicly releasing these shows. Second, she said these requests make her uncomfortable even though the interaction is fantasy and the client gives her permission to say these things to him. On the one hand, we must respect a performer's right to decline services to clients because it makes them uncomfortable or violates their ethics. Sex must always be consensual. On the other hand, race play is, especially for some Black men, empowering and pleasures them by pushing the boundaries of race. What are the implications of White performers denying Black men this service? This question, again, highlights the importance of a sociological theory of pleasure. Pleasure is imbued with power and sociologists must examine the implications of who has the power to deny or grant others pleasure.

Additionally, performers could provide race play to the best of their ability and, if they are genuinely concerned about their client, provide what BDSM practitioners commonly call "aftercare"—the attention, pampering, and nurturing given to a partner (usually the sub/bottom) after a play scene. Usually, partners will negotiate just what aftercare they will engage in. Aftercare is an essential aspect of safe BDSM play. As one White cam model posted on a discussion board:

> I do it [race play], but it never gets to the point where I'm like a Nazi KKK freak. After, I always let them know that it was all a fantasy and that I am not like that at all in IRL [in real life], and I ask if they feel ok. Aftercare is important both for your own psyche and your customer.

Race play, like all BDSM play, should be carried out only by experienced models. Part of the reason for some models' lack of comfort and the inability of some to carry out these services is that they haven't been properly trained in doing fetish work. Performers who are highly specialized and trained in kink work, like Elizabeth and Rebecca, may personally struggle with scenes such as race play, but they can still try to help their clients in a sane, safe, and consensual way and, crucially, in a way that doesn't judge them. If society already tells a person their sexual desires are deviant, pathological, and perverted, having a sex professional insinuate the same by refusing service can further exacerbate a client's feelings of internalized shame.

A sociological analysis of pleasure suggests that pleasure can exist in saying and doing things that societies prohibit. Given the taboos around race, there can be pleasure for marginalized people in taking control of racist cultural scripts and deciding when and how people call them a racial slur. In everyday life, people of color do not have the power to control when people hurl racial epithets at them. In race play, people who are disadvantaged by the system of White supremacy can escape that system momentarily when they take control over the racial scripts in their interactions with a White person. The affectual pleasures of this escape and reclaiming of power can be cathartic. Moreover, perhaps, for performers, especially White women, it is also possible that performing race play with their Black male clients, and doing proper aftercare with them, can help demystify the oppressive systems and social and political (not psychological) forces that shape why Black men seek catharsis in this way.

Kink Work and the Diffuse Life

The kink work that performers do in the context of private shows is not merely about delivering an economic service to a stranger. Performers build intimate relationships with regular clients. Their interactions affect the lives of the performers and clients even after they get off and log off. In examining the diffuse lives of cam performers and their clients, I demonstrate that a symbiotic relationship exists between people's cam lives and offline lives. Elizabeth and I were talking about one of her regulars and the relationship they have cultivated over a period of two years:

> I had this one customer; he's a hockey player, and has a really good, high-end job, [and] makes decent money. He gets all kinky and sissy for me, and I humiliate him, and then he cums and then he cries. Then I comfort him for like half an hour. It's gotten better now, but he's, like, I'll never be able to have a normal life being submissive! I'm, like, what? I said do you think that you need to be totally vanilla to have a wife and kids someday? I'm, like, you can find a girl that will kick the shit out of you and fuck you in your ass, and then have your kids. It doesn't have to be [this way], but people are so ingrained [into] *normal* [sexuality], they're made to feel guilty. You don't even understand, dude! Like, you can have it all! . . . But they just have this image in their head, that they're wrong, and that they'll never have a normal life because they're kinky. . . . They never go see a therapist. I've worried about him before. I've said maybe you should you go talk to someone. I'm not a healthcare professional, love. Yeah, I've taken a ton of psych classes, but I'm not qualified. . . . He's doing so much better now, too; I'm so happy. I've been working with him for two years, and now, he's gone on [a kink website]; he's meeting up with some dom, and he's exploring now. And he's not feeling guilt about it. And I'll pat myself on the back for helping with that, but honestly, I'm honored. If I can do that for people, then I can't think of a more important thing to

teach people than to not feel bad for their urges. As long as it's consensual and you're not hurting anyone, who the fuck cares? Like, do it up!

This story exemplifies how kink work is about so much more than just a service worker delivering a sexual service. Elizabeth cared about this man. He cared about her. She helped him become more comfortable with his desires. In their sessions, they developed an intimate relationship. She assisted him to become more at peace with himself. Their interactions affected him outside of their sessions. Kink performers often provide clients with emotional, instrumental, and informational support. Especially in BDSM shows, the informational support models provide to clients can be just as important as the sexual service they provide, which is why it is crucial that cam models be skilled in and knowledgeable about BDSM before offering services online.

In my conversations with Rebecca, we discussed the importance of her training and the education that she provides clients:

I'm usually pretty personable, even when I'm doing dom shows, like, my regular slave guys will come to me and ask me questions because I'm an open book. I also know a lot about what I'm talking about. So, if we talk about lifestyle BDSM, I was in a collared relationship for two years—a polyamorous collared relationship. So I can sit there and talk about that all day long. I've been classically trained as a dom. . . . Also, me doing as much fetish modeling beforehand here and there out here . . . and I think people automatically knew who I was or they'd come across me, oh, I watched your videos on such and such site, and that helped because I already kind of had a name before even starting to cam. . . . I've also gotten some dom/sub couples where . . . it's a male dom and a female submissive, so that's been pretty interesting. I had a regular client; I haven't seen him for a few months, but he would come and he would ask how, how like what he should do with her, and I was part of their role play, so that was kind of neat. I've watched couples and, like, instructed them on what to do together, so that was always interesting.

Being successful as a kink performer requires skill and cultural capital. Rebecca was able to educate single clients as well as couples exploring

BDSM. She does more than educate; she works to validate people's desires and to support them in their sexual journeys. She continued:

> I feel that I help people a lot to realize that they're not weird, they're not strange, and the things that they are into are just things they are into and that it doesn't say anything bad about them. That's just what turns them on! And what right do I have to judge someone for what they get turned on by? Or I've had guys who were really into feet and then realized, like, after talking to me for so long, they're, like, it's okay if you're wanting to go, like, to a foot party and worship someone's feet. Like, I can actually, like, actualize my fantasy and not hurt anyone and the other person's into it. So that's pretty cool, too.

Rebecca performs an immediate service, but the long-term value of her work cannot be underestimated. She helps change people's everyday lives and helps them to acquire the skills they need to practice BDSM in safe, consensual, and sane ways. She helps them come to terms with who they are and become comfortable practicing BDSM offline. In addition to the benefits of these interactions for clients, I want to also focus on the benefits of performing kink online to performers themselves.

Finding Myself: On Being a Sub

Cam performers can use kink work to explore their desires. Their interactions with clients are not just about fulfilling the clients' sexual needs. By performing for clients, models can have more than their immediate sexual needs met; they can also learn more about their sexual subjectivities. While performing BDSM shows for clients, performers shape their own identities and find their truths. Adeline, a 25-year-old polyamorous White trans woman from the United States whom we've met before, told me, "I didn't really realize that I was like, a sub, so . . . the whole submissive BDSM thing developed from camming." As Adeline received requests from dom clients to perform and interact in shows as a submissive, she entered onto a path of self-discovery.

Adeline's sexual journey is not just about discovering her submissive self; it is also about pushing boundaries related to her gender identity in ways that bring her multiple and overlapping pleasures.

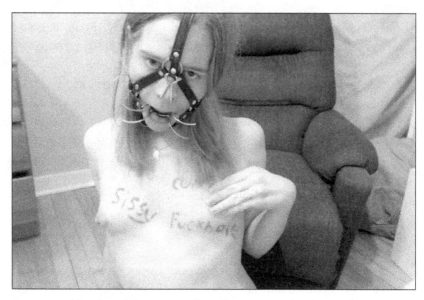

Figure 9.1. Adeline degraded in a private show. She is wearing a bondage mask with spikes and has the words "sissy," "fuckhole," and "cunt" written on her chest in red lipstick.

Figure 9.2. Adeline degraded in a private show. She is sitting on the floor naked. Her left thigh has the word "pain" written in red lipstick and her right thigh, "slut." Her forehead has the word "cunt" written on it and her chest has the phrases "cheap fuck meat," "abuse me," and "humiliate me."

In the show from which figure 9.1 was taken, Adeline was told to write "sissy" on her own chest. She explained to me: "I never identified as a sissy. I think as a result, I felt less restricted by my own gender-related insecurities." In the experience represented by figure 9.2, Adeline recalled that the client told her:

> Now for the rest of the show, and it's going to be a long one, you're going to have to stare at the word "cunt" on your forehead. Shortly after, as punishment, I was asked to write every number 1–100 on a piece of paper.

Adeline and I discussed her experience of these shows. She continued:

> In both pics, I was in subspace, and I am a subspace junkie. Throughout my camming career, I would have my soft limits pushed farther away. Being called the word "sissy" was a soft limit for me because I worked so hard in real life to be treated equally with other women, and I did not like the implications of being called a sissy. That being said, the entire act was not about me or what I want. In camming and submitting, it is about pleasing the dom and making their fantasies come to life. Perhaps this guy had a strong emasculation urge. My role as a submissive cam artist is not to judge one's kinks but to let them come alive. I liked this guy, too; he always tipped well and gave me really long shows, and sometimes after roleplaying, we would watch YouTube videos together while the token clock was still turning. Having that trust between us is what makes our cam sex like real sex and not just a service I provide. Working through my soft limits on cam is comparable to working through my soft limits off cam.

Adeline has the opportunity to explore her sexuality through submissive role play and to get paid well for doing it. She called herself a subspace junkie. In BDSM communities, subspace refers to a psychological state achieved by a submissive in a bottoming play scene. No singular affective state is achieved by entering subspace; the feelings one experiences while in subspace are highly individualized. For Adeline, being in subspace means she can push her boundaries, which produces a feeling of freedom.

Importantly, Adeline noted that it is the rapport and trust that she and her client have built over time that makes their play more than just a service. Their intimate bond is why she can push her own limits and enjoy exploring her desires for submissive role play. Notice that after shows, Adeline and this regular client decompress together. Again, aftercare is an essential part of having consensual, sane, and safe BDSM play. Adeline's story also highlighted the symbiotic relationship between a person's cam life and offline life. When performers practice safe, sane, and consensual BDSM play with regular clients in nonjudgmental ways, it can lead to incredibly pleasurable experiences for cam models. Adeline elaborated on her experiences of pleasure in the play scene described above:

> After he said that line about "cunt" on my forehead, I felt endorphins in my chest that meant I am entering further into subspace. It is one of my favorite feelings, subspace. Being a sub on cam was a score for me because sometimes I would have to be a dom or vanilla-y, and those cases were sometimes more like acting to me. When I got to be a sub, I would feel lots of pleasure from the experience.

Adeline will perform vanilla shows, but she experiences pleasure camming when she explores her desires through submissive role play with a dom. She spoke of endorphins, but her pleasure was not just physiological. Societal norms regarding gender and sexuality conditioned the role play enacted by Adeline and her client. By allowing a cis man to dominate her, Adeline was pushing her boundaries. Her experiences underscore that pleasure is often simultaneously bound up in physiological responses, as well as affectual states, that are both shaped by the social context and the cultural scripts that Adeline and her client's interactions challenge. When cam models cultivate long-term relationships with regular clients, they can, in the process, develop the trust necessary to have transformative, meaningful, and pleasurable experiences with them.

Conclusion

Performing kink online has numerous rewards for cam models. First, given that BDSM play is taboo and highly stigmatized, performers can charge a premium for these services. Models who perform kink well can make a great deal of money by branding and marketing themselves as fetish or kink performers. Second, models can use their interactions with clients in BDSM shows to explore their sexual subjectivities. For Adeline, doing kink work meant she could explore and enjoy submissive role play in ways that produced pleasure for her and helped her become even more comfortable with herself and her womanhood. Third, the work that kink performers do with clients can have positive effects on both the lives of the client and the performer. In exploring sexual desires, and by pushing sociocultural boundaries through role play, people can find ephemeral moments of freedom from regulatory forces in society that control human sexual behavior. Sociologically, it is these ephemeral moments that create the basis of pleasure. However, there are two crucial problems with this reading of kink online.

First, BDSM play on- or offline can feel like a radical experience of alterity—that is an escape from the social systems that confine our desires and restrict our bodies, which does produce pleasure. As anthropologist Margot Weiss has argued, BDSM play feels freeing to many, but it still exists within the realm of social relations and various overlapping systems of oppression.[10] Race play, for example, is a pleasurable fantasy and experience for some people. The use of racially charged epithets such as "nigger" during sex and role play involving slave narratives is a way that some Black men, for example, take control and ownership over how these words are used in their interactions with White people, thus helping them manage both historical and current racial trauma. Transgressing social boundaries and playing with race in ways that we are not supposed to can feel empowering and liberating. On the other hand, various forms of BDSM play, not just race play, also reinforce systems of oppression such as White supremacy, patriarchy, and cissexism. Despite the presence of consent, and the pleasurable outcomes for Adeline, What are the politics of Adeline's domination by a cis man who calls her a sissy? These types of play scenes may reinforce forms of racial, gendered, and class-based power arrangements and entitlements.

The second issue with reading kink online as a utopian story is that not all kinky play online produces positive effects for clients and performers. Some of the interactions described in this chapter could potentially cause harm. Increasingly, due to market saturation, many cam performers strategically market themselves using tags such as #fetish to drive additional traffic to their rooms. This hashtag can have a positive effect by creating more visibility for kinky sex and, thus, help to discursively push sociocultural boundaries regulating sex. However, performing kink work often involves highly specialized cultural capital. As demonstrated in Margot Weiss's study of BDSM, practicing BDSM requires highly specialized techniques.[11] Performers who do not correctly execute BDSM practices may not only lose clients but cause harm to clients and themselves. In other words, poorly performed BDSM can cause economic harm to the model, and psychological harm to both model and client. Even in an online context, BDSM play should still always be safe, sane, and consensual.

Two overlapping issues likely caused the lack of comfort many of the people in this chapter felt performing race play. First, regardless of the virtual context, we cannot remove ourselves from systems of social relations or oppression. People can say that calling someone a "nigger," "kike," or "spic" is just harmless talk in the context of consensual play, but it is difficult to divorce this language from its socially constructed meanings. Performers' subjectivities and social positions within existing power regimes no doubt condition how they experience race play and if they can find it pleasurable. One web forum poster said:

> I personally can't do race play because I live in the south [in the US], and I'm so incredibly used to that word having such an awful connotation. I've met so many racist fucks who use it in a degrading way. It's incredible how many people here use it casually, as if it's nothing.

For people who have lived in environments, for example, the US South, where words such as "nigger" are deployed in violent ways every day, words cannot be separated from that context—even online. People who live in so-called "shitholes" throughout the world, whose lives have been so negatively affected by imperialism and colonialism, often cannot divorce racist language from their political, economic, and social realities.[12] Again, people live diffuse lives; their offline selves and online selves shape one another.

Second, many of the performers asked by random customers to practice BDSM online have no training or background participating in BDSM subculture. BDSM play requires skill and knowledge. As a result of lack of training, performers are practicing BDSM online in ways that are not safe, sane, and consensual. If a person is not trained in what Weiss calls "the techniques of pleasure," they often cannot perform such fantasy work in safe, sane, and consensual ways. If many performers are untrained in how to do race play safely and sanely, even if it is consensual, it is no wonder that many reported not liking to perform it.

Finally, offering kink services online can be very lucrative for performers. The idea that someone could rake in $15 per minute or hundreds of dollars for one show is understandably enticing to performers. But when cam models agree to perform BDSM shows for clients without proper training, this can cause various forms of harm to themselves and their clients. Working with equipment that one is not trained to use is not safe and can cause physical harm. Engaging in role plays that one is not trained to facilitate and failing to engage in aftercare is unsafe and can cause psychological harm. When performers untrained in BDSM market themselves as doing fetish or kink work, and then turn down clients' requests they find too uncomfortable, such rejections can reify clients' possible feelings of shame. My analysis is not meant as a baseless condemnation; cam models' economic motivations are not lost on me. Clients, as consumers, also have a responsibility to do research and find skilled BDSM practitioners with whom to work. As a Black woman earlier told us quite clearly, she has it written on her profile that she does not do fetish work and especially will not do race play. Clients should always respect performers' boundaries and, for their benefit, conduct better research on performers when seeking BDSM services.[13]

Conclusion

Belle Knox: The Duke Porn Star

In 2013, Miriam Weeks, better known as Belle Knox, began shooting pornographic films to pay her exorbitant tuition bill at Duke University. In early 2014, a male student attending Duke recognized Knox from a pornographic film she starred in and outed her. Weeks first spoke out under a pseudonym, Lauren A, in an article in the *Duke Chronicle* student newspaper. Duke University imposed no sanctions because Week's employment occurred off campus, but she suffered other consequences. In February 2014, she wrote an xoJane blog post telling her story and discussing the harassment she had faced since she was outed.[1] She described how she had been doxed, harassed, and terrorized, receiving death and rape threats. When Weeks reported this harassment to the police, she was belittled and told that they were just "childish threats." No action was taken by law enforcement to find or prosecute any of the people who terrorized Weeks.

The Oregon State Library Girl

In 2015, 19-year-old Kendra Jane Sunderland became known on the Internet as "The Oregon State Library Girl." In the fall semester of 2014, Sunderland had been working on MyFreeCams for only two weeks when she decided to broadcast a show from her college library. Later, in January 2015, people posted capped videos of her performance to porn tube sites and social media. As a result, the college and police eventually learned of the performance. Sunderland was cited with public indecency and initially faced a maximum jail sentence of one year, a potential $6,250 fine, and possible registration as a sex offender. In September 2015, she was convicted of public indecency, which is a misdemeanor;

she paid a $1,000 fine, received no jail time, and did not have to register as a sex offender.

Rentboy.com

On August 25, 2015, Homeland Security and other federal agents raided the offices of Rentboy.com in New York City. They arrested the CEO, Jeffery Hurant, and six other employees. Rentboy itself, the largest online website for male escorts to safely advertise their services, was seized by the FBI and shut down. Rentboy had over 500,000 unique visitors a day and earned $10 million in revenues in just the five years before its seizure.[2] In June 2016, Hurant was sentenced to six months in prison for promoting prostitution (federal guidelines recommended 15 to 21 months). Judge Margo Brodie also ordered that he undergo a mental health treatment program, as well as pay a $7,500 fine.

Backpage.com

On April 6, 2018, federal agents raided the home of Backpage.com co-founder Michael Lacey. Lacey and six other executives were arrested and faced a 93-count indictment, which was sealed. Backpage was an online classified advertising website best known for its sex work advertisements. In 2014, Backpage's revenues were said to be $135 million annually.[3] The site had been part of an ongoing federal sex trafficking investigation. "The National Center for Missing and Exploited Children has told Congress that nearly three quarters of the cases submitted to the center related to ads posted on [Backpage]."[4] Backpage had been sued numerous times both civilly and criminally for charges related to sex trafficking. For example, Backpage was named in a wrongful-death suit filed by Yvonne Ambrose, after her 16-year-old daughter, Desiree, was beaten and stabbed to death by a person whom she met after her pimp posted an ad on the site.[5] Once unsealed, the federal indictment also revealed accounts of sex trafficking. For example, a young woman said from the age of 14 to 19 she was forcibly prostituted on Backpage and was gang-raped, choked to near death, and forced to perform sex acts at gunpoint. Evidence, meanwhile, also shows that Backpage actively assisted law enforcement in cases and reports of sex trafficking.[6] While

Carl Ferrer, the CEO and cofounder of Backpage, had pleaded guilty to money laundering and facilitating prostitution before the raid that forced the site's shutdown, the fates of Lacey and several other Backpage executives are still pending.

* * *

On April 11, 2018, President Donald J. Trump signed the Fight Online Sex Trafficking Act (FOSTA) into law. It combined elements from the original FOSTA bill, drafted in the House of Representatives, and the Senate's similar Stop Enabling Sex Traffickers Act (SESTA) bill. The original House bill had focused only on websites such as Backpage, while the Senate bill targeted all websites. Section 2 of the final act states:

It is the sense of Congress that—

(1) section 230 of the Communications Act of 1934 (47 U.S.C. 230; commonly known as the "Communications Decency Act of 1996") was never intended to provide legal protection to websites that unlawfully promote and facilitate prostitution and websites that facilitate traffickers in advertising the sale of unlawful sex acts with sex trafficking victims;

(2) websites that promote and facilitate prostitution have been reckless in allowing the sale of sex trafficking victims and have done nothing to prevent the trafficking of children and victims of force, fraud, and coercion; and

(3) clarification of such section is warranted to ensure that such section does not provide such protection to such websites.

In effect, Congress rewrote the 1996 Communications Decency Act, arguing that it was written before lawmakers could have foreseen the growth of online adult websites and their role in facilitating prostitution and sex trafficking. According to Congress, adult website owners have been "reckless" and knowingly allowed sex traffickers to use their sites. In addition, FOSTA also updated the Mann Act, which prohibits the interstate prostitution of another person, by adding new language that explicitly prohibits the use of a website to facilitate the prostitution of another person. FOSTA was a massive win for the rescue industry and anti-trafficking organizations and advocates. But how will this new legislation and the continued momentum of the anti-trafficking movement affect voluntary sex workers?

Following FOSTA's passage, and before President Trump even signed the bill into law, several websites with adult classifieds begun shutting down the adult sections used by sex workers. Craigslist, for example, said it was taking down its personals sections because "[a]ny tool or service can be misused. We can't take such risk without jeopardizing all our other services, so we are regretfully taking craigslist personals offline" (figure C.1). The popular Reddit site also quickly removed all subreddits related to sex work. And such preemptive reactions to FOSTA were not limited to just a couple of websites.

Vice reported that sex workers' pornographic content has disappeared from Google Drive, as the company begins to more ardently enforce its sexual content policy, which states, "Do not publish sexually explicit or pornographic images or videos . . . we do not allow content that drives traffic to commercial pornography."[7] Sex workers are seeing their social media accounts suspended.[8] Cam models have had their emails locked because they have pornographic content and third-party billing companies have suspended their accounts for receiving payments for sex work. Elizabeth, whom I've quoted several times, is one of a few models I keep in contact with. She told me her professional email was locked after FOSTA, leading to the loss of clients and bookings.

Crucially, FOSTA may affect sex workers' ability to organize and politically mobilize themselves. Due to FOSTA, Switter, which was sex workers' alternative to Twitter, was shut down by its content delivery service, Cloudflare.[9] In June 2018, in response to FOSTA, the Desiree Alliance[10] cancelled its planned 2019 conference, which was going to be held in Las Vegas. Since 2006, every two or three years the Desiree Alliance had hosted a conference, the largest one for sex workers and sex work advocates. The Desiree Alliance posted the following message on its website:

> It is with great sadness and much consideration that Desiree Alliance announces the cancellation of our July 2019 conference Transcending Borders: Immigration, Migration, and Sex Work. Due to FOSTA/SESTA enactments, our leadership made the decision that we cannot put our organization and our attendees at risk. We hope you understand our grave concerns and continue to resist every law that exists to harm sex workers! Keep fighting!

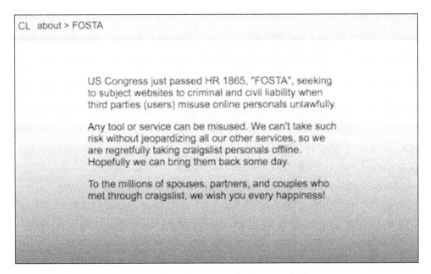

Figure C.1. Craigslist message about the removal of personal ads.

The shifts in US immigration policy, alongside FOSTA, led to concern among the organizers that meeting publicly could compromise the safety of the more than 500 sex worker attendees they expected. The point is, FOSTA and the efforts of the rescue industry to address sex trafficking have had deleterious effects on voluntary sex workers.

ISPs, civil liberties organizations, and sex worker advocacy organizations are challenging FOSTA in the courts, and hopefully the law will be repealed. The International Entertainment Adult Union is proposing a bill to Congress called the Red Collar Workers Act calling for the amendment of FOSTA.[11] In the interim, the current anti–sex work climate in the United States and the fear of litigation created by FOSTA is reverberating throughout the global network of sex work industries.

Several questions need to be asked about this watershed moment. How will FOSTA continue to affect online sex work globally? It is too reductive to say, Well, FOSTA applies only to sex entrepreneurs in the US. It is naïve to think FOSTA will not affect the entire online global sex industry. Additionally, we must ask, How will adult websites continue to operate if they must function under the perpetual fear that at any moment content posted on their sites will violate FOSTA? How, specifically, will FOSTA affect cam sites?

Based on the preventive measures already implemented in response to FOSTA, I anticipate many issues will arise in the camming market. First, as I noted earlier, it is plausible that people are forced to perform against their will in camming studios. If law enforcement implicated one cam studio in a sex-trafficking case, it could potentially take down an entire cam-site network. For example, given that Streamate and Live-Jasmin actively work with studios, and both have extensive networks of cam sites, if a studio was seized because of FOSTA, it is possible that the cam site(s) the trafficked cam models performed on could be brought up on charges and shut down. This would be a worst-case scenario.

Another possible effect of FOSTA on cam sites relates to intellectual property and copyright infringements. If FOSTA no longer protects ISPs, music companies and other entities may sue sex entrepreneurs for copyright violations because models frequently use copyrighted music and other trademarked products in their shows. Music companies would likely not go after individual models; models who said that these companies will now "have bigger fish to fry" are right. Why sue a cam model who makes $40,000 a year when music companies can sue a cam site owner who makes millions a year? If safe harbor no longer exists in the US, cam sites may begin to implement stricter policies regarding the use of copyrighted materials in cam shows. Changes in policies regarding copyrighted content will create even more work for cam models. One solution suggested by models I interviewed was for cam sites to initiate license agreements with music companies. Models may need to start restricting their use of music only to that which has been released under Creative Commons licenses or is otherwise royalty-free.

Even if safe harbor no longer protects cam sites, I do not believe sex entrepreneurs will be rushing to shut down their multimillion-dollar-a-year businesses. Will these companies find ways to move overseas to protect themselves? Relocation is also problematic. Given the relatively liberal laws regarding pornography in the US, it is unclear where in the world it is practical for cam site owners to move their companies. Moreover, as we have seen with the online gambling market, there will likely be laws that prevent easy relocation. Even if relocation is possible, say to the UK, which has laws similar to those in the US regarding pornography, how would relocation affect the camming market? For those in the US who cannot safely relocate or choose not to, as a result of FOSTA and the rescue industries mobilization around sites such as Backpage, cam-site owners and moderators will assuredly be under greater scrutiny.

It is highly likely, then, that cam sites will begin to monitor cam models' pages and performances more heavily. Moreover, given models' accounts of how race, nationality, and gender shape cam site moderators' surveillance practices, it is also plausible that cam models will not evenly feel the increased surveillance resulting from FOSTA. The act will no doubt add to the discriminatory experiences of cam models of color, trans women, and cis men who service other men. Heavy policing of models' performances will likely lead to more censoring of content and suspensions of models. The most economically, socially, and politically vulnerable sex workers will continue to be the most severely affected.

In addition to hyperpolicing on cam sites, other sites, such as ManyVids, where models post content will likely become stricter about pornographic content sold by models. In May 2018, Microsoft and Skype implemented changes to their policies and now use auto-detection filters to search for sexual content. The new Microsoft policy states, "Don't publicly display or use the Services to share inappropriate content or material (involving, for example, nudity, bestiality, pornography, offensive language, graphic violence, or criminal activity)."[12] Cam models who use Skype will be heavily monitored, and I suspect some will lose their accounts. Models could move to Skype Private, which is not a US company and thus not affected directly by FOSTA. However, whereas on regular Skype models keep 100% of their earnings, Skype Private takes a commission to Skype Private. Models will also have more significant problems with third-party billers who are afraid of being charged by law enforcement with facilitating prostitution. In sum, FOSTA will harm many cam models, especially those already the most marginalized. It has not been my intention to downplay the importance of anti-sex-trafficking advocacy—sex trafficking is a global human rights problem. However, it is essential to consider how new policies targeting sex trafficking will affect voluntary sex workers in many different segments of the online global sex trade.

With FOSTA in mind, let's return to the four cases that introduced this conclusion. Each raised critical issues about the growth of online sex work and how since the introduction of the Internet the law has not been adequately updated. First, millions of sex workers like Belle

Knox face rampant stigma, which shapes how they are treated by law enforcement. Knox told police she was terrorized after she had been outed as a porn star. The police did nothing. While the moral entrepreneurs argue that they want to protect sex workers from harm, evidence suggests their benevolence extends only to those sex workers coerced into the sex trade. How do we address violence against and harassment of voluntary sex workers in a digital age?

Sunderland's case raised important questions about privacy and piracy. She did not release the video of her library performance. It was capped and posted on porn tube sites by other parties. If the court found Sunderland guilty of public indecency, aren't the people who capped the video without her permission and disseminated it also culpable? In addition, people now use the Internet everywhere, including public spaces. When a person uses a private server or one that does not belong to them, say on a college campus, students are responsible for abiding by the terms and conditions set by the network owner. Will sex workers and clients who use servers and networks that do not belong to them be criminalized further? How will the law continue to adapt to the ubiquity of the Internet and the reality that sex work is being negotiated, sold, and performed in nonphysical spaces?

Importantly, we must ask how contemporary attempts to regulate a global network of sex work industries will affect sex workers who work offline as well. When Rentboy and Backpage were shut down by law enforcement agencies, what happened to the voluntary sex workers that used these websites? The Internet has helped reduce the harm and violence sex workers, especially street-based sex workers, face. The literature that documents the benefits of the Internet for sex workers tends to come from four different sources: cultural studies, criminology, psychology and health studies, and sociology. While the theoretical underpinnings of these fields and their methodologies may differ, their work ends up sharing one common theme—it all highlights the ability of the Internet to safeguard sex workers and their clients. Online sex work has increased because of the numerous benefits of sex work that occurs when all or some part of the erotic labor is performed by sex workers in an online environment, including promoting physical safety, fostering better wages, assisting workers with advertising, screening clients, and reputation building.[13] Considerable research has documented that the

backpage.com and affiliated websites have been seized

as part of an enforcement action by the Federal Bureau of Investigation, the U.S. Postal Inspection Service, and the Internal Revenue Service Criminal Investigation Division, with analytical assistance from the Joint Regional Intelligence Center.

Other agencies participating in and supporting the enforcement action include the U.S. Attorney's Office for the District of Arizona, the U.S. Department of Justice's Child Exploitation and Obscenity Section, the U.S. Attorney's Office for the Central District of California, the office of the California Attorney General, and the office of the Texas Attorney General.

Additional information will be provided at around 6:00 pm EST on Friday, April 6, by the U.S. Department of Justice, and all media inquiries should be directed to the U.S. Department of Justice's Office of Public Affairs at 202-514-2007 and press@usdoj.gov.

April 6, 2018

Figure C.2. Backpage.com homepage after the site was seized and shut down by US law enforcement agencies.

Internet helps to reduce the possibility of harm to escorts. If the moral entrepreneurs continue to take platforms such as Rentboy offline, that puts voluntary sex workers at significant risk. Policies such as FOSTA will only create more criminalization and result in even more sex workers getting bound up in the prison industrial complex.

FOSTA will lead to greater policing of sex workers on- and offline. We must ask how gender, race, nationality, and sexuality will influence this overpolicing. In this book, I have explored how moderators monitored cam models' performances on cam sites and how the models' embodiment and subjectivity influenced moderators' interventions. The case of Rentboy suggests that law enforcement agents may also target sites that cater to non-normative sexualities. The increased regulation and criminalization of voluntary sex workers will have a devastating effect on the most marginalized.

Why would the United States government knowingly pass a law that would harm so many people, especially when even the Federal Bureau of Investigation has noted that sex trafficking convictions have decreased and of all the prostitution and disorderly conduct arrests from 1981 until 2013, only 1.8% involved minors?[14] The answer is that the US government does not care about protecting voluntary sex workers. As the Desiree Alliance put it in speaking out against FOSTA:

> The Desiree Alliance has serious concerns over the ongoing attacks against sexual freedoms of adult-oriented industries. We view the right for consensual sexual freedoms as fundamental civil liberties every citizen is afforded to engage in without legal recourse, without policing, and without moral repercussions. These intrusions and deprivations debase personal privacy and equality that censor the First Amendment right guaranteed to every citizen. The targeting, profiling, arrests, and convictions against vulnerable populations inherently impair the health and well-being of communities that have limited or no access to services that provide safe working environments and protections against state-sanctioned violence. When government begins to criminalize sex in the guise of morality and jettisons legal language, we question the validity and reasoning as to why government interference belongs in the consensual labor of sex and online advertising sites that provide safety from second and third party interferences and exploitations.[15]

The government's intent is not only to save victims of trafficking—moral entrepreneurs attempt to forcibly stop people from voluntarily working in any sex industry, despite the billions of dollars in revenue sex industries create. The global criminalization and hyperregulation of sex work is a unique case insofar as states place religious and neo-Victorian moral agendas before even capitalism and economic growth. This underscores the main theoretical point of this book, that the regulation of pleasure is a central task of major social institutions—governments will strip citizens of fundamental human and civil rights in order to control pleasure. Societies are built around forcing people (often violently) to sacrifice pleasure. The sacrifice of pleasure provides structure and order to society and its institutions, yet the sacrifice of pleasure is embedded with power, and in this process, human freedoms are limited, and these moralistic structures subjugate people.

Beyond FOSTA: What's Next?

Will legislators and legal systems implement further measures to regulate the online sex industry? Will politicians update laws to adapt to the digital age? FOSTA has created a groundswell of activism among sex work activists and civil liberties organizations. The Electronic Frontier Federation, a nonprofit defending digital privacy, free speech, and innovation, launched the Stop SESTA campaign.[16] *Gizmodo*'s Melanie Ehrenkranz, reporting on sex worker protests on International Whores Day,[17] June 2, 2018, wrote:

> The groundswell of resistance in response to SESTA/FOSTA has increasingly put the need for sex workers' rights on people's radar. It's a law that represents state violence and police brutality against sex working people and survivors, and it's evident all around me at the International Whores' Day demonstration that this law has transformed and united the community.[18]

Sex workers' rights activists have not ceased fighting paternalistic laws that put their lives in danger and stigmatize them. As Ehrenkranz noted, "this law has transformed and united the community." How will cam models respond to FOSTA, the increased saturation of the market, and the various forms of discrimination and exploitation they face? Will many cam models join the existing sex workers' rights movement? In what follows, I take up both of these questions.

Law: Revisiting the Miller Test

Lawmakers are beginning to realize that laws and policies that regulate sex work industries must be updated for the digital age. Will they favor amending and creating new laws, such as FOSTA, that impose more punitive regulations and restrictions on sex workers? As cases under these new laws come before the courts, how will judges deal with them and the many gaps in the law that remain? Whatever new precedents the courts set, and whatever new laws legislatures create, one thing is clear—the US legal system must recognize the global impact of US policies in shaping global online sex work industries. Laws regarding pornography, such as obscenity laws and the Miller test, will be scrutinized in US courts, and the outcomes will affect the entire online global sex work industry.

As I discussed in chapter 3, *Miller v. California*, 413 US 15 (1973), declared that the First Amendment does not protect material deemed obscene. The Miller test was adopted to help lower courts and law enforcement distinguish between legally pornographic material and obscene material. In assessing pornographic material, the Miller test poses three questions: (1) Would "'the average person, applying contemporary community [i.e., local] standards' . . . find that the work, taken as a whole, appeals to the prurient interest"? (2) Does "the work depict or describe, in a patently offensive way, sexual conduct specifically defined by the applicable state law"? (3) Would "the work, taken as a whole, lack serious literary, artistic, political, or scientific value"? The Miller test was developed when pornography was primarily consumed as print media and in VHS- and DVD-formatted films. Given the growth of online pornography, the Miller test is now more problematic than ever.

The Miller test needs to be updated to take into account the amount of pornographic content disseminated online. Specifically, the language regarding a "whole work" and local "community standards" requires updating. First, How can a court determine what a whole work is? When the Miller test was established, the "whole work" language was adopted to ensure that a prosecutor or judge could not simply take one piece of a larger work and use it out of context. In the context of camming, is a "whole work" an entire show? Say, for example, a cam model performs a show, and law enforcement agencies charge the model (or cam site) with obscenity, is the whole work the cam model's performance on that entire given day? Is the performance considered within the context of all the performances on the cam site? In addition, where do the boundaries of cam sites begin and end? When considering the whole work, does all the content on a model's page count as part of the work? If so, do all the links on a model's page count? Some cam models may have links to social media accounts or pornographic clips on another site or links to their fan page. Where does a cam models' room begin and end? The point is, all this content is connected online, and the law needs to grapple with this complicated issue.

There is another problem with the Miller test and current US obscenity law: *Miller* held that a work should be evaluated for obscenity by local and not national standards. In an online context, how do we define the "local community"? The Miller test was crafted in a time when people's consumption of pornography was confined to limited and objective spaces. While the Miller test was designed to give the individual states the freedom to handle obscenity cases, online pornography dissemination complicates this rationale. In the global camming industry, there is no local community, and the law needs to address this point. Recent events suggest that the persecution and criminalization of sex workers will not cease and, in fact, will likely worsen. How the law will continue to unfold and how sex workers and their allies will respond is a question that only time can answer.

Camily and the Potential for Political Mobilization

Historically, the sex industry's most vulnerable, those who trade sex under the most deplorable conditions, have generally been at the helm of sex work activism. Given that cam models report high rates of job satisfaction and report that they find their work pleasurable, will cam models politically mobilize themselves? Will cam models use the social capital developed by participating in the camily as a resource for political action? The conditions created by FOSTA, alongside the existing exploitation, discrimination, and harassment cam models regularly face, will perhaps be the catalyst for political mobilization.

Put yet another way, will cam models join the struggle for sex workers' rights? Will they join organizations such as the International Entertainment Adult Union[19] or become involved with advocacy in the Sex Workers Outreach Project[20] or attend conferences hosted by the Desiree Alliance (if any more such conferences are ever held)? Will they unionize as women in San Francisco strip clubs did as the Exotic Dancers Union, SEIU Local 790, or the performers at the famous Lusty Lady peep show, also in San Francisco, did despite being independent contractors?[21] Will cam models step up and challenge exploitative payment structures, especially in studio work? Will they demand better protection from trolls and online harassment? With the enactment of punitive legislation and the renewed power of the rescue industry, do cam models actually need or want more regulation?

I was struck by the community that has developed alongside the camming industry. The camming community that I documented in chapter 6 is a vital resource for this group of marginalized workers. It is crucial that sex workers support one another. For those with access, the camily provides critical support, and the development of social capital can help improve workers' wages. Networked performers may help drive traffic into other performers' rooms or provide informational support that helps them improve their shows, which, in turn, can boost their wages. Amelia, a 29-year-old straight White cis woman from England, stressed the importance of cam performers using the social capital they've developed politically:

> I always feel like camgirls need to unionize; this is my thing. It's just that, camgirls do so much physically demanding work, and the sites do not pay them enough. They do not! They don't regulate the men enough! . . . You can get a load of freeloaders on the site that just come and abuse me [and other] women, and the sites don't really do anything about it? They don't force them to pay a monthly fee to be members. They don't force them to buy tokens. So they can just come in, view shows, [and] be abusive to women and leave. The girls just don't get paid enough for that, ya know? . . . And like, they wouldn't have sites without us; so I wish there was some sort of way for sex workers and camgirls to unionize in general without the stigma so that we could negotiate better rates with the site. Because I feel like the sites take advantage of a lot of their [performers] by under-underpaying. Like Streamate, I think, at one point, it was something like 10% they were paying girls. So they were taking like a 90% profit, and they would, just like I said, they just wouldn't have anything without the women. . . . I wish something could be done about in the industry, 'cause I feel like it's gross . . . the girls deserve to be making [more] for what they're actually doing.

I spoke with several other performers who, like Amelia, wished the camily would politically mobilize itself, as other sex workers have. At this point, there are no indications that any movement toward unionization or collective struggle to challenge capitalist exploitation is afoot. Moreover, the data that I present in this book points to several challenges any effort to forge a political movement among cam models faces.

First, job satisfaction rates were high in my sample of cam models. Workers overwhelmingly found the work less alienating, more rewarding, and more pleasurable than other jobs available to them. These factors may well diminish the likelihood of workers organizing. However, the adverse changes in working conditions prompted by FOSTA could change this. While changes in the law could mean cam models (and pornographers) will be more concerned with their day-to-day survival than broader political battles, if the new legislation leads to attacks on the pleasures of camming, perhaps these workers will push back. FOSTA may create the conditions under which many cam models will join existing sex workers' movements.

Second, given the exclusion that also takes place in the camily, should performers decide to mobilize and orient their social capital toward politics, and not just toward the economics of the camming industry, they will need to grapple with how they can engage in better intersectional coalition building. Sex workers' movements have a long, rich history of mobilizing in the interests of the most vulnerable and the most exploited. Poor migrant women, people of color, and trans people have led sex workers' movements. Perhaps the overlap between the on- and offline sex work communities—cam models who are also porn stars, pro-dommes, escorts, and phone sex operators—will encourage online sex workers to join the ranks of offline sex workers' organizations. Given the atypical demographics of this sex work industry and the privileged experience of sex work that many in the cam industry enjoy, it will be interesting to see if these camily members politically mobilize themselves. If they do, will they draw boundaries between themselves and other sex workers?

Given that the industry is still in its early stages, only time will provide the answers to these questions. If political mobilization occurs among cam models, they will need to devise and propose a set of resolutions strategically. Another critical question thus emerges: If cam models organized, what would resolve their experiences of exploitation, discrimination, doxing, harassment, and privacy violations? In other words, would cam models call for more regulation of their market?

To Regulate or Not Regulate: Learning from Decriminalization

Sex workers have been calling for governments to decriminalize prostitution for decades.[22] Politicians must take the empirical data about the horrific effects of criminalization on sex workers seriously and respond to their demands. In 2003, New Zealand became the first country to recognize the research and acknowledge activists' calls by decriminalizing sex work through the enactment of the Prostitution Reform Act, which was largely due to the efforts of sex work activists in the New Zealand Prostitutes' Collective (NZPC).[23] The act decriminalizes the sale and purchase of sexual services by consenting individuals over the age of 18. Although, under the Act, prostitution remains illegal for migrant workers, the New Zealand case is an excellent example of full decriminalization that avoids many of the problems with legalization, where while the sale and consumption of sex are legal, there are also mandatory regulations imposed by the state.[24] The full-decriminalization model adopted in New Zealand is also different than the so-called "Nordic model" adopted in Sweden, where only the buyers of sex are prosecuted. By criminalizing "Johns," the moral entrepreneurs attempt to minimize demand for sex, and thus aim to regulate the consumption of pleasure. In New Zealand, full decriminalization has helped workers operate their businesses safely, reduced violence against sex workers, improved sex workers' relations with law enforcement, and helped reduce the harms caused by criminalization and the prison industrial complex.[25]

In 2016, Amnesty International (AI) published an official policy on sex work that advocates decriminalization:

> Amnesty International's policy is the culmination of extensive worldwide consultations, a considered review of substantive evidence and international human rights standards and first-hand research, carried out over more than two years. . . . The policy makes several calls on governments including for them to ensure protection from harm, exploitation and coercion; the participation of sex workers in the development of laws that affect their lives and safety; an end to discrimination and access to education and employment options for all. It recommends the decriminalization of consensual sex work, including those laws that prohibit associated activities—such as bans on buying, solicitation and

general organization of sex work. This is based on evidence that these laws often make sex workers less safe and provide impunity for abusers with sex workers often too scared of being penalized to report crime to the police. Laws on sex work should focus on protecting people from exploitation and abuse, rather than trying to ban all sex work and penalize sex workers.[26]

The World Health Organization supports the AI policy, as do UNAIDS, the Global Alliance Against Traffic in Women (GAATW), Human Rights Watch, Lambda Legal, and the American Civil Liberties Union. This list includes anti-sex-trafficking advocates, reflecting the fact that there is a continually growing movement among sex workers and their political allies to decriminalize prostitution. Unlike the moral entrepreneurs' policy decisions about sex work, sex worker advocates developed the AI policy based on the needs reported by sex workers and sound empirical data from research conducted all over the globe.

As Amnesty notes, the criminalization of sex work aims to "penalize sex workers." The criminalization of sex work is a concrete example of how the state regulates pleasure. Why should consenting people not have the ability to engage in sex for money? What is the state's interest in regulating sex work? Regulating the sex lives of consenting partners is paternalistic and a breach of fundamental human rights. The moral entrepreneurs would likely argue that they are concerned about trafficking and the safety of all sex workers. However, if governments around the world decriminalized all forms of sex work, it would expand help and assistance to all sex workers, including victims of sex trafficking.[27] Moral entrepreneurs must recognize that we are not playing a zero-sum game, and they need to start talking to voluntary sex workers. The state can simultaneously help victims of trafficking, while not persecuting voluntary sex workers. I asked Naomi, a 28-year-old queer White trans woman from the United States, what she thought people should know about sex work. She said:

> For me personally . . . [it] is the whole trafficking component. . . . I can't even fathom how awful it is for them to be trapped. . . . So I'm an advocate for helping people who are trafficked and helping them and I think that the worst way to do that is make sex work illegal, like prostitution . . .

it's wasting resources and it's limiting options and that to me is the most important thing about any kind of sex work, is helping the people who don't wanna be doing it.

Moving forward, as Naomi said, the state must no longer devote precious funds to criminalizing people and instead redirect them to providing resources that actually help people. Sex workers need access to free medical clinics. They need protection from myriad forms of violence, including the doxing and harassment that models in this book discussed. The rescue industry can create free access to such services and protections if they are genuinely concerned about the safety of sex workers and public health.

There are additional social policy and public health implications of my research. As camming is a safer form of sex work that requires no physical encounters, why not provide grants to NGOs and sex workers to open free camming studios where people can still sell sex from the physical safety of an enclosed room. Not all people will want to leave escorting, and they should not have to. Many workers will not want to concede the pleasures they often experience from physical sexual encounters. I am not making this suggestion as a means by which to stop prostitution; I am not an abolitionist, and I favor decriminalization. However, as I have discussed, some people do not have access to a private space or the money needed to begin camming. Some people choose to escort, often in deplorable working conditions, because this is their only option. The Internet has expanded sex worker industries, and all people should have unfettered access to the work opportunities they provide. Sex workers need safe working conditions and governments that work for them as citizens. What they don't need are governments that deprive them of basic civil liberties— governments that act as if the state must regulate and control pleasure.

The movement to decriminalize prostitution is an instructive case. Scholars should apply the rationales for decriminalizing prostitution to all sex industries, including the camming industry. The argument for decriminalization relies heavily on a neoliberal focus on individual rights and freedoms. Meanwhile, critiques of neoliberalism are often reductive and leave many questions unanswered about the potential benefits of such ideologies for the marginalized subjects who adopt them.

Political scientist Kristin Bumiller's *In an Abusive State* astutely examines state-sponsored policies aimed at thwarting violence against
women.[28] As she describes, in the 1980s, US feminists' mounting fight
against rape and domestic violence succeeded in prompting government intervention. Reforms within the criminal legal and social welfare
systems were instituted that ostensibly aimed to help women. The new
policies aimed at helping female victims ultimately gave the state more
control over women's bodies and lives. Rape victims may now be more
likely to see their attackers brought before the criminal legal system,
which is crucial, but these new policies have also increased surveillance
by social-service bureaucracies, which have had a disproportionately adverse effect on poor women of color.[29] Drawing from research on other
policies created to help survivors of gendered violence and the argument
made by sex workers that full decriminalization and not legalization is
ideal, it is clear that state intervention is not always the best solution,
particularly for sex workers.

Sociologist Elizabeth Bernstein has examined the rise of carceral
feminism and how anti-trafficking advocacy groups call for policies that
increase the presence and role of the state and the criminal legal system
in the lives of sex workers. She writes:

> Within the United States, although some anti-trafficking activists con-
> tinue to pay lip service to the goal of decriminalizing and securing
> economic rights for sex workers, the overwhelming thrust of current
> feminist attention has been similarly oriented towards widening—rather
> than eliminating—the sphere of criminal justice intervention in the sex
> industry.[30]

Interventions made by the state or its agencies often have adverse effects
on sex workers' lives and their ability to perform their work free from
surveillance, harassment, and overpolicing.

Thinking about the deleterious effects of carceral feminism on sex
workers raises several questions regarding the camming industry. What
type of interventions would help protect cam models from privacy violations and online harassment? To protect cam models from capping, who
would enforce stricter copyright laws? Who would police and punish the
trolls? In addition, we know that workplace privilege and exploitation is

never felt evenly. In this book, I empirically show that race, nationality, gender, sexuality, age, and ability shape cam models' experiences and the discrimination, exploitation, and harassment these workers face every day. How would any top-down interventions into this online market contend with the intersectional nature of exploitation, discrimination, and harassment?

My concern is that more regulation will mean closer monitoring of models' performances and more surveillance of their already highly scrutinized and stigmatized bodies. This added oversight would likely mean less bodily autonomy for models and more regulation of the intimate relationships between performers and customers. In addition, the heightened surveillance under FOSTA has already multiplied cam models' problems with third-party billers and social-media sites. These conditions can affect their wages. If models' rooms were to be policed more intensively by cam-site moderators, under the rationale that they want to protect models from trolls, this would take power away from models who currently can ban trolls who harass them. In addition, does heightened surveillance decrease the pleasure cam models' find in their work? If cam sites force all customers to purchase tokens, as Amelia suggested, then crowd sizes will decrease, which could affect how cam models on sites such as Chaturbate make money. Models gain fame by having thousands of viewers, even if all do not tip. Decreased crowd sizes could also affect the acquisition of pleasure. For many cam models, there is pleasure in being watched by large crowds of people—again, pleasure is a contextual social experience. Part of the pleasure of camming is the public nature of most cam sites—clients are crowned "king tippers" publicly, models get to have crowds of thousands shower them with compliments and tips. Externally imposed regulations that serve to make the camming experience more exclusively private might then also restrict the acquisition of pleasure among both models and clients.

Interestingly, decriminalization advocates make demands for deregulation by drawing on neoliberal arguments, which are generally rebuked by activists on the left when dealing with other social ills. Perhaps neoliberal ideologies are political tools that have uses beyond capitalists' deployment of them to exploit workers or dehumanize people. Marginalized people often develop an ethos of resiliency and build communities because of neoliberal economic policies. Various groups of marginalized people are constantly under attack by the systems of capitalism, White supremacy, patriarchy, cissexism, and ableism, and thus fight for fewer government interventions in their lives.

At the risk of sounding like I have been seduced by the promise of freedom in neoliberal-inspired individualism, I am only asking readers not to frame neoliberalism in solely negative ways. Subjectivity matters—we need less theorizing around what neoliberalism *does* to people and more theorizing around what people *do* with neoliberalism. On the one hand, in the current unchallenged neoliberal capitalist system, cam-site owners take very little responsibility for protecting workers' fundamental human rights; as a result, cam models are subject to regular violations of privacy and various forms of harassment. In the face of this, workers use neoliberal strategies to navigate their working environment and still report high levels of pleasure and empowerment. Also, affect matters—progressives cannot afford to miss the point that the expressions and effects of neoliberalism are incredibly diverse and we need more empirical studies to understand this point better. Finally, context matters—sex workers are working in a highly stigmatized form of labor, and they are not mere handmaids, victims, or vectors of capitalism and other overlapping systems of oppression. As Alison Bass has shown, sex workers face more regulation, criminalization, and state-sponsored violence in the 21st century than they did in the 19th century.[31] Politically drawing on neoliberal ideologies about individual freedom and liberties helps many sex workers survive state-sponsored violence. Sex workers are resilient people, who remain on the frontlines of the struggle for human and sexual freedom—their work ensures greater access to more and diverse forms of pleasure, despite societal institutions' attempts to control our embodiments and how we access and experience various forms of pleasure.

ACKNOWLEDGMENTS

First, and most importantly, I would like to thank all the cam models who participated in my research and who shared their lives with me. I especially want to thank Elizabeth, a cam model who appears in this book, who read a chapter and provided me with invaluable feedback. I want to express my heartfelt gratitude to my students, especially Alyssa for first introducing me to the world of camming. This book is for them, and I feel privileged to tell their stories—and my only hope is that I do their stories justice.

I want to express gratitude to Georgiann Davis, Clare Forstie, Erica J. Freidman, Kristen Lawler, Tey Meadow, and Laurel Westbrook for reading draft chapters and providing me with vital criticism and notes that undoubtedly pushed my thinking and elevated my writing. Thank you to Shantel Gabriel Buggs, Jason Ronald Orne, Brandon Andrew Robinson, and Salvador Vidal-Ortiz for reviewing earlier writing that eventually became a part of this book. Finally, I am indebted to Aaron J. Howell, who assisted me with the statistical analyses of my survey data.

I am thankful to Liz Coston, who worked with me as a graduate research assistant, running statistical analyses of the first data set in my research. I want to also express appreciation to Palma Palacio-Colon, who for two years worked with me as an undergraduate research assistant, and to Matthew Roth, another undergraduate student who assisted me with this project. At Farmingdale State College, I am also grateful to various administrators who supported my research and provided me with much-needed course release time in which to conduct my research and write this book.

I am grateful to my editor, Ilene Kalish, for her meticulous notes—cutting so many of my "little darlings" was challenging, but her notes indeed improved the quality and readability of my book. Ilene, thank you for your support and commitment to my work. I would also like to thank Sonia Tsuruoka, NYU Press assistant editor, for shepherding me through the publication process. Also at NYU, thank you, Dan Geist; you are an amazing copyeditor.

Finally, to my friends, and family—thank you. Thank you for your unwavering support. Thank you for your encouraging words and hugs when I felt overwhelmed and for your excitement and enthusiasm as I completed this book. To Erica J. Friedman, you were my rock and I am beyond grateful for all the love and support you gave me through-out this process. To my favorite human on the planet: Jordan, while it will likely be a while before you ever read Mama's work—whenever you do—I need you to know that I am so thankful for you. When I took time from playing with you to write, you *usually* did not complain. When you woke up late at night after having a bad dream and I was interviewing someone on Skype, you patiently waited for me to finish. Thank you, my baby, for supporting your mama.

I also want to acknowledge that portions of this book have appeared in various scholarly journals and books:

"Kink Work Online: The Diffuse Lives of Erotic Webcam Performers and Their Clients." In *Expanding the Rainbow: Exploring the Relationships of Bi+, Trans, Polyamorous, Asexual, Kinky, and Intersex People*, edited by Brandy L. Simula, J. E. Sumerau, and Andrea Miller. Sense Publishers, forthcoming.

"Pornographics as Queer Method." In *Other, Please Specify: Queer Methods in Sociology*, edited by D'Lane Compton, Tey Meadow, and Kristen Schilt. Berkeley: University of California Press, 2018.

The Unfinished Queer Agenda after Marriage Equality, edited by Angela Jones, Joseph Nicholas DeFilippis, and Michael W. Yarbrough. After Marriage Equality 3. Oxfordshire: Routledge, 2018.

"'I Get Paid to Have Orgasms': Adult Webcam Models' Negotiation of Pleasure and Danger." *Signs: Journal of Women in Culture and Society* 42, no. 1 (2016): 227–56.

"For Black Models Scroll Down: Web-Cam Modeling and the Racialization of Erotic Labor." *Sexuality and Culture* 19, no. 4 (2015): 776–99.

"Sex Work in a Digital Era." *Sociology Compass* 9 no. 7 (2015): 558–70.

APPENDIX A

Cam Models in the Study

TABLE AA.1. Survey Participants and Demographic Responses, $N = 105$

Name	What is your age in years?	What is your gender identity?	What is your race?	What is your nationality?	What country do you currently live in?	Do you live in a:	What is the highest level of education you have achieved?	What is your sexual identity?	What is your relationship status?
Lisa	30	cis woman	White	American	USA	major city	completed an advanced degree	queer	in a relationship(s)
Alvaro	32	cis man	White	Spanish	Spain	major city	completed an advanced degree	straight	in a relationship(s)
Marsha	42	cis woman	White	Canadian	Canada	major city	some college	queer	in a relationship(s)
Rita	26	cis woman	Black	American	USA	suburban area	some college	straight	single
Clarissa	19	cis woman	White	American	USA	suburban area	did not complete high school/ secondary school	bisexual	single
Cata	34	cis woman	These categories are not used in my country	Costa Rican	Costa Rica	major city	completed college	bisexual	single
Aarav	25	cis man	Asian	Indian	India	major city	completed an advanced degree	straight	in a relationship(s)

TABLE AA.1. (*cont.*)

Name	What is your age in years?	What is your gender identity?	What is your race?	What is your nationality?	What country do you currently live in?	Do you live in a:	What is the highest level of education you have achieved?	What is your sexual identity?	What is your relationship status?
Kate	24	cis woman	White	American	USA	suburban area	some college	bisexual	in a relationship(s)
Carla	32	cis woman	White	American	USA	suburban area	completed college	bisexual	married or domestic partnership
Kim	33	cis woman	White	American	USAS	major city	did not complete high school/ secondary school	straight	single
Elena	27	cis woman	White	Bulgarian	Bulgaria	major city	some advanced degree but not completed	bisexual	in a relationship(s)
Maggie	29	cis woman	White	American	USA	major city	completed college	straight	in a relationship(s)
Ruth	46	cis woman	White	American	USA	rural area	some college	bisexual	married or domestic partnership
Candice	23	cis woman	Biracial	American	USA	suburban area	some college	doesn't matter	in a relationship(s)
Chrissy	40	cis woman	White	American	USA	suburban area	some college	bisexual	in a relationship(s)
Theresa	20	cis woman	White	American	United States	major city	some college	bisexual	single
Michelle	21	trans woman	White	American	USA	suburban area	some college	straight	single
Francisco	21	cis man	Other/ Hispanic is not a race.	Mexican	Mexico	major city	some college	queer	single
Amelia	29	cis woman	White	British	England	major city	some college	straight	in a relationship(s)
Rene	25	cis woman	White	American	USA	major city	some college	bisexual	single

TABLE AA.1. (*cont.*)

Name	What is your age in years?	What is your gender identity?	What is your race?	What is your nationality?	What country do you currently live in?	Do you live in a:	What is the highest level of education you have achieved?	What is your sexual identity?	What is your relationship status?
Samuel	70	cis man	White	USA	USA	suburban area	some advanced degree but not completed	straight	married or domestic partnership
Lukas	21	cis man	White	German	USA	suburban area	some college	straight	single
Chloe	25	cis woman	These categories are not used in my country	French	France	major city	completed college	bisexual	in a relationship(s)
Martina	27	cis woman	White	Spanish	Spain	major city	some advanced degree but not completed	bisexual	married or domestic partnership
Rachel	36	trans woman	White	American	USA	rural area	completed high school/ secondary school or equivalency degree	straight	in a relationship(s)
Erica	28	cis woman	White	American	USA	rural area	completed an advanced degree	Polyamorous	married or domestic partnership
Mike	32	cis man	White	American	USA	suburban area	some college	queer	single
Alexandra	28	cis woman	White	American	USA	major city	some college	bisexual and polyamorous	in a relationship(s)

TABLE AA.1. (*cont.*)

Name	What is your age in years?	What is your gender identity?	What is your race?	What is your nationality?	What country do you currently live in?	Do you live in a:	What is the highest level of education you have achieved?	What is your sexual identity?	What is your relationship status?
Leah	37	cis woman	White	American	USA	suburban area	completed high school/ secondary school or equivalency degree	straight	in a relationship(s)
Daniel	32	cis man	White	Spanish	Poland	major city	completed an advanced degree	straight	in a relationship(s)
Freya	32	cis woman	White	British	U.K.	rural area	completed college	bisexual	in a relationship(s)
Sofia	22	cis woman	These categories are not used in my country	Greek	America	rural area	did not complete high school/ secondary school	I would prefer not to say	married or domestic partnership
Matt	23	cis man	White	American	Mexico	major city	some college	straight	single
Robin	40	cis woman	White	Canadian	Canada	rural area	completed college	straight	married or domestic partnership
Kaya	23	cis woman	Black	Black British	England	major city	some advanced degree but not completed	straight	single
Lucia	22	cis woman	Hispanic	Spanish	Spain	rural area	completed high school/ secondary school or equivalency degree	queer	in a relationship(s)
Charlotte	52	trans woman	White	Australian	Australia	suburban area	completed college	lesbian	single

TABLE AA.1. (*cont.*)

Name	What is your age in years?	What is your gender identity?	What is your race?	What is your nationality?	What country do you currently live in?	Do you live in a:	What is the highest level of education you have achieved?	What is your sexual identity?	What is your relationship status?
Tiffany	23	cis woman	Black	American	USA	suburban area	some college	lesbian	married or domestic partnership
Mya	44	cis woman	White	American	USA	suburban area	did not complete high school/ secondary school	bisexual	single
Dominique	24	cis woman	White	American	USA	major city	completed college	bisexual	single
Denise	28	cis woman	White	American	United States	rural area	some college	lesbian	single
Myra	28	cis woman	White	American	United States	suburban area	completed college	bisexual	married or domestic partnership
Luiza	32	cis woman	White	Brazilian	Brazil	major city	completed college	straight	married or domestic partnership
Sarah	25	cis woman	White	American	USA	suburban area	completed high school/ secondary school or equivalency degree	bisexual	in a relationship(s)
Jen	25	cis woman	White	American	USA	suburban area	some college	bisexual	in a relationship(s)
Evie	28	cis woman	White	Australian	Australia	suburban area	some college	bisexual	in a relationship(s)
Audrey	24	cis woman	White	American	USA	suburban area	some college	straight	in a relationship(s)
Melinda	32	cis woman	White	Canadian	Canada	major city	completed college	queer	married or domestic partnership
Aron	31	cis man	White	Hungarian	Hungary	major city	some college	bi-curious	in a relationship(s)
Elizabeth	38	cis woman	White	American	USA	rural area	some college	bisexual	in a relationship(s)

TABLE AA.1. (*cont.*)

Name	What is your age in years?	What is your gender identity?	What is your race?	What is your nationality?	What country do you currently live in?	Do you live in a:	What is the highest level of education you have achieved?	What is your sexual identity?	What is your relationship status?
Mariam	23	trans woman	Middle eastern	Tunisian	France	major city	completed an advanced degree	straight	single
Madeline	30	cis woman	White	American	USA	major city	completed college	straight	single
Coral	36	cis woman	White	American	USA	rural area	completed an advanced degree	straight	divorced
Brianna	20	cis woman	White	American	USA	major city	completed high school/ secondary school or equivalency degree	bisexual	in a relationship(s)
Rick	27	cis man	White	American	USA	major city	completed college	bisexual	in a relationship(s)
Ronnie	35	cis man	White	American	USA	suburban area	completed high school/ secondary school or equivalency degree	Polyamorous	in a relationship(s)
Steve	43	cis man	White	American	USA	suburban area	completed college	straight	married or domestic partnership
Emma	29	cis woman	White	Canadian	Canada	major city	some college	straight	married or domestic partnership
Viktorija	19	cis woman	White	Latvian	Latvia	major city	completed high school/ secondary school or equivalency degree	bisexual	single

TABLE AA.1. (*cont.*)

Name	What is your age in years?	What is your gender identity?	What is your race?	What is your nationality?	What country do you currently live in?	Do you live in a:	What is the highest level of education you have achieved?	What is your sexual identity?	What is your relationship status?
Florence	46	trans woman	White	English	England	major city	did not complete high school/ secondary school	gay	single
Lenny	34	cis man	Black	British	U.K.	major city	completed an advanced degree	polyamorous	in a relationship(s)
Marta	27	cis woman	White	Latvian	Latvia	major city	completed an advanced degree	straight	single
Halona	32	woman	Native American	American	USA	major city	some college	queer	single
Timothy	20	cis man	White	American	USA	major city	completed high school/ secondary school or equivalency degree	gay	in a relationship(s)
Lily	31	cis woman	White	British	U.K.	major city	completed high school/ secondary school or equivalency degree	bisexual	single
Katrina	20	cis woman	White	American	USA	major city	some college	queer	in a relationship(s)
Rebecca	34	cis woman	White	American	USA	major city	completed college	polyamorous	divorced
Mindy	46	cis woman	White	American	USA	major city	completed an advanced degree	straight	single

Table AA.1. (*cont.*)

Name	What is your age in years?	What is your gender identity?	What is your race?	What is your nationality?	What country do you currently live in?	Do you live in a:	What is the highest level of education you have achieved?	What is your sexual identity?	What is your relationship status?
Jose	24	cis man	White	Canadian	Canada	major city	completed college	gay	in a relationship(s)
Natalie	26	trans woman	White	American	USA	major city	did not complete high school/ secondary school	demi asexual poly romantic	single
Mihaela	29	cis woman	White	Romanian	Romania	major city	completed an advanced degree	straight	in a relationship(s)
Hannah	18	cis woman	White	South African	South Africa	suburban area	completed high school/ secondary school or equivalency degree	straight	married or domestic partnership
Allison	20	cis woman	White	American	USA	suburban area	some college	bisexual	single
Kendra	28	cis woman	White	American	USA	rural area	completed college	bisexual	married or domestic partnership
Daan	35	cis man	White	Dutch	Netherlands	suburban area	completed an advanced degree	straight	single
Oivia	20	cis woman	White	English	England	major city	some advanced degree but not completed	bisexual	in a relationship(s)
Tayna	27	cis woman	White	American	USA	major city	completed high school/ secondary school or equivalency degree	polyamorous	single

TABLE AA.1. (*cont.*)

Name	What is your age in years?	What is your gender identity?	What is your race?	What is your nationality?	What country do you currently live in?	Do you live in a:	What is the highest level of education you have achieved?	What is your sexual identity?	What is your relationship status?
Felicity	23	cis woman	White	English	England	suburban area	completed an advanced degree	bisexual	in a relationship(s)
Vanessa	34	cis woman	White	American	USA	major city	completed an advanced degree	straight	single
Taryn	26	cis woman	White	American	USA	major city	completed high school/ secondary school or equivalency degree	straight	married or domestic partnership
Crista	27	cis woman	White	American	USA	major city	completed college	polyamorous	in a relationship(s)
Carmen	19	cis woman	Black	American	USA	suburban area	some college	queer	single
Alexei	21	cis man	White	Russian	Russia	major city	some advanced degree but not completed	straight	in a relationship(s)
Bridget	29	cis woman	White	Scottish	Scotland	major city	completed high school/ secondary school or equivalency degree	straight	single
Anca	31	cis woman	White	Romanian	Romania	major city	completed college	straight	in a relationship(s)
Jason	24	cis man	White	American	USA	major city	some college	bisexual	single
Deidra	26	cis woman	White	American	USA	rural area	completed college	bisexual	married or domestic partnership

TABLE AA.1. (*cont.*)

Name	What is your age in years?	What is your gender identity?	What is your race?	What is your nationality?	What country do you currently live in?	Do you live in a:	What is the highest level of education you have achieved?	What is your sexual identity?	What is your relationship status?
Claudia	28	cis woman	White	American	USA	rural area	completed college	bisexual	married or domestic partnership
Whitney	28	cis woman	White	American	USA	rural area	some college	bisexual	in a relationship(s)
Georgia	22	cis woman	White	American	USA	suburban area	completed college	bisexual	in a relationship(s)
Milena	28	cis woman	White	German	U.K.	suburban area	completed college	polyamorous	in a relationship(s)
Romey	33	cis woman	White	Canadian	Canada	rural area	completed high school/ secondary school or equivalency degree	bisexual	married or domestic partnership
Camille	24	cis woman	White	American	USA	major city	some college	bisexual	married or domestic partnership
Gia	26	trans woman	White	American	USA	major city	did not complete high school/ secondary school	queer	in a relationship(s)
Gian	55	cis man	White	Swiss	Germany	rural area	completed an advanced degree	straight	single

TABLE AA.1. (*cont.*)

Name	What is your age in years?	What is your gender identity?	What is your race?	What is your nationality?	What country do you currently live in?	Do you live in a:	What is the highest level of education you have achieved?	What is your sexual identity?	What is your relationship status?
Stella	33	cis woman	White	American	Australia	suburban area	completed college	queer	married or domestic partnership
Rochelle	55	cis woman	White	American	USA	rural area	some college	bisexual	married or domestic partnership
Adeline	25	trans woman	White	American	USA	major city	some college	polyamorous	in a relationship(s)
Carl	31	cis man	Black	American	USA	major city	completed college	bisexual	in a relationship(s)
Marcy	42	cis man	White	American	USA	rural area	some college	queer	married or domestic partnership
Dylan	42	cis woman	White	American	USA	rural area	some college	queer	married or domestic partnership
Naomi	38	trans woman	White	American	USA	major city	completed high school/ secondary school or equivalency degree	queer	single
Andres	20	cis man	Hispanic	Colombian	Colombia	suburban area	some college	pansexual	single
Matías	23	cis man	Hispanic	Colombian	Colombia	Major City	completed HS	straight	single
Jimena	33	trans woman	Hispanic	Colombian	Colombia	Suburban area	completed HS	Gay	single

TABLE AA.2. Survey Demographics

Gender identification	Percent	Race	Percent
trans woman	9.5	Black	5.7
cis woman	68.6	Native American	1.0
cis man	21.9	Hispanic	4.8
		Biracial	1.0
Nativity		Asian	1.0
Non-USA/UK	36.2	Other	3.8
USA/UK	63.8	White	82.9
Age		**Education**	
50 and up	3.8	Less than college degree	56.2
36–49	14.3	College degree	29.5
31–35	21.0	Graduate degree	14.3
27–30	21.0		
22–26	25.7	**Sexual orientation**	
Under 22	14.3	Queer	13.3
		Bisexual	34.3
Community Type		Polyamorous	7.6
Rural	18.1	Lesbian	2.9
Suburban	29.5	Gay	3.8
Major city	52.4	Other	5.7
		Straight	32.4

n=105 for all variables

Nationality and Race

Including profiles used in the statistical analyses of data on MyFree-Cams, along with survey participants the cam models in this book come from countries all over the world: Australia, the Bahamas, Bermuda, Brazil, Bulgaria, Canada, Colombia, Costa Rica, the Czech Republic, Denmark, France, French Polynesia, Germany, Greece, Hungary, India,

Italy, Iraq, Japan, Kazakhstan, Latvia, Lebanon, Lithuania, Mexico, Netherlands, New Zealand, Panama, Philippines, Poland, Romania, the Russian Federation, Scotland, Slovakia, Slovenia, South Africa, Spain, Ukraine, the United Kingdom, and the United States. In this book, I focused my analyses on the nationality of models, alongside race when applicable.

While cam models from all racial backgrounds work in the camming industry, my research suggests White cam models dominate the industry. White people were also overrepresented in my sample. Applying the limited US system of racial categorization to an international sample of cam models was problematic. In my survey sample, there were cam models from Costa Rica, Greece, and France who selected the survey answer "These racial identities are not used in my country." There were cam models in my sample who used ethnic identities in their offline lives and only used racial identities when camming because White supremacy plays a significant role in shaping the camming field.[1] There are light-skinned people of color around the world who identify as White.[2] As an example, a respondent from Brazil identified as White because she has light skin and her country, like many others, has a complicated history of race, colorism, and colonialism.[3] Throughout this book, I have relied less on analyses based on a US system of racial categorization and instead explored how colorism within the system of global White supremacy affects the market experiences of an international sample of cam models.[4]

Class, Education, Age, and Community Type

Cam models also come from widely different socioeconomic backgrounds. I spoke with models who began camming to escape dire poverty. I spoke with middle-class college students. I spoke with relatively affluent people who cam primarily as exhibitionists. Cam models come from widely disparate educational backgrounds, as well. While the majority of cam models in my survey sample (56.2%) did not have college degrees, nearly half did, and about one in seven (14.3%) had one or more graduate degrees. While the mean age of the cam models in my survey sample was 29.9 years old, there was significant diversity in age. While respondents reported that customers value youthfulness in the field, cam models of various ages worked in the industry and made money. This quantitative data (alongside the qualitative data presented throughout the book) buttresses my claim that online sex work is appealing to workers who previously have not been involved in sex work, or who due to factors such as age have been marginalized by sex entrepreneurs from other forms of sex work.

Finally, cam models come from communities of various sizes and types. While a slight majority of models in the sample came from large cities, many also lived in rural and suburban places. My qualitative analyses complemented this quantitative data, because where cam models resided often shaped their motivations and experiences camming. Cam models who lived in rural areas often described having a hard time finding work close to their homes and how they used camming for intimacy due to feeling geographically isolated.

Sexuality and Gender

The majority of survey respondents (68%) identified as not straight. Bisexual respondents comprised 34% of the sample, queer people made up 13%, polyamorous people were 8% of the sample, 6% identified as other, 3% identified as lesbians, and gay men made up 4% of the sample. While this data is not representative, these findings were not surprising. As Kate D'Adamo succinctly states, "The story of LGBTQ survival has always included the story of sex work."[5] LGBTQ folks face persistent, unchecked, and often legal employment discrimination in many nations throughout the world. People frequently trade sex in the absence of other decent-paying and legal forms of labor. Camming is also a way for people to explore their sexualities. It is crucial for scholars of sex work to consider the complex ways that an individuals' sexual identities influence their motivations to perform erotic labor, the wages they earn, their job satisfaction, and their experiences of actual labor. Future lines of inquiry should further consider this question beyond the tentative conclusions based on the data presented in this study.

The majority of survey respondents were cis women, but the sample also includes trans women and cis men. In the survey, I provided respondents the opportunity to provide their gender identities using a range of categories and an open-ended field. I did not have any respondents that identified as non-binary, genderqueer, agender, genderfluid, two-spirit, etc. Cam sites either employ binary gender options with only the choices female and male or they have three gender options: transgender, female, and male. My respondents used only these three options to identify their gender identities. I believe the limited gender options on cam sites may have influenced how some cam models identified in the survey. I realize that the absence of non-binary, two-spirit, genderqueer, or agender people from my study may unintentionally reify a trans/cis binary. I did, however, make sure to examine respondents' diverse lived experiences of gender and how other aspects of their identities mediate those experiences. I hope it is clear to readers that gender is fluid and not binary.

Crucially, there were no trans men in my survey sample. This was not due to limitations in recruitment or other research design flaws. There is a distinct underrepresentation of trans men in the camming industry. Throughout my five years of participant observation, I observed only a handful of trans men who worked as cam models. Based on my field notes, I found inactive trans men's accounts on various cam sites but very rarely did I see trans men actively performing. In 2016, I found one account on Chaturbate (CB) for a performer who identified as a trans man, whose profile said he was saving money for top surgery and appreciated offline tips to support his transition. During my participant observation, this performer was also the only trans man of color that I observed on a major cam site. In the most recent instance, in 2018, I observed two trans men performing on CB. At the time of this observation, 340 trans people were performing on CB. Of all the trans cam models performing, fewer than 1% were transmasculine. These numbers are striking given that cam models perceived CB as the most diverse cam site and the most welcoming of trans and gender-nonconforming people. Per my field notes, on another occasion in 2018, I observed only one active trans man's account on Streamate (SM), and that was out of 1,700 cam models online—under .05%. As a final example, I noted the absence of trans men in my field notes on many occasions while doing participant observation on LiveJasmin (LJ). LJ uses a binary gender system and has tags for both "transgirl" and "transboy," but I've only ever observed trans women performing under either of these tags.

While there have been calls for more attention to be paid to trans men's sexualities, there is still a paucity of research.[6] Future lines of inquiry should explore the experiences of trans men in various sex work industries. This research must also avoid the trap of using only medicalized frameworks for analysis that pathologize trans people and sex workers. I so wish I had the opportunity to survey trans men who work in camming or who have left camming.[7] I plan to study the experiences of trans men in sex work in the future and hope to see other researchers also take up this important line of inquiry.

APPENDIX B

Methods

Camming draws from a five-year mixed-methods study of the erotic webcam industry. I used multiple methodologies, which included web analytics, participant observation on cam sites, statistical analyses of data collected from cam model profiles, content/discourse analyses of web forums for cam models, survey data, in-depth interviews, and auto-ethnography. The use of multiple data collection strategies has become standard practice in sociological research because it increases the reliability and generalizability of the findings.[1] The methods I employed as part of my five-year study of the adult webcam industry are described below and I end with a brief discussion of recruitment procedures for the survey and interviews and limitations of the study design.

I launched my study of the erotic webcam industry in 2013. I began my research with approximately a year of intensive participant observation between 2013 and 2014; thereafter, I continued participant observation throughout the entire span of the project. After that first year, I had a good understanding of how the camming industry functioned, and I began to use other strategies to collect data about the industry. First, I collected and analyzed demographic and camscore[2] data on the cam site MyFreeCams (N=343). Second, I conducted content analyses on four major web forums for cam models, which included analyzing hundreds of threads and ultimately led to the inclusion of the voices of many cam models who did not participate in the survey or interviews. Third, I researched the history of the webcam industry. At the conclusion of this data collection, and after analysis was complete, I began writing up my findings. The journal articles published as a result are the foundation of several chapters in this book.

Next, I developed a survey instrument and interview schedule, which I experienced significant delays launching due to unnecessary postponements caused by Institutional Review Board procedures and moralistic issues raised by individual IRB members.[3] After finally receiving IRB approval, I officially launched the online survey in December 2016. The survey, available for approximately one year, consisted of both quantitative and qualitative questions. The survey was taken by a nonrepresentative international sample of cam models (N=105, see appendix A). Participants in the survey and interview portions of this research project included any responding individual who was either currently working as a webcam performer or who had done so within 12 months before the study. Participants were required to be 18 years of age or older and have worked voluntarily as a webcam performer (screening questions preceded the survey).

I conducted a total of 30 in-depth interviews, which included 23 cam performers and 7 other market participants. These additional market participants included one cam-site creator, two studio owners, two web forum creators and moderators, the founder of the Live Cam Awards, and a lawyer who specializes in pornography law. Interviews with cam models were conducted via Skype and ranged from 30 minutes to two and a half hours. Most interviews with cam models lasted one hour. In a few cases, I continued conversation with models via email. Interviews with other market participants were conducted via phone and asynchronously.

During the writing of this book, I chose to include autoethnographic data based on my personal experiences as a former sex worker. In May 2018, when the initial draft of the book was almost complete, I completed the web analytics portion of the study. While I regularly observed and kept track of cam-site traffic scores to document any significant shifts in the market, given that I wanted to present the most current data about website traffic and cam-site usage, I waited until the latest possible date to construct tables about cam-site usage and traffic.

Survey and Interview Recruitment

The population under study was hard to reach because they are considered a "deviant" social group. Recruitment was challenging. Following standard procedures in the recruitment of hard-to-reach or highly stigmatized groups,[4] I tried to incentivize participation to increase response rates. Unfortunately, despite my best efforts to acquire funding for this research through competitive grants, I had no funding to pay all participants. All I could offer was to enter each survey participant into a lottery for a chance to win an electronic $100 gift card for Amazon.com. The lack of compensation for participation was a serious problem, and it was an issue that likely biased my data.

This project used a hybrid of nonrandom sampling techniques to generate the highest response rate possible and to include diverse participants. First, I developed an IRB-approved recruitment advertisement, which I planned to send to individual cam models and post on cam models' web forums. Initially, cam models seemed skeptical of participating in the study and response rates were very low. I had to pivot early in my research and, deviating slightly from my IRB-approved invitation script, adjusted my email so it began by informing performers that I was a retired sex worker and now a sociologist studying the camming industry. This disclosure helped increased response rates. Especially with hard-to-reach populations, it is crucial that we remain open to sharing ourselves with respondents—just as we expect them to share with us. While strict positivists would say that the researcher must remain entirely objective and conventionally "professional," sometimes the most professional thing we can do is be honest with our respondents about ourselves.

First, I posted these invitations to participate in the study on the public web forums for cam models. I requested permission from the website moderators before posting any invitations. In general, I did not post invitations on any website or contact models that explicitly said that they do not want to be contacted by the public or by researchers. Next, I also sent invitations to models directly. I attempted probability sampling. I sent performers invitations to participate in the study directly through cam sites' instant messaging systems. As I learned over time, this technique was problematic and led to low response rates.

There were several issues with this recruitment strategy. First, cam performers are inundated with unwanted messages from customers; as a result, many do not even open their direct messages on the sites where they perform. In the MyFreeCams message center, you can see if the other person has opened your message and I could see that models were overwhelmingly not even opening my recruitment invitations. Second, cam sites such as CAM4 were monitored closely for spam. I sent one message that was flagged as spam, and I lost my messaging privileges. Other websites had hard limits on the number of direct messages that I could send. If there were, say, 1,200 performers online and I wanted to reach them all, this was impossible—in a common scenario, I could contact only ten before being cut off for the day. In addition, given that many cam models use Twitter, I also sent invitations to performers using Twitter, which also monitors spam, and I would often no longer be able to send invitations after I had sent approximately 25 in a day. In addition, many models do not respond to "DMs" (direct messages) on Twitter. I sent direct invitations, as well, to cam models who are also popular bloggers. I found several webcam performers who blog about their workplace experiences. Finally, I used a snowball recruitment technique: all participants were asked to share information about the study with their colleagues.

Limitations

There were two significant limitations of this study's research design. First, I conducted almost all the interviews in English. I also designed the survey in Spanish, and I had two respondents complete the survey in Spanish. One of these respondents also participated in an asynchronous interview in Spanish. My written Spanish skills are good, but my conversational skills are weak. I did not think it was appropriate to attempt to conduct interviews via Skype.

Most importantly, I studied a global workplace, and collecting data almost exclusively in English biased the data. There are cam models whom I could not reach because I do not speak multiple languages and could not afford to hire a research team to create surveys and conduct interviews in other languages. When I began this project, I investigated how this language barrier might affect my research. Given that BongaCams caters to the European market, I logged on to the site to test the potential bias that only collecting data in English might cause. Of the 205 models online, 182 could communicate in English—only 11% communicated exclusively in Russian or other languages. (This data was available on cam models' profiles). Given that English is the dominant language in the industry, this limitation only minimally affected recruitment, data collection, and findings. In future studies, I hope to see multilingual researchers reach more cam models around the world, especially those working in physical studios.

Second, the use of Skype was a significant limitation of this study's research design. Given that many cam models perform shows on Skype, I chose it as the platform I used for interviews. I thought this was the most convenient option for them. Nonetheless, I experienced regular technical issues with Skype. While I always I used a grounded connection for interviews, there were frequent service disruptions. Once the interviews had been transcribed (by a hired company called Qualitative Health Research Consultants),[5] it became clear that portions of many were inaudible. I lost quite a bit of data due to poor-quality-connection issues with Skype. In one case, because we could not get a good connection no matter how many times we tried, I was not able to interview a certain respondent. When I tried to reschedule, they no longer wanted to participate and rightfully so. They had set aside time for me once for an unpaid interview; I understood why they wouldn't do it again.

Ethical Considerations

The Internet has affected social research. The migration of sex work online necessitates that scholars incorporate web-based methodological strategies into their research. Suzanne Jenkins has written about how "Internet technology can offer an opportunity to extend the scope of sex work research into new territories by providing a platform for the voices of people working in areas of the industry about which little is known."[1] Given that the population under study operated online, all of the data collection strategies I used were web-based. Doing online research raises important issues for social scientists. Digital technologies have affected the research questions we ask, our field sites, our methods, ethical issues, and the conclusions we reach.[2] In what follows, I discuss three critical ethical issues that my online research raised and make suggestions to researchers doing online ethnographic work.

Collecting Data Online: Participant Observation and Web Forums

There is something voyeuristic and almost creepy about doing online participant observation. In the offline context, my embodiment is visible. In an offline field site, people can see me, even if they are unaware that I am a researcher. In an online context, it is vital that we make ourselves visible and when possible not anonymously lurk. Doing virtual world fieldwork often requires creating an online embodiment or avatar of ourselves.[3] In many cases, creating an avatar is not possible. In my research, I always registered on cam sites and logged in under my screenname, profjones. I intentionally chose this screenname, hoping that the "prof" might give people an indication that I was a professor. If sites allow researchers to upload a photo, we should. As Eynon, Fry, and Schroeder assert, "[E]ven if online virtual worlds are prima facie public spaces, it is nevertheless important to be sensitive to the social context . . . in online worlds the possibilities of recording, reproducing, and analyzing interactions, especially covertly, are more powerful."[4] It is imperative that researchers do not deceptively and covertly gather data online.

In the camming industry, on cam sites there is generally a clear division between public and private spaces. All shows on Chaturbate are public, and cam models are aware of this and sign a contract when they sign up acknowledging the public nature of their performances. On a cam site such as MyFreeCams, while many cam models perform while in public chat, some cam models do perform in private. In addition, on MFC, I could have paid to spy on private shows in order to gain access to private shows. My screenname would tell the model I was watching, but despite the "prof" in my screenname, the cam model would not know I was conducting research and in the context of a show marked as "private" the model has a reasonable expectation of privacy that they do not have while performing in spaces marked "public." In order to act ethically, I only conducted participant observation in spaces marked as public and relied on qualitative data to report on private shows. There was likely a wealth of data about the services rendered, and the relationships between clients and workers that I could not document as a result. While having data from participant observation in private shows would have enhanced my data and study, gaining access would have required unethical conduct.

Collecting data online requires that scholars be respectful of people's privacy, even in public spaces. There has been much debate among researchers about whether collecting data from message boards and web forums constitute ethical research.[5] One group says these posts are in public domain and fair game. The other camp says people post there with an expectation of privacy. In addition, people often form these online communities as safe spaces or because they are a marginalized group seeking community and safety among their peers. As Boellstroff et al. observe, "virtual world ethnographers have long noted that we must be diligent about how the people we study define the distinction between 'private' and 'public' with reference to particular communities and activities."[6] When collecting data on web forums and discussion boards, it is vital for researchers to ask themselves: Would this population consider their posts public or private?

The founders and moderators of web forums structured these websites similar to cam sites. There are public sections of the web forum that are open to the public and where clients post as well. There are also private sections of the forum for models only. This means that I did not have access to private sections of public forums, and thus did not have access to essential data. Acquiring access to this data would have required that I engage in deceptive behavior in order to gain access to the models-only sections. This was a limitation, but yet a necessary feature of ethical data collection. Given that I also administered a survey and conducted interviews, I was able to gain insight about the industry directly from cam models—this data is likely similar to what I would have found in the private, models-only sections of the web forums.

When conducting online research on web forums, I strongly suggest to all researchers that we follow Boellstroff et al.'s suggestion that we conduct participant observation and use data from websites and web forums regarding communications that the population under study would see as publicly shared. When publishing this data all names should be anonymized. I firmly believe that is best to err on the side of caution when using data from web forums, even when that data came from a public discussion board. Yes, a person could ostensibly google the quotation and find the forum and model but why unnecessarily publish identifying information about an online user who did not give written consent to participate? I see no good reason for publishing people's screennames or other identifying material posted on web forums without their consent.

Online Recruitment

Online recruitment can be a fantastic low-cost tool to contact hard-to-reach populations, and researchers can use the Internet to reach people all over the globe. However, most web-based surveys produce low response rates. My study suffered from low response rates. First, 147 people completed the consent form, but only 105 people took the survey. So, there was significant roll-off. I suspect that some people completed the consent form, and then either saw questions that they didn't want to answer or because of a large number of open-ended questions, did not want to invest the time to complete the survey for no compensation. Research has suggested that "respondents appear to drop out more often when presented with open-ended questions."[7]

Another issue that frequently plays a role in low response rates to web-based surveys is that "the invitation is easily overlooked by intended respondents, or treated as spam."[8] Respondents often treat recruitment emails as spam.[9] During my research, I thought a lot about the ethics of spamming people in the name of research. I would like to raise two critical points regarding online recruitment and spam. First, I never emailed a performer more than once and kept records of email recruitment to avoid (to the best of my ability) duplicate emails—this is an essential best practice for online researchers.

Second, during recruitment I had my account suspended on two sites for spam. A researcher could be tempted to create a new account under a different email or adopt covert methods to change their IP address to regain access to a website; however, this is a serious ethics violation. Consider this: a researcher is conducting fieldwork offline, say at a bar, and due to patrons' complaints the manager tells the researcher to leave and that they do not have permission to conduct research there. Should the researcher go back to the bar? Of course not. Well, the online context should not change how researchers view the answer to this question. If a cam site or web forum ever terminated my account, I did not create a new one, and I discontinued recruitment on those sites. Given the design of my study, I already had data from participant observation on those sites, and this termination only meant that I could not continue recruitment for the survey and interviews on these sites. Given that I used nonrandom sampling methods, terminating recruitment on these sites did not present issues to my sampling procedures that did not already exist.

It is also crucial that we think and talk more about how people respond to recruitment emails that they perceive as spam, even when researchers are conducting ethical online recruitment. I received several angry email responses from cam models to my recruitment emails—one called me a "dizzy bitch," and all sternly told me never to email them again. These responses generally made sense to me. I know how annoyed I feel receiving endless emails from people looking to sell me things and tell me about their "opportunities." Yes, as scholars, we see our emails to potential respondents as being different from the for-profit journals that spam us regularly. However, to many people, our research recruitment emails are spam.

Now, I received messages from performers who were excited about my research, and even a few who thanked me for doing this work. However, I want to focus on those responses that saw my emails as spam. There was one particular response that made me very upset—it was a response I thought about for weeks. This cam model not only saw my email as spam, but they found it offensive. I want to focus on these responses because an analysis of these responses can lead to the development of useful best practices for researchers doing online research, especially those in sexualities.

Again, there was one response to a recruitment email that I will never forget. This cam model berated me and laid into me. The cam model said that I was awful and despicable for asking sex workers to participate in research with no compensation. In their email, they said that everyone knows researchers have grants and get money from their institutions to conduct research, and then rhetorically, they asked why I was not offering to pay them. They said, because I used to perform sex work, something I disclosed in my recruitment email, that I should know better as a former sex worker and thus I should be ashamed of myself. Now, it was not the choice language they used in the email that upset me—instead I was upset by the assumptions they made about my motivations and position in academia. People may assume that we all have large NSF grants and 25-person research teams. They may not know that in sexualities research unless you are studying disease and public health, most funding agencies want nothing to do with you. People may think of researchers and picture professors working at Ivy League research institutions.

So how do online researchers grapple with the issues related to online recruitment that I have introduced here? Scholars conducting online research must craft recruitment emails strategically and thoughtfully. It is crucial that in recruitment material if we cannot pay respondents that we add a line or two telling them why. If there are respondents who see our emails as spam, the least we can do is add a line to recruitment emails apologizing to respondents if they perceive the email as spam. The point is, ethical online research requires that we act in ways that reduce harm to participants and more carefully crafting recruitment emails is one way that researchers can accomplish this.

Observing Sex Online

Qualitative researchers must be reflexive about how our identities shape the research process and our experiences in the field. I engaged in frequent reflexive note-taking in which I described my feelings and erotic desires in the field, which, as Rooke suggests, tends to produce "a slightly embarrassed, uneasy silence."[10] It is essential that researchers, especially those who study sex remain reflexive throughout the research process. Cam pages usually have over a thousand thumbnail pictures of cam models that the customer clicks on to enter the performer's room. My sexual desires often affected how I navigated these cam pages. On several occasions, I noted that I was drawn to the rooms of people who were genderqueer and women with lots of tattoos. Therefore, when observing cam models rooms, I intentionally navigated to all different cam models' rooms. As a researcher, I tried to be mindful of how my sexuality and desires might bias my research. When I conducted participant observation, I was frequently turned on. There were occasions where I stopped collecting data and logged off because I felt my sexual desires and the pleasure I was experiencing during participant observation was compromising my ability to act as a researcher. Using this pornographic type of queer reflexivity, will allow researchers to make adjustments that protect our research participants and help us act more ethically.

To sexualities researchers I say, we need less silence, and more reflexive writing and discussion around sexual desire and sexual practice. As Ester Newton has discussed, we need to write more honestly about how desire shapes fieldwork. This is especially true when we are online and our presence is not known to others. Perhaps, as sociologist Tey Meadow suggests, sexualities researchers often remain silent about this issue and fail to embrace "the mess" because we don't have to implicate ourselves—to publicly expose our sexual desires and identities. Meadow writes:

> It's about leaning into rather than away from the complexities of being a
> sexual and gendered subject in the field. It's about embracing a particular

type of vulnerability—the risk of being dismissed as unprofessional, over-determined, politically motivated, subjective—about being in "the mess" of gender and sexual material with our subjects and, by extension, with our colleagues. This engagement requires unlearning some of the reflexive habits we pick up in our training, and allowing our sexual and gender subjectivities to be queerly messy, unruly, and difficult to affix.[11]

As Meadow has shown, leaning into the mess can help researchers unpack and better understand the social worlds they study. My goal here, too, has been to show the benefits of intimately involving myself in my research and speaking openly about my sexuality as part of my reflexive process. Doing so contributes to an ethical research process.

NOTES

PREFACE

1 I intentionally use a vague date to protect Alyssa's anonymity. Like all the names that appear in this book, Alyssa is an alias.

2 Throughout this book, I report earnings in USD. I do so only because companies in the United States dominate the industry, and models' earnings are computed using USD.

3 Exotic dancers are independent contractors and pay club owners per diem fees to work.

INTRODUCTION

1 The "gig economy" refers to temporary jobs that employers hire independent contractors to perform. While the gig economy has increased dramatically, sex work is perhaps one of the oldest forms of labor in the gig economy.

2 Throughout this book, I use the terms "erotic webcam industry" and "adult webcam industry" interchangeably to avoid repetition and most often use the shorthand term "camming" to refer to the form of sex work in which people broadcast live-streaming, interactive, sexually explicit performances online.

3 Harcourt and Donovan (2005) demonstrated that there are at least 25 different types of sex work. Further, they divided these labor activities into two groups: the direct sex industry and the indirect sex industry. Direct sex work refers to direct genital contact (as when an escort has penetrative sex for a fee); indirect sex work refers to sex work where there is no genital contact. Therefore, the erotic webcam industry is a new form of indirect sex work and a unique development.

4 In *Righteous Discontent* (1993), Evelyn Brooks Higginbotham famously coined the term "politics of respectability." She argued that, after the end of slavery and the institutionalization of Jim Crow, African American women fought to achieve a higher social status and combat negative stereotypes by reforming their behavior— that is, by demonstrating their respectability to Whites, African Americans would have greater access to quality education, work, and other vital resources. Respectability politics was a strategy embraced by many 20th-century political movements including the civil rights movement, women's movements, and lesbian and gay movements. In social movements, activists often advocate for access to civil rights by arguing that they are respectable, just like people who already have access to a particular set of rights, and thus are worthy of those rights, as well.

5 Bernstein, 2007; Bimbi, 2007; Walby, 2012.

6 Throughout this book, I use the term "cisgender" and the shorthand "cis" to refer to people whose gender identity corresponds with the one assigned to them at birth. I use the term "transgender" and the shorthand "trans" to refer to people whose gender identity does not correspond with the one assigned to them at birth.

7 This project was originally solely focused on cam models, and thus my research design limited my ability to study consumers. While readers will encounter anecdotal evidence about consumer desires and motivations from cam models, alongside a few comments from male clients who participated on web forums, this book is not focused on consumers. I do hope that my data and the questions I raise will influence future research that focuses not only on sex workers but sexual consumers, as well.

Cam models told me that consumption in the camming industry is driven primarily by cis male consumers from the United States. Cam models of different genders told me they primarily serviced cis men; some who had been camming for long periods of time shared stories with me about the few times they serviced women. Also, cam models who specialize in BDSM sometimes work with straight couples who are seeking education or role plays involving more than two people. Interestingly, cam models often know the actual identities only of those clients for whom they perform private shows, where both cams have been turned on. It is quite possible that people other than cis men are, in fact, active patrons in the industry.

My data suggests that gender is an essential variable in understanding sexual consumption. Historically, sex industries were created as places for satisfying men's desires, and for propagating hegemonic masculinity and bolstering men's sense of masculinity through the consumption of women's bodies. Most cam models said they designed their performances for the male gaze. The underrepresentation of consumers who are not cis men is likely caused by the perception that the camming industry is an erotic marketplace that like so many other sex markets caters to cis men only. Future lines of inquiry should explore how gender shapes sexual consumption—and not only how cis women consume sex; we also need to understand how people with non-binary and transgender identities consume sex.

8 Weisman, 2015; Davies, 2013; Bertrand, 2014; Trout, 2017.

9 Mathews, 2017.

10 Nayar, 2017a.

11 Van Doorn and Velthuis, 2018.

12 Sanders, 2005a.

13 "Doxing" refers to acquiring, through research or hacking, identifiable information about a model (or other person) and then sharing it.

14 Jones, 2016.

15 Frank, 2002.

16 Bernstein, 2007.

17 Jones, 2015a.

18 Allen, 2017.

19 Jones, 2016.

20 Parsons, Koken, and Bimbi, 2004, 2007; Pruitt, 2005; Quinn and Forsyth, 2005; Sanders, 2005b, 2008; Weitzer, 2005; Bernstein, 2007; Holt and Blevins, 2007; Murphy and Venkatesh, 2006; Castle and Lee, 2008; Phua and Caras, 2008; Ashford, 2009; Cunningham and Kendall, 2011; Walby, 2012; Minichiello, Scott, and Callander, 2013; Feldman, 2014; Jonsson, Svedin, and Hydén, 2014.

21 For exceptions, see Bernstein, 2007; Walby, 2012.

22 Hine, 2000, 2005.

23 Brim and Ghaziani, 2016; Compton, Meadow, and Schilt, 2018; Browne and Nash, 2010.

24 Flaherty, 2017a, 2017b.

25 Hegarty, Lemieux, and McQueen, 2010; Hegarty and Buechel, 2006.

26 Ellis and Bochner, 2000, pg. 739.

27 For examples of excellent use of autoethnography in contemporary sociology, see Vidal-Ortiz, 2004; Buggs, 2017; Schippers, 2016.

28 Orne and Bell, 2015, pg. 148.

29 Ellis, Adams, and Bochner, 2011.

30 Sontag, [1967] 2002, pg. 59.

31 Duggan and Hunter, 1995.

32 Dworkin and MacKinnon, 1988; Dworkin, 1981.

33 Rubin, 1984; Willis, [1992] 2012a, [1992] 2012b.

34 Vance, 1984; Snitow, Stansell, and Thompson, 1983.

35 Weitzer, 2010, pg. 6.

36 See, for example, Roscingo, 2007.

37 Crenshaw, 1989, pg. 140.

38 Collins, 1990. "Gynocentrism" refers to the idea that all women share similar experiences of economic, political, and social oppression, and as result share an intrinsic sisterhood.

39 Davis, 1981; hooks, 1981; Lorde, 1984; Crenshaw, 1991; Hull, Bell Scott, and Smith, 1993; Guy-Sheftall, 1995; Moore, 2011.

40 See, for example, Ehrenreich, 2002.

41 McCall, 2005, pg. 1782.

42 Choo and Ferree, 2010; McCall, 2005.

CHAPTER 1. THE PLEASURE DEFICIT

1 See, for example, Goodwin, Jasper, and Polletta, 2000; Goodwin, 1997.

2 Dixon-Mueller, 1993.

3 Higgins and Hirsch, 2007.

4 Jones, 2018a.

5 O'Malley and Valverde, 2004, pg. 26.

6 For excellent accounts, see, for example, MacLean, 2005; Pennay, 2012; Zajdow, 2010.

7 As a practice, I do not assume anyone's gender based on their name. If I do not know how someone identifies, I use the gender-neutral pronoun "they."

8 Duff, 2008, pg. 386.

9 Green, 2008.

10 Veblen, 1899; Bourdieu, 1984.

11 Schulman, 2012.

12 For example, see Orne, 2017. In the book *Boystown*, Orne discusses racial exclusion and sexual racism in what they call sexy communities or gay spaces devoted to sexual pleasure.

13 Ahmed, 2010, pg. 212.

14 Geertz, 1973, pg. 89.

15 In the stripping industry, a "money shower" refers to the act of a customer giving a large amount of money in small denominations to the bartender, who then, in a fanning motion, tosses the bills over the dancer's body. This tipping practice is colloquially referred to as "making it rain."

16 Wallenstein, 2009, pg. 208.

17 Ibid., pg. 209.

18 Ibid., pg. 97.

19 Bloom, 2010, pg. 205.

20 Kringelbach and Berridge, 2010.

21 Foucault, 1985, pgs. 66–67.

22 Plato, *Phaedrus* (ca. 370 BCE). In De Botton, 1999, pg. 794.

23 Epicurus, *Letter to Menoeceus* (ca. 4th c. BCE). In Shafer-Landau, 2012, pg. 13.

24 Mill, *Utilitarianism* (1863). In Shafer-Landau, 2012, pg. 20.

25 Bentham, 1907, pg. 14.

26 Davies, 1982.

27 Rubin, 1984.

28 See world map based on Aengus Carroll and Lucas Ramón Mendos, "Sponsored Homophobia: A World Survey of Sexual Orientation Laws: Criminalisation, Protection and Recognition" (May 2017), *ILGA*, https://ilga.org (accessed May 25, 2018).

29 While not just related to sex acts, for a great analysis of worldwide trends in the criminalization of sex, see Frank, Camp, and Boutcher, 2010.

30 Foucault, 1994.

31 Foucault, 1978, pg. 95.

32 See, as an example, Orne, 2017.

CHAPTER 2. INTRODUCTION TO CAMMING

1 Attwood, 2010.

2 See Flowers, 1998; Selmi, 2012.

3 Attwood, 2010.

4 Murphy and Roser, 2018.

5 Senft, 2008, pg. 1.

6 Ibid., pg. 20.

7 Bartlett, 2014.

8 Paasonen, 2011.

9 Comella, 2017.

10 In 2013, in a *New York Times* article, "Intimacy on the Web, with a Crowd," Matt Richtel, based on his early research on the industry, argued that the cam industry was a billion-dollar industry. Given the growth documented here, there is no doubt that it is now a multibillion-dollar industry.

CHAPTER 3. THE CONTEMPORARY CAMMING MARKET

1 In her famous book *Sex at the Margins: Migration, Labour Markets and the Rescue Industry*, Laura Agustín argued that workers around the world make rational choices to sell and trade sexual services. However, the rescue industry, which is composed of a range of anti-trafficking activists, politicians, and social service agencies, labels all sex workers, especially women, as victims who need to be saved.

2 Walters, 2013.

3 This is why California is the hub of the porn industry in the United States.

4 Morris, 1884.

5 See appendix A for a discussion of the underrepresentation of trans men in camming.

6 Alexa Website Analytics computes data about Internet traffic patterns, tracking the websites visited by Internet users who have installed the Alexa toolbar on their browsers. This group amounts to millions of Internet users; however, because the Alexa toolbar is not installed on all Internet users' browsers, the data is based on a nonrandomly sampled population of Internet users. Despite this limitation, the Alexa Website Analytics data does provide a general idea of how frequently visited or popular a particular website is and generates a reliable estimate of web traffic (Vaughan and Yang, 2012). Alexa calculates traffic scores by using the number of average daily visitors to a website, combined with the number of page views a website receives over a three-month period. Given the limitations of the Alexa data, it is used herein only to document overall trends in the webcam marketplace. I also rely on qualitative data to support claims about the popularity of various cam sites.

7 As I note at other points herein, there is no evidence to support the idea that almost all men who visit male cam models' rooms identify as gay. In fact, I suspect that many men who visit male cam models' rooms identify as straight. See Ward, 2015.

8 Pascoe, 2007.

9 Due to the limitations imposed by my survey's sample size, I use the quantitative data that follows only to draw tentative conclusions about the relationships

between wages and various demographic variables. I rely primarily on my qualitative data throughout the rest of the book to make more definitive claims about each of the study's independent variables.

10 In my sample, the mean monthly earnings were $2,012, but some outliers were skewing the mean to yield a higher average that is not representative of most models' monthly earnings. Thus, here I present the median.

11 Nayar, 2017b.

CHAPTER 4. GLOBAL MOTIVATIONS TO CAM

1 Jenness, 1990.

2 Agustín, 2007.

3 Kempadoo and Doezema, 1998.

4 Holloway, 2010.

5 See Hochshild, 1983.

6 James, et al. 2016. The NTDS showed that transfeminine survey participants were twice more likely to trade sex than transmasculine respondents, 13.1% versus 7.1%, respectively. However, transmasculine participants still comprised 26.4% of all participants who reported trading sex. As the NTDS noted, "While most discussions of sex work and trans people focus on transgender women, this finding shows that many transmasculine people are engaged in the sex trade" (13). It is thus unfortunate that there is almost no research on transmasculine sex workers. While I was not able to capture the voices of trans men who cam, my forthcoming research project focuses entirely on transmasculine sex workers.

7 Beatty, 2012.

8 Mainstream accounts suggest that multilevel marketing businesses fail for as many as 99% of individual participants. See Williams, 2017.

9 In "Estranged Labour" (1844), Karl Marx argued that, under capitalism, workers are estranged from their humanity. The more humans work, the more degraded they become. According to Marx, workers, the proletariat, are alienated and estranged from the objects they produce, from the process of labor, from their human essence, and from other workers. Capitalism causes workers to be complicit in the degradation of their bodies, minds, and souls—complicit in the removal of life's pleasures.

As Marx noted, the conditions of labor under capitalism cause workers displeasure. Capitalist labor degrades our bodies and minds and makes us unhappy. Under capitalism, we can never reach our full potential as humans and as a society because we are reduced to animals. Importantly, while Marx's work could have been more attentive to corporeality, the effects of capitalism on our affective states, and pleasure specifically, his work in "Estranged Labour" was clear—alienation under capitalism deprives workers of their human essence. What Marx did not highlight enough was that an essential aspect of the human essence is the desire to experience pleasure through work and social intercourse.

Marx assumed that humans would regain their "singular essence" when alienation ceases to exist under communism. What Marx missed is that the deprivation of humanity through alienation is not singular, and worker subjectivity will influence our needs as individuals. Again, other systems of oppression such as White supremacy overlap with capitalist production and reconfigure experiences of alienation. While humanity means different things to each worker, what is common to all workers is that they long for corporeal pleasure and affective states of happiness that are fostered by having dignity and autonomy. I argue that the deprivation of pleasure is a central component of the human experience of alienation, and not only is alienation changing, it is getting worse.

10 Bernstein, 2007.
11 Welter, 1966.
12 Morris, 1884.
13 Lawler, 2017.
14 Krugh, 2014.
15 McCaughey and French, 2001.
16 Rodgers and Taves, 2017.

CHAPTER 5. "I GET PAID TO HAVE ORGASMS"

1 Vance, 1984, pg. 1.
2 Ibid., pg. 3.
3 Lamm and Meeks, 2009.
4 Bernstein, 2007; Walby, 2012.
5 Walby, 2012, pg. 169.
6 Bernstein, 2007; Walby, 2012.
7 Sanders, 2008.
8 Kik is a free instant-messaging app.
9 Though I had the opportunity to interview Sherry, she did not participate in the survey. Thus, she is not represented in the tables in appendix A, which present survey participant data.
10 See Ferguson, 2003.
11 Scott, 2010, pg. 164.
12 Ibid., pg. 165.
13 Vance, 1984, pg. 5.
14 Carol Wolkowitz (2002, 2006) argues that the sociology of work has ignored the corporeal experiences of work. Specifically, she posits that labor scholars have focused on the role of the worker's own body in work, but have missed the importance of how workers manipulate, train, and please other people's bodies. The term "body work" has come to refer to "work that focuses directly on the bodies of others: assessing, diagnosing, handling, treating, manipulating, and monitoring bodies, that thus become the object of the worker's labour" (Twigg et al., 2011, pg. 171). Body work scholarship has focused on an expansive range of work that

people do on other's bodies and the venues for such work: healthcare (e.g., Twigg et al., 2011; Cacchioni and Wolkowitz, 2011); nail salons (Kang, 2003); beauty salons (Black, 2004); therapeutic massage (Oerton, 2004); personal trainers in gyms (George, 2008); body work in funeral homes (Howarth, 1996). As it involves the manipulation and/or pleasuring of others' bodies, sex work is a prime example of body work (e.g., Sanders, 2005a; Bott, 2006; Wolkowitz, 2006).

15 Beloso, 2012, pgs. 65–66.

CHAPTER 6. WE ARE CAMILY

1 Hunter, 1974, 2006.
2 See Castells, 1983; Ghaziani, 2014; Orne, 2017.
3 Foley, 1995.
4 Weinstock and Rothblum, 1996; Nardi, 1999.
5 McPherson, Smith-Lovin, and Cook, 2001.
6 This is my note, not Putnam's.
7 Oldenburg, 1999.
8 Small, 2009; Ruef, 2010.
9 Kwon, Heflin, and Ruef, 2013, pg. 985.
10 This thread contained 65 posts, with 13 different people—including the moderator—commenting in total.
11 Butler, 1990.
12 For a brilliant and well-documented history of transmisogyny in radical lesbian feminism, as well as in the broader society, see Stryker, 2008.
13 The Michigan Womyn's Music Festival, often simply referred to as Michfest, was a music festival held every August from 1976 to 2015. The event was created as a woman-only space. It was created, organized, run, and attended exclusively by women. As noted in this chapter, women have often sought to create safe spaces where they can feel free from male oppression and harassment. Michfest had a "womyn-born-womyn" policy that meant that only women assigned female at birth could attend. The policy and the event was boycotted by many activists groups who denounced Michfest for its transmisogyny.

CHAPTER 7. PERFORMING IN A SEXUAL FIELD

1 Mears and Connell, 2016, pg. 353.
2 Green, 2014.
3 Ibid., pgs. 27–28.
4 Ibid., pg. 15.
5 Sanders, 2005a.
6 "Colorism" refers to the system of advantages given to people with light skin, and the disadvantages that befall people with dark skin. Racial groups are often reductively seen as monolithic, and in turn people miss the differences in people's lived experiences caused by colorism. For examples of research in the social sciences on colorism, see Hunter, 1998, 2002; Hunter, Allen, and Telles, 2001; Hill, 2000,

2002; Telles, 2004; Herring, Keith, and Horton, 2004; Dixon and Maddox, 2005; Hochschild and Weaver, 2007; Glenn, 2008.

7 Woodward, 2006.

8 Utrata, 2011.

9 Melina, 2008.

10 Woodward, 2006, pg. 163.

11 For academic examples, see Escoffier, 2003; Laing, Pilcher, and Smith, 2016. For a mainstream account, see James Michael Nichols, "Here's What This Straight Man Who Does 'Gay for Pay' Porn Wants You to Know" (December 16, 2015), *Huffington Post*, www.huffingtonpost.com.

12 It is important that many of their clients may not be gay men at all. These performers assume this, but it is likely that their clients have a range of gender and sexual identities, which also no doubt includes straight-identified men. See Ward, 2015.

13 Connell and Messerschmidt, 2005.

14 Parsons et al., 2012; Van Eeden-Moorefield, Malloy, and Benson, 2016; Bonello and Cross, 2010.

15 Schippers, 2016; Moors et al., 2014.

16 Douglas, 1966.

17 Kessler and McKenna, 1978.

18 As I've noted elsewhere, I realize that my comparisons of trans and cis women may reify a trans/cis binary that does not acknowledge the fluidity of gender. Unfortunately, because I had no participants who were non-binary, genderqueer, etc., I am not able to include a wider range of gender identities in this analysis.

19 Bordo, 1993, pg. 193.

20 Hennen, 2005; Whitesel, 2014.

21 For a fuller discussion of the experiences of BBW cam models, see my article "The Pleasures of Fetishization" (2018b).

22 Here I am anonymizing the first part of Jose's name only, so that his explanation of his manufactured identity still makes sense to readers.

23 Walby, 2012.

24 Johnson, 2010, pgs. 238–39.

25 Hakim, 2010; Green, 2014.

CHAPTER 8. FOR BLACK MODELS SCROLL DOWN

1 Steinblatt, 2015; Wager, 2015.

2 Bedi, 2015, pg. 998.

3 Orne, 2017, pg. 67.

4 Callander, Newman, and Holt, 2015.

5 Robinson, 2015.

6 For notable exceptions, see Phua and Caras, 2008; Miller-Young 2008; Koken, Bimbi, and Parsons, 2009; Brooks, 1997, 2010; Minichiello, Scott, and Callander, 2013; Nash, 2014.

7 For further information about this data set and statistical analyses, see my article "For Black Models Scroll Down: Web-Cam Modeling and the Racialization of Erotic Labor," *Sexuality and Culture* 19, no. 4 (2015): 776–99.

8 I created ranged variables for camscores used in the statistical analyses: camscores under 500 were categorized as "low"; 500–7,499, "medium"; and 7500-plus, "high."

9 Bonilla-Silva, 2009, pgs. 2–3.

10 Brooks, 2010, pg. 99.

11 Mears, 2011, pg. 207.

12 Orne, 2017, pg. 68.

13 Mears, 2011, pg. 196.

14 Brooks, 2010, pg. 7.

15 Koken, Bimbi, and Parsons, 2009, pgs. 220–21.

16 Orne, 2017, pgs. 67–68.

17 Yarbrough and Bennett, 2000; Collins, 2004.

18 Collins, 1986.

19 Noble, 2018.

CHAPTER 9. GETTING KINKY ONLINE

1 "Safe, sane, and consensual" is a phrase used in BDSM communities to emphasize that all play should be performed safely by individuals who have taken care to become educated and skilled in these practices, so they do not harm their partners. Second, play should be sane. This means all play should be practiced by individuals with the capacity to exercise sound and responsible judgment. Finally, all play should be consensual and negotiated before its initiation.

2 Weiss, 2011; Cruz, 2016; Simula, 2013.

3 Lindemann, 2010, 2012; Levey and Pinsky, 2015.

4 Connell and Messerschmidt, 2005.

5 Cruz, 2016, pg. 50.

6 Miller-Young, 2014, pg. 49.

7 "Other performers" here anonymizes the actual names of the models referenced.

8 Bederman, 1995; Collins, 2004; Partridge, 2008; Meszaros and Bazzaroni, 2014.

9 Russell, 2010.

10 Weiss, 2011, pg. 6.

11 Ibid.

12 In January 2018, United States president Donald Trump referred to Haiti and African nations as "shithole countries" during a meeting with senators at the White House.

13 Further research exploring the client side of these sexual arrangements is needed to better understand the outcomes of these interactions.

CONCLUSION

1 The webpage xoJane and the original blog post are no longer available on the Internet.

2 Feuer, 2017.

3 Porter, 2018.

4 Ibid.
5 Jackman and O'Connell, 2017.
6 Jackman, 2017.
7 Cole, 2018a.
8 Tierney, 2018.
9 Cole, 2018b.
10 "About Us," Desiree Alliance, http://desireealliance.org (accessed April 27, 2018).
11 "About I.E.A.U.," *Int'l Entertainment Adult Union*, http://entertainmentadultunion.com (accessed April 27, 2018).
12 "Microsoft Services Agreement" (March 1, 2018), *Microsoft*, www.microsoft.com (accessed April 27, 2018).
13 Jonsson, Svedin, and Hydén, 2014; Feldman, 2014; Minichiello, Scott, and Callander, 2013; Walby, 2012; Cunningham and Kendall, 2011; Lee-Gonyea, Castle, and Gonyea, 2009; Weitzer, 2005, 2010; Ashford, 2009; Castle and Lee, 2008; Senft, 2008; Phua and Caras, 2008; Holt and Blevins, 2007; Bernstein, 2007; Murphy and Venkatesh, 2006; Parsons, Koken, and Bimbi, 2004, 2007; Pruitt, 2005; Quinn and Forsyth, 2005.
14 "Sex Worker's Rights Joint Statement," *Desiree Alliance*, https://docs.google.com/document/d/1n0lvaK_PQEfrcnNlmjoJos37RMtvHRGLQlrjKqwo3xk/edit (accessed May 4, 2018).
15 Ibid.
16 *Stop Sesta and Fosta*, https://stopsesta.org (accessed May 4, 2018).
17 International Whore's Day (IWD) began in 1975, and now consists of protests that commemorate the occupation of Église Saint-Nizier in Lyon, France, and five additional churches by thousands of sex workers. See McGowan, 2018.
18 Ehrenkranz, 2018.
19 "About I.E.A.U."
20 "About Us," *Sex Workers Outreach Program*, www.new.swopusa.org (accessed April 27, 2018).
21 "Exotic Dancers Union, SEIU Local 790," *Sex Workers Education Network*, http://bayswan.org (accessed May 4, 2018); "A Brief History of the Lusty Lady Theater," *The Lusty Lady*, www.lustyladysf.com (accessed May 4, 2018); "About," *Stripper Labor Rights*, http://stripperlaborrights.com (accessed May 4, 2018).
22 Albright and D'Adamo, 2017.
23 For an excellent discussion of the NZPC's efforts and the positive effects of decriminalization, see Abel, 2014.
24 See Armstrong, 2017a, 2017b.
25 Abel, Fitzgerald, and Brunton, 2009; Armstrong, 2014.
26 Amnesty International, 2016.
27 Albright and D'Adamo, 2017.
28 Bumiller, 2008.
29 Interested readers should also see Dewey and St. Germain's recent book, *Women of the Street: How the Criminal Justice Social Services Alliance Fails Women in Prostitu-*

tion. They analyze the dynamic and often hostile relationship between sex workers and law enforcement agents, judges, lawyers, probation and parole officers, and the social workers and drug treatment providers that sex workers are often mandated by courts to see. Coining the term "criminal justice-social services alliance," the authors, like Bumiller, show how government policing and regulation too often harm, not help, women, many of whom are poor women of color.

30 Bernstein, 2012, pg. 242.
31 Bass, 2015.

APPENDIX A. CAM MODELS IN THE STUDY

1 There were a significant number of cam models that selected the racial category they use while camming on the survey and revealed to me their ethnicities in qualitative data.
2 See Vidal-Ortiz, 2004, for an excellent account of the limitations of the US system of race.
3 Telles, 2004. For an excellent account of race and identity formation in the Dominican Republic, see Candelario, 2007.
4 Although, as readers will see, race was a salient topic in my conversations with Black models from the US and UK.
5 D'Adamo, 2018, pg. 36.
6 Cromwell, 1999; Pfeffer, 2014; Tompkins, 2014; Latham, 2016.
7 I sent recruitment emails to the trans men I saw performing in the field. None of these men responded. In addition, when I interviewed Buck Angel for this book, the survey had long been closed and interviews transcribed and analyzed.

APPENDIX B. METHODS

1 Creswell, 2014.
2 Camscore is a sorting and ranking mechanism used by MyFreeCams. This algorithmically derived score is a reflection of performer success on the website. Performers who make the most tokens in the least amount of time online have higher camscores.
3 See my article "Pornographics as Queer Method," in D'Lane Compton, Tey Meadow, and Kristen Schilt, eds., *Other, Please Specify: Queer Methods in Sociology* (Berkeley: University of California Press, 2018), for a full discussion of my experiences with the IRB.
4 Church, 1993.
5 See the company's website for further information: "About," *Qualitative Health Research Consultants*, https://qhrconsultants.com (accessed May 25, 2018).

APPENDIX C. ETHICAL CONSIDERATIONS

1 Jenkins, 2010, pg. 92.
2 McKee and DeVoss, 2007.
3 For a great discussion of participant observation in the virtual world, see Boellstroff et al., 2012.

4 Eynon, Fry, and Schroeder, 2008, pg. 31.
5 Flicker, Haans, and Skinner, 2012.
6 Boellstroff et al., 2012, pg. 135.
7 Best and Krueger, 2008, pg. 229.
8 Vehovar and Lozar Manfreda, 2008, pg. 182.
9 Fricker, 2008.
10 Rooke, 2016, pg. 34.
11 Meadow, 2018, pg. 156.

BIBLIOGRAPHY

Abel, Gillian M. 2014. "A Decade of Decriminalization: Sex Work 'Down Under' but Not Underground." *Criminology & Criminal Justice: An International Journal* 14, no. 5: 580–92.

Abel, Gillian M., Lisa J. Fitzgerald, and Cheryl Brunton. 2009. "The Impact of Decriminalisation on the Number of Sex Workers in New Zealand." *Journal of Social Policy* 38, no. 3: 515–31.

Adams, Rebecca G., and Graham Allan, eds. 1998. *Placing Friendship in Context*. New York: Cambridge University Press.

Agustín, Laura Maria. 2007. *Sex at the Margins: Migration, Labour Markets and the Rescue Industry*. London: Zed Books.

Ahmed, Sara. 2010. *The Promise of Happiness*. Durham, NC: Duke University Press.

Albright, Erin, and Kate D'Adamo. 2017. "Decreasing Human Trafficking through Sex Work Decriminalization." *AMA Journal of Ethics* 19, no. 1: 122–26.

Allen, Tyler. 2017. "Amber Rose Embraces Adult Webcam Platform, CAM4, as an Official Sponsor of the 2017 Amber Rose SlutWalk." *Business Wire*, September 28.

Amnesty International. 2016. "Amnesty International Publishes Policy and Research on Protection of Sex Workers' Rights." May 26.

Armstrong, Lynzi. 2014. "Screening Clients in a Decriminalised Street-Based Sex Industry: Insights into the Experiences in New Zealand." *Australian & New Zealand Journal of Criminology* 47, no. 2: 207–22.

———. 2017a. "Decriminalisation and the Rights of Migrant Sex Workers in Aotearoa/ New Zealand: Making a Case for Change." *Women's Studies Journal* 31, no. 2: 69–76.

———. 2017b. "From Law Enforcement to Protection? Interactions between Sex Workers and Police in a Decriminalized Street-Based Sex Industry." *British Journal of Criminology* 57, no. 3: 570–88.

Ashford, Chris. 2009. "Male Sex Work and the Internet Effect: Time to Re-evaluate the Criminal Law." *Journal of Criminal Law* 73, no. 3: 258–80.

———. 2012. "Carceral Politics as Gender Justice? The 'Traffic in Women' and Neoliberal Circuits of Crime, Sex, and Rights." *Theory and Society* 41, no. 3: 233–59.

Attwood, Feona. 2010. *Porn.Com: Making Sense of Online Pornography*. New York: Peter Lang.

Bartlett, Jamie. 2014. *The Dark Net: Inside the Digital Underworld*. New York: Melville House.

Barton, Bernadette. 2007. "Managing the Toll of Stripping: Boundary Setting among Exotic Dancers." *Journal of Contemporary Ethnography* 36, no. 5: 571–96.

Bass, Alison. 2015. *Getting Screwed: Sex Workers and the Law*. Lebanon, NH: ForeEdge Press.

Beasly, Chris. 2008. "The Challenge of Pleasure: Re-imagining Sexuality and Sexual Health." *Health Sociology Review* 17: 151–63.

Beatty, J. E. 2012. "Career Barriers Experienced by People with Chronic Illness: A U.S. Study." *Employee Responsibilities and Rights Journal* 24: 91–110.

Bederman, Gail. 1995. *Manliness and Civilization: A Cultural History of Gender and Race in the United States, 1880–1917*. Chicago: University of Chicago Press.

Bedi, Sonu. 2015. "Sexual Racism: Intimacy as a Matter of Justice." *Journal of Politics* 77, no. 4: 998–1011.

Beloso, Brooke M. 2012. "Sex, Work, and the Feminist Erasure of Class." *Signs: Journal of Women in Culture and Society* 38, no. 1: 47–70.

Bentham, Jeremy. 1907. *An Introduction to the Principles of Morals and Legislation*. Oxford: Clarendon Press.

Berardi, Franco. 2009. *The Soul at Work: From Alienation to Autonomy*. South Pasadena, CA: Semiotext(e).

Bernstein, Elizabeth. 2007. *Temporarily Yours: Intimacy, Authenticity, and the Commerce of Sex*. Chicago: University of Chicago Press.

———. 2012. "Carceral Politics as Gender Justice? The 'Traffic in Women' and Neoliberal Circuits of Crime, Sex, and Rights." *Theory and Society* 41, no. 3: 233–59.

Bertrand, Natasha. 2014. "How Webcam Models Make Money." *Business Insider*, November 18.

Best, Samuel J., and Brian S. Krueger. 2008. "Internet Survey Design." In *The SAGE Handbook of Online Research Methods*, edited by Nigel G. Fielding, Raymond M. Lee, and Grant Blank, 217–29. Los Angeles: SAGE.

Bimbi, David S. 2007. "Male Prostitution: Pathology, Paradigms and Progress in Research." *Journal of Homosexuality* 53, nos. 1–2: 7–35.

Black, Paula. 2004. *The Beauty Industry: Gender, Culture, Pleasure*. New York: Routledge.

Bloom, Paul. 2010. *How Pleasure Works: The New Science of Why We Like What We Like*. New York: W. W. Norton.

Boellstroff, Tom, Bonnie Nardi, Celia Pearce, and T. L. Taylor. 2012. *Ethnography and Virtual Worlds: A Handbook of Method*. Princeton, NJ: Princeton University Press.

Bonello, Kristoff, and Malcolm C. Cross. 2010. "Gay Monogamy: I Love You but I Can't Have Sex with Only You." *Journal of Homosexuality* 57, no. 1: 117–39.

Bonilla-Silva, Eduardo. 2009. *Racism without Racists: Color-Blind Racism and the Persistence of Racial Inequality in the United States*, 3rd ed. Lanham, MD: Rowman & Littlefield.

Bordo, Susan. 1993. *Unbearable Weight: Feminism, Western Culture, and the Body*. Berkeley: University of California Press.

Bott, Esther. 2006. "Pole Position: Migrant British Women Producing Selves through Lap Dancing Work." *Feminist Review*, no. 83: 23–41.

Bourdieu, Pierre. 1984. *Distinction: A Social Critique of the Judgement of Taste*. New York: Routledge.

Brim, Matt, and Amin Ghaziani. 2016. "Introduction: Queer Methods." *Women's Studies Quarterly* 44, nos. 3–4: 14–27.

Brooks, Siobhan. 1997. "Dancing towards Freedom," In *Whores and Other Feminists*, edited by Jill Nagle, 57–65. New York: Routledge.

———. 2010. *Unequal Desires: Race and Erotic Capital in the Stripping Industry*. Albany: State University of New York Press.

Browne, Kath, and Catherine J. Nash. 2010. *Queer Methods and Methodologies: Intersecting Queer Theories and Social Science Research*. New York: Routledge.

Buggs, Shantel G. 2017. "'Your Momma Is Day-Glow White': Questioning the Politics of Racial Identity, Loyalty, and Obligation." *Identities: Global Studies in Culture and Power* 24, no. 4: 379–97.

Bumiller, Kristen. 2008. *In an Abusive State: How Neoliberalism Appropriated the Feminist Movement against Sexual Violence*. Durham, NC: Duke University Press.

Butler, Judith. 1990. *Gender Trouble*. New York: Routledge.

Cacchioni, Thea, and Carol Wolkowitz. 2011. "Treating Women's Sexual Difficulties: The Body Work of Sexual Therapy." *Sociology of Health & Illness* 33, no. 2: 266–79.

Callander, Denton, Christy Newman, and Martin Holt. 2015. "Is Sexual Racism Really Racism?: Distinguishing Attitudes toward Sexual Racism and Generic Racism among Gay and Bisexual Men." *Archives of Sexual Behavior* 44, no. 7: 1991–2000.

Candelario, Ginetta E. B. 2007. *Black behind the Ears: Dominican Racial Identity from Museums to Beauty Shops*. Durham, NC: Duke University Press.

Castells, Manuel. 1983. *The City and the Grassroots: A Cross-Cultural Theory of Urban Social Movements*. London: E. Arnold.

Castle, Tammy, and Jennifer Lee. 2008. "Ordering Sex in Cyberspace: A Content Analysis of Escort Websites." *International Journal of Cultural Studies* 11, no. 1: 107–21.

Choo, Hae Yeon, and Myra Marx Ferree. 2010. "Practicing Intersectionality in Sociological Research: A Critical Analysis of Inclusions, Interactions, and Institutions in the Study of Inequalities." *Sociological Theory* 28, no. 2: 129–49.

Church, Allan H. 1993. "Estimating the Effect of Incentives on Mail Survey Response Rates: A Meta-Analysis." *Public Opinion Quarterly* 57: 62–79.

Cole, Samantha. 2018a. "Sex Workers Say Porn on Google Drive Is Suddenly Disappearing." *Motherboard*, March 21, https://motherboard.vice.com.

———. 2018b. "Cloudflare Just Banned a Social Media Refuge for Thousands of Sex Workers." *Motherboard*, April 19, https://motherboard.vice.com.

Collins, Patricia Hill. 1986. "Learning from the Outsider Within: The Sociological Significance of Black Feminist Thought." *Social Problems* 33, no. 6: S14–S32.

———. 1990. *Black Feminist Thought: Knowledge, Consciousness and the Politics of Empowerment*. New York: Routledge.

———. 2004. *Black Sexual Politics: African Americans, Gender, and the New Racism*. New York: Routledge.

Comella, Lynn. 2017. *Vibrator Nation: How Feminist Sex-Toy Stores Changed the Business of Pleasure*. Durham, NC: Duke University Press.

Comella, Lynn, and Shira Tarrant, eds. 2015. *New Views on Pornography: Sexuality, Politics, and the Law*. Santa Barbara, CA: Praeger.

Compton, D'Lane, Tey Meadow, and Kristen Schilt, eds. 2018. *Other, Please Specify: Queer Methods in Sociology*. Berkeley: University of California Press.

Connell, R. W., and James W. Messerschmidt. 2005. "Hegemonic Masculinity: Rethinking the Concept." *Gender and Society* 19, no. 6: 829–59.

Crenshaw, Kimberlé. 1989. "Demarginalizing the Intersection of Race and Sex: A Black Feminist Critique of Antidiscrimination Doctrine, Feminist Theory and Antiracist Politics." *University of Chicago Legal Forum*, no. 140: 139–67.

———. 1991. "Mapping the Margins: Intersectionality, Identity Politics, and Violence against Women of Color." *Stanford Law Review* 43, no. 6: 1241–99.

Creswell, John W. 2014. *Research Design: Qualitative, Quantitative, and Mixed Methods Approaches*. Los Angeles: SAGE.

Cromwell, Jason. 1999. *Transmen and FTMs: Identities, Bodies, Genders, and Sexualities*. Champaign: University of Illinois Press.

Cruz, Arianne. 2016. *The Color of Kink: Black Women, BDSM, and Pornography*. New York: NYU Press.

Cunningham, Scott, and Todd D. Kendall. 2011. "Prostitution 2.0: The Changing Face of Sex Work." *Journal of Urban Economics* 69, no. 3: 273–87.

D'Adamo, Kate. 2018. "Queering the Trade: Intersections of the Sex Worker and LGBTQ Movements." In *The Unfinished Queer Agenda after Marriage Equality*, edited by Angela Jones, Joseph Nicholas DeFilippis, and Michael W. Yarbrough, 35–52. After Marriage Equality 3. Oxfordshire: Routledge.

Davies, Christie. 1982. "Sexual Taboos and Social Boundaries." *American Journal of Sociology* 87, no. 5: 1032–63.

Davies, Jack. 2013. "I Spent a Month Living in a Romanian Sexcam Studio." *Vice*, December 9, www.vice.com.

Davis, Angela Y. 1981. *Women, Race, and Class*. New York: Vintage Books.

De Botton, Alain, ed. 1999. *The Essential Plato*. New York: Quality Paperback Book Club.

Dewey, Susan, and Tonia St. Germain. 2016. *Women of the Street: How the Criminal Justice Social Services Alliance Fails Women in Prostitution*. New York: New York University Press.

Dixon, Travis, and Keith Maddox. 2005. "Skin Tone, Crime News, and Social Reality Judgments: Priming the Stereotype of the Dark and Dangerous Black Criminal." *Journal of Applied Social Psychology* 35, no. 8: 1555–70.

Dixon-Mueller, Ruth. 1993. "The Sexuality Connection in Reproductive Health." *Studies in Family Planning* 24, no. 5: 269–82.

Douglas, Mary. 1966. *Purity and Danger: An Analysis of Pollution and Taboo*. London: Routledge & Kegan Paul.

Duff, Cameron. 2008. "The Pleasure in Context." *International Journal of Drug Policy* 19: 384–392.

Duggan, Lisa, and Nan D. Hunter. 1995. *Sex Wars: Sexual Dissent and Political Culture.* New York: Routledge.

Dworkin, Andrea. 1981. *Pornography: Men Possessing Women.* New York: Perigee.

Dworkin, Andrea, and Catharine MacKinnon. 1988. *Pornography and Civil Rights: A New Day for Women's Equality.* Minneapolis: Organizing Against Pornography.

Egan, Danielle. 2006. *Dancing for Dollars and Paying for Love: The Relationships between Exotic Dancers and Their Regulars.* New York: Palgrave Macmillan.

Ehrenkranz, Melanie. 2018. "Sex Workers Fight Back against a Dangerous Law by Stepping into the Spotlight." *Gizmodo,* June 4, www.gizmodo.com.

Ehrenreich, Nancy. 2002. "Subordination and Symbiosis: Mechanisms of Mutual Support Between Subordinating Systems." *UMKC Law Review* 71: 251–324.

Ellis, Carolyn, and Arthur P. Bochner. 2000. "Autoethnography, Personal Narrative, Reflexivity: Researcher as Subject." In *Handbook of Qualitative Research,* 2nd ed., edited by Norman K. Denzin and Yvonna S. Lincoln, 733–68. Thousand Oaks, CA: SAGE.

Ellis, Carolyn, Tony E. Adams, and Arthur P. Bochner. 2011. "Autoethnography: An Overview." *Forum: Qualitative Social Research,* 12, no. 1: art. 10.

Escoffier, Jeffery. 2003. "Gay-for-Pay: Straight Men and the Making of Gay Pornography." *Qualitative Sociology* 26, no. 4: 531–55.

Eynon, Rebecca, Jenny Fry, and Ralph Schroeder. 2008 "The Ethics of Internet Research." In *The SAGE Handbook of Online Research Methods,* edited by Nigel Fielding, Raymond M. Lee, and Grant Blank, 23–41. Los Angeles: SAGE.

Feldman, Valerie. 2014. "Sex Work Politics and the Internet." In *Negotiating Sex Work: Unintended Consequences of Policy and Activism,* edited by Carisa R. Showden and Samantha Majic, 243–66. Minneapolis: University of Minnesota Press.

Ferguson, Roderick. 2003. *Aberrations in Black: Toward a Queer of Color Critique.* Minneapolis: University of Minnesota Press.

Feuer, Alan. 2017. "Owner of Rentboy.com Is Sentenced to 6 Months in Prison." *New York Times,* August 2.

Flaherty, Colleen. 2017. "A Pedagogy Questioned." *Inside Higher Ed,* October 20, www.insidehighered.com.

———. 2017. "'Progressive Stacking' Teaching Technique Sparks Debate." *Times Higher Education,* October 23, www.timeshighereducation.com.

Flicker, Sarah, Dave Haans, and Harvey Skinner. 2012. "Ethical Dilemmas in Research on Internet Communities." In *Core Issues, Debates and Controversies in Internet Research,* Volume 1, *SAGE Internet Research Methods,* edited by Jason Hughes, 221–32. Washington, DC: SAGE.

Flowers, Amy. 1998. *The Fantasy Factory: An Insider's View of the Phone Sex Industry.* Philadelphia: University of Pennsylvania Press.

Foley, Kevin. 1995. "Slick S.F. Posters Advocate Decriminalizing Prostitution." *San Francisco Chronicle,* August 14.

Foucault, Michel. 1978. *Discipline and Punish: The Birth of the Prison.* New York: Vintage Books.

———. 1985. *The History of Sexuality, Vol. 2: The Use of Pleasure.* New York: Vintage Books.

———. 1994. *The Birth of the Clinic: An Archaeology of Medical Perception.* New York: Vintage Books.

Frank, David John, Bayliss J. Camp, and Steven A. Boutcher. 2010. "Worldwide Trends in the Criminal Regulation of Sex, 1945 to 2005." *American Sociological Review* 75, no. 6: 867–93.

Frank, Katherine. 2002. *G-Strings and Sympathy: Strip Club Regulars and Male Desire.* Durham, NC: Duke University Press.

———. 2003. "Just Trying to Relax: Masculinity, Masculinizing Practices, and Strip Club Regulars." *Journal of Sex Research* 40, no. 1: 61–75.

Freud, Sigmund. (1930) 1961. *Civilization and Its Discontents.* New York: W. W. Norton.

Fricker, Ronald, Jr. 2008. "Sampling Methods for Web and Email Surveys." In *The SAGE Handbook of Online Research Methods,* edited by Nigel G. Fielding, Raymond M. Lee, and Grant Blank, 195–216. Los Angeles: SAGE.

Geertz, Clifford. 1973. *The Interpretations of Cultures.* New York: Basic Books.

George, Molly. 2008. "Interactions in Expert Service Work: Demonstrating Professionalism in Personal Training." *Journal of Contemporary Ethnography* 37, no. 1: 108–31.

Ghaziani, Amin. 2014. *There Goes the Gayborhood?* Princeton, NJ: Princeton University Press.

Glenn, Evelyn Nakano. 2008. "Yearning for Lightness: Transnational Circuits in the Marketing and Consumption of Skin Lighteners." *Gender and Society* 22, no. 3: 281–302.

Goodwin, Jeff. 1997. "The Libidinal Constitution of a High-Risk Social Movement: Affectual Ties and Solidarity in the Huk Rebellion, 1946 to 1954." *American Sociological Review* 62: 53–69.

Goodwin, Jeff, James M. Jasper, and Francesca Polletta. 2000. "The Return of the Repressed: The Fall and Rise of Emotions in Social Movement Theory." *Mobilization: An International Journal* 5, no. 1: 65–83.

Green, Adam Isaiah. 2008. "Erotic Habitus: Toward a Sociology of Desire." *Theory and Society* 37, no. 6: 597–626.

———. 2014. *Sexual Fields: Toward a Sociology of Collective Sexual Life.* Chicago: University of Chicago Press.

Guy-Sheftall, Beverly. 1995. *Words of Fire: An Anthology of African American Feminist Thought.* New York: New Press.

Hakim, Catherine. 2010. "Erotic Capital." *European Sociological Review* 26, no. 5: 499–518.

Harcourt, Christine, and Basil Donovan. 2005. "The Many Faces of Sex Work." *Sexually Transmitted Infections* 81, no. 3: 201–6.

Hawkes, Gail. 2004. *Sex & Pleasure in Western Culture.* Malden, MA: Polity Press.

Hegarty, Peter, and Carmen Buechel. 2006. "Androcentric Reporting of Gender Differences in APA Journals: 1965–2004." *Review of General Psychology* 10: 377–89.

Hegarty, Peter, Anthony Lemieux, and Grant McQueen. 2010. "Graphing the Order of the Sexes: Constructing, Recalling, Interpreting, and Putting the Self in Gender Difference Graphs." *Journal of Personality and Social Psychology* 98: 375–91.

Hennen, Peter. 2005. "Bear Bodies, Bear Masculinity: Recuperation, Resistance, or Retreat?" *Gender and Society* 19, no. 1: 25–43.

Herring, Cedric, Verna M. Keith, and Hayward Derrick Horton, eds. 2004. *Skin Deep: How Race and Complexion Matter in the "Color-Blind" Era.* Chicago: University of Illinois Press.

Higginbotham, Evelyn Brooks. 1993. *Righteous Discontent: The Women's Movement in the Black Baptist Church, 1880–1920.* Cambridge, MA: Harvard University Press.

Higgins, Jenny A., and Jennifer S. Hirsch. 2007. "The Pleasure Deficit: Revisiting the 'Sexuality Connection' in Reproductive Health." *Perspectives on Sexual and Reproductive Health* 39: 240–47.

Hill, Mark E. 2000. "Color Differences in the Socioeconomic Status of African American Men: Results of a Longitudinal Study." *Social Forces* 78, no. 4: 1437–60.

———. 2002. "Skin Color and the Perception of Attractiveness among African Americans: Does Gender Make a Difference?" *Social Psychology Quarterly* 65, no. 1: 77–91.

Hine, Christine. 2000. *Virtual Ethnography.* Thousand Oaks, CA: SAGE.

———. 2005. *Virtual Methods: Issues in Social Research on the Internet.* New York: Berg.

Hochschild, Arlie Russell. 1983. *The Managed Heart: Commercialization of Human Feeling.* Berkeley: University of California Press.

Hochschild, Jennifer L., and Vesla Weaver. 2007. "The Skin Color Paradox and the American Racial Order." *Social Forces* 86, no. 2: 643–70.

Holloway, John. 2010. *Crack Capitalism.* New York: Pluto Press.

Holt, Thomas, and Kristie Blevins. 2007. "Examining Sex Work from the Client's Perspective: Assessing Johns Using Online Data." *Deviant Behavior* 28, no. 4: 333–54.

hooks, bell. 1981. *Ain't I a Woman: Black Women and Feminism.* Boston: South End Press.

Howarth, Glennys. 1996. *Last Rites: The Work of the Modern Funeral Director.* New York: Baywood Press.

Hull, Gloria T., Patricia Bell Scott, and Barbara Smith, eds. 1993. *All the Women Are White, All the Blacks Are Men, but Some of Us Are Brave.* New York: Feminist Press.

Hunter, Albert. 1974. *Symbolic Communities: The Persistence and Change of Chicago's Local Communities.* Chicago: University of Chicago Press.

———. 2006. "Contemporary Conceptions of Community." In *Handbook of Community Movements and Local Organization,* edited by Ram A. Cnaan and Carl Milofsky, 20–33. Oxford: Blackwell.

Hunter, Margaret. 1998. "Colorstruck: Skin Color Stratification in the Lives of African American Women." *Sociological Inquiry* 68, no. 4: 517–35.

———. 2002. "'If You're Light You're Alright': Light Skin Color as Social Capital for Women of Color." *Gender and Society* 16, no. 2: 175–93.

Hunter, Margaret, Walter Allen, and Edward Telles. 2001. "The Significance of Skin Color among African Americans and Mexican Americans." *African American Research Perspectives* 7, no. 1: 173–84.

Internet Society. 2015. "Global Internet Report 2014: Open and Sustainable Access for All." Reston, VA: Internet Society (accessible via Analysis & Policy Observatory, https://apo.org.au).

Jackman, Tom. 2017. "Under Attack, Backpage.com Has Its Supporters as Anti-trafficking Tool. But Many Differ." *Washington Post*, July 18.

Jackman, Tom, and Jonathan O'Connell. 2017. "16-Year-Old Was Found Beaten, Stabbed to Death after Being Advertised as Prostitute on Backpage." *Washington Post*, July 11.

James, Sandy E., Jody L. Herman, Susan Rankin, Mara Keisling, Lisa Mottet, and Ma'ayan Anafi. 2016. "The Report of the 2015 U.S. Transgender Survey." Washington, DC: National Center for Transgender Equality.

Jenkins, Suzanne. 2010. "New Technologies, New Territories: Using the Internet to Connect with Sex Workers and Sex Industry Organizers." In *New Sociologies of Sex Work*, edited by Kate Hardy, Sarah Kingston, and Teela Sanders, 91–108. Burlington, VT: Ashgate.

Jenness, Valerie. 1990. "From Sex as Sin to Sex as Work: COYOTE and the Reorganization of Prostitution as a Social Problem." *Social Problems* 37, no. 3: 403–20.

Johnson, Michael, Jr. 2010. "'Just Getting Off': The Inseparability of Ejaculation and Hegemonic Masculinity." *Journal of Men's Studies* 18, no. 3: 238–39.

Jones, Angela. 2015a. "For Black Models Scroll Down: Web-Cam Modeling and the Racialization of Erotic Labor." *Sexuality and Culture* 19, no. 4: 776–99.

———. 2015b. "Sex Work in a Digital Era." *Sociology Compass* 9, no. 7: 558–70.

———. 2016. "'I Get Paid to Have Orgasms': Adult Webcam Models' Negotiation of Pleasure and Danger." *Signs: Journal of Women in Culture and Society* 42, no. 1: 227–56.

———. 2018a. "Sex Is Not a Problem: The Erasure of Pleasure in the Sexual Sciences." *Sexualities* 22, no. 4: 643–68.

———. 2018b. "The Pleasures of Fetishization: BBW Erotic Webcam Performers, Empowerment, and Pleasure." *Fat Studies: An Interdisciplinary Journal of Body Weight and Society*. doi: 10.1080/21604851.2019.1551697.

Jonsson, Linda S., Carl Göran Svedin, and Margareta Hydén. 2014. "Without the Internet, I Never Would Have Sold Sex: Young Women Selling Sex Online." *Cyberpscyhology: Journal of Psychosocial Research on Cybersapce* 8, no. 1: 1–14.

Kang, Miliann. 2003. "The Managed Hand: The Commercialization of Bodies and Emotions in Korean Immigrant-Owned Nail Salons." *Gender and Society* 17, no. 6: 820–39.

Kempadoo, Kamala, and Jo Doezema. 1998. *Global Sex Workers*. New York: Routledge.

Kessler, Suzanne J., and Wendy McKenna. 1978. *Gender: An Ethnomethodological Approach*. Chicago: University of Chicago Press.

Koken, Juline A., David S. Bimbi, and Jeffrey T. Parsons. 2009. "Male and Female Escorts: A Comparative Analysis." In *Sex for Sale: Prostitution, Pornography, and the Sex Industry*, 2nd ed., edited by Ronald Weitzer, 205–32. New York: Routledge.

Kringelbach, Morten L., and Kent C. Berridge. 2010. "The Neuroscience of Happiness and Pleasure." *Social Research* 77, no. 2: 659–78.

Krugh, Michele. 2014. "Joy in Labour: The Politicization of Craft from the Arts and Crafts Movement to Etsy." *Canadian Review of American Studies* 44, no. 2: 281–301.

Kwon, Seok-Woo, Colleen Heflin, and Martin Ruef. 2013. "Community Social Capital and Entrepreneurship." *American Sociological Review* 78, no. 6: 980–1008.

Laing, Mary, Katy Pilcher, and Nicola Smith, eds. 2016. *Queer Sex Work*. New York: Routledge.

Lamm, Eric, and Michael D. Meeks. 2009. "Workplace Fun: The Moderating Effects of Generational Differences." *Employee Relations* 31, no. 6: 613–31.

Latham, J. R. 2016. "Trans Men's Sexual Narrative-Practices: Introducing STS to Trans and Sexuality Studies." *Sexualities* 19, no. 3: 347–68.

Lawler, Kristen. 2017. "Free Ride: The Food Stamp Surfer, American Counterculture, and the Refusal to Work." In *The Critical Surf Studies Reader*, edited by Dexter Zavalza Hough-Snee and Alexander Sotelo Eastman, 305–17. Durham, NC: Duke University Press.

Lee-Gonyea, Jennifer. A., Tammy Castle, and Nathan E. Gonyea. 2009. "Laid to Order: Male Escorts Advertising on the Internet." *Deviant Behavior* 30, no. 4: 321–48.

Levey, Tania G., and Dina Pinsky. 2015. "A Constellation of Stigmas: Intersectional Stigma Management and the Professional Dominatrix." *Deviant Behavior* 36, no. 5: 1–21.

Lindemann, Danielle J. 2010. "Will the Real Dominatrix Please Stand Up: Artistic Purity and Professionalism in the S&M Dungeon." *Sociological Forum* 25, no. 3: 588–606.

———. 2012. *Dominatrix: Gender, Eroticism, and Control in the Dungeon*. Chicago: University of Chicago Press.

Lorde, Audre. 1984. *Sister Outsider: Essays and Speeches*. New York: Crossing Press.

MacLean, Sarah. 2005. "'It Might Be a Scummy-Arsed Drug but It's a Sick Buzz': Chroming and Pleasure." *Contemporary Drug Problems* 32, no. 2: 295–318.

Marx, Karl. 1844. "Estranged Labour" (sections XXII–XXVII of *The Economic and Philosophical Manuscripts of 1844*). Marxists Internet Archive, www.marxists.org.

Mathews, Paul William. 2017. "Cam Models, Sex Work, and Job Immobility in the Philippines." *Feminist Economics* 23, no. 3: 160–83.

McCall, Leslie. 2005. "The Complexity of Intersectionality." *Signs: Journal of Women in Culture and Society* 30: 1771–800.

McCaughey, Martha, and Christina French. 2001. "Women's Sex-Toy Parties: Technology, Orgasm, and Commodification." *Sexuality & Culture* 5, no. 3: 77–96.

McGowan, Emma. 2018. "What Is International Whore's Day? Sex Workers Are Marching for Their Rights on June 2." *Bustle*, June 1.

McKee, Heidi A., and Danielle Nicole DeVoss. 2007. *Digital Writing Research: Technologies, Methodologies and Ethical Issues*. New York: Hampton Press.

McPherson, Miller, Lynn Smith-Lovin, and James M. Cook. 2001. "Birds of a Feather: Homophily in Social Networks." *Annual Review of Sociology* 27: 415–44.

Meadow, Tey. 2018. "The Mess: Vulnerability as Ethnographic Practice." In *Other, Please Specify: Queer Methods in Sociology*, edited by D'Lane Compton, Tey Meadow, and Kristen Schilt, 154–66. Berkeley: University of California Press.

Mears, Ashley. 2011. *Pricing Beauty: The Making of a Fashion Model*. Berkeley: University of California Press.

Mears, Ashley, and Catherine Connell. 2016. "The Paradoxical Value of Deviant Cases: Toward a Gendered Theory of Display Work." *Signs: Journal of Women in Culture & Society* 41, no. 2: 333–59.

Melina, Lois Ruskai. 2008. "Backstage with The Hot Flashes: Performing Gender, Performing Age, Performing Rock 'n' Roll." *Qualitative Inquiry* 14, no. 1: 90–110.

Meszaros, Julia, and Christina Bazzaroni. 2014. "From Taboo to Tourist Industry: The Construction of Interracial Intimacies between Black Men and White Women in Colonial and Contemporary Times." *Sociology Compass* 8: 1256–68.

Miller-Young, Mireille. 2014. *A Taste for Brown Sugar: Black Women in Pornography*. Durham, NC: Duke University Press.

Minichiello, Victor, John Scott, and Denton Callander. 2013. "New Pleasures and Old Dangers: Reinventing Male Sex Work." *Journal of Sex Research* 50, nos. 3–4: 263–75.

Moore, Mignon. 2011. *Invisible Families: Gay Identities, Relationships, and Motherhood among Black Women*. Berkeley: University of California Press.

Moors, Amy C., Jennifer D. Rubin, Jes L. Matsick, Ali Ziegler, and Terri D. Conley. 2014. "It's Not Just a Gay Male Thing: Sexual Minority Women and Men Are Equally Attracted to Consensual Non-monogamy." *Journal für Psychologie* 22, no. 1: 38–51.

Morris, William. 1884. "Architecture and History." Marxists Internet Archive, www.marxists.org.

Murphy, Alexandra, and Sudhir Venkatesh. 2006. "Vice Careers: The Changing Contours of Sex Work in New York City." *Qualitative Sociology* 29, no. 2: 129–54.

Murphy, Julia, and Max Roser. 2018. "Internet." Our World in Data, https://ourworldindata.org.

Nardi, Peter. 1999. *Gay Men's Friendships: Invincible Communities*. Chicago: University of Chicago Press.

Nash, Jennifer C. 2014. *The Black Body in Ecstasy: Reading Race, Reading Pornography*. Durham, NC: Duke University Press.

Nayar, Kavita Ilona. 2017a. "Working It: The Professionalization of Amateurism in Digital Adult Entertainment." *Feminist Media Studies* 17, no. 3: 473–88.

———. 2017b. "Sweetening the Deal: Dating for Compensation in the Digital Age." *Journal of Gender Studies* 26, no. 3: 335–46.

Noble, Safiya Umoja. 2018. *Algorithms of Oppression: How Search Engines Reinforce Racism*. New York: NYU Press.

Oerton, Sarah. 2004. "Bodywork Boundaries: Power, Politics and the Professionalism in Therapuetic Massage." *Gender, Work, and Organization* 11, no. 5: 544–65.

Oldenburg, Ray. 1999. *The Great Good Place: Cafes, Coffee Shops, Bookstores, Bars, Hair Salons, and Other Hangouts at the Heart of a Community*. New York: Marlowe & Company.

O'Malley, Pat, and Mariana Valverde. 2004. "Pleasure, Freedom and Drugs: The Uses of 'Pleasure' in Liberal Governance of Drug and Alcohol Consumption." *Sociology* 38, no. 1: 25–42.

Orne, Jason. 2017. *Boystown: Sex & Community in Chicago*. Chicago: University of Chicago Press.

Orne, Jason, and Michael Bell. 2015. *An Invitation to Qualitative Fieldwork: A Multilogical Approach*. New York: Routledge.

Paasonen, Susanna. 2011. *Carnal Resonance: Affect and Online Pornography*. Cambridge, MA: MIT Press.

Parsons, Jeffery T., Juline Koken, and David S. Bimbi. 2004. "The Use of the Internet by Gay and Bisexual Male Escorts: Sex Workers as Sex Educators." *AIDS Care* 16, no. 8: 1021–35.

———. 2007. "Looking beyond HIV: Eliciting Individual and Community Needs of Internet Escorts." *Journal of Homosexuality* 53, nos. 1–2: 219–40.

Parsons, Jeffrey T., Tyrel J. Starks, Kristi E. Gamarel, and Christian Grov. 2012. "Non-monogamy and Sexual Relationship Quality among Same-Sex Male Couples." *Journal of Family Psychology* 26, no. 5: 669–77.

Partridge, D. J. 2008. "We Were Dancing in the Club, Not on the Berlin Wall: Black Bodies, Street Bureaucrats, and Exclusionary Incorporation into the New Europe." *Cultural Anthropology* 23: 660–87.

Pascoe, C. J. 2007. *Dude, You're a Fag*. Berkeley: University of California Press.

Pennay, Amy. 2012. "Carnal Pleasures and Grotesque Bodies: Regulating the Body during a 'Big Night Out' of Alcohol and Party Drug Use." *Contemporary Drug Problems* 39: 397–428.

Pfeffer, Carla A. 2014. "Making Space for Trans Sexualities." *Journal of Homosexuality* 61, no. 5: 597–604.

Phua, Voon Chin, and Allison Caras. 2008. "Personal Brand in Online Advertisements: Comparing White and Brazilian Male Sex Workers." *Sociological Focus* 41, no. 3: 238–55.

Plumridge, Elizabeth, Jane Chetwynd, Anna Reed, and Sandra Gifford. 1997. "Discourses of Emotionality in Commercial Sex: The Missing Client Voice." *Feminism and Psychology* 7, no. 2: 165–81.

Porter, Tom (and Reuters). 2018. "Backpage Website Shut Down, Founder Charged with 93 Counts by FBI in Sealed Indictment." *Newsweek*, April 7.

Pruitt, Mathew. 2005. "Online Boys: Male for Male Internet Escorts." *Sociological Focus* 38, no. 3: 189–203.

Quinn, James, and Craig Forsyth. 2005. "Describing Sexual Behavior in the Era of the Internet: A Typology for Empirical Research." *Deviant Behavior* 26, no. 3: 191–207.

Richtel, Matt. 2013. "Intimacy on the Web, with a Crowd." *New York Times*, September 21.

Robinson, Brandon A. 2015. "'Personal Preference' as the New Racism: Gay Desire and Racial Cleansing in Cyberspace." *Sociology of Race and Ethnicity* 1, no. 2: 317–30.

Robinson, Brandon A., and Salvador Vidal-Ortiz. 2013. "Displacing the Dominant 'Down Low' Discourse: Deviance, Same-Sex Desire, and Craigslist.org." *Deviant Behavior* 34, no. 3: 224–41.

Rodgers, Diane M., and Ryan Taves. 2017. "The Epistemic Culture of Homebrewers and Microbrewers." *Sociological Spectrum* 37, no. 3: 127–48.

Rooke, Alison. 2016. "Queer in the Field: On Emotions, Temporality and Performativity in Ethnography." In *Queer Methods and Methodologies: Intersecting Queer Theories and Social Science Research*, edited by Catherine J. Nash, 25–40. New York: Routledge.

Rubin, Gayle. 1984. "Thinking Sex: Notes for a Radical Theory of the Politics of Sexuality." In *Pleasure and Danger: Exploring Female Sexuality*, edited by Carole S. Vance, 267–319. New York: Routledge & Kegan Paul.

Ruef, Martin. 2010. *The Entrepreneurial Group: Social Identities, Relations, and Collective Action*. Princeton, NJ: Princeton University Press.

Russell, Thaddeus. 2010. *Renegade History of the United States*. New York: Free Press.

Rust, Paula, ed. 2000. *Bisexuality in the United States: A Social Science Reader*. New York: Columbia University Press.

Sanders, Teela. 2005a. "It's Just Acting: Sex Workers' Strategies for Capitalising on Sexuality." *Gender, Work and Organization* 12, no. 4: 319–42.

———. 2005b. *Sex Work: A Risky Business*. Portland, OR: Willan.

———. 2008. "Male Sexual Scripts: Intimacy, Sexuality and Pleasure in the Purchase of Commercial Sex." *Sociology* 42, no. 3: 400–17.

Sanders, Teela, Jane Scoular, Rosie Campbell, Jane Pitcher, and Stewart Cunningham. 2018. *Internet Sex Work: Beyond the Gaze*. Oxford: Palgrave.

Schippers, Mimi. 2016. *Beyond Monogamy: Polyamory and the Future of Polyqueer Sexualities*. New York: NYU Press.

Schulman, Sarah. 2012. *Ties That Bind: Familial Homophobia and Its Consequences*. New York: New Press.

Scott, Darieck. 2010. *Extravagant Abjection: Blackness, Power, and Sexuality in the African American Literary Imagination*. New York: NYU Press.

Selmi, Giulia. 2012. "Dirty Talks and Gender Cleanliness: An Account of Identity Management Practices in Phone Sex Work." In *Dirty Work: Identity Studies in the Social Sciences*, edited by Ruth Simpson, Natasha Slutskaya, Patricia Lewis, and Heather Höpfl, 113–25. London: Palgrave Macmillan.

Senft, Theresa M. 2008. *Camgirls: Celebrity and Community in the Age of Social Networks*. New York: Peter Lang.

Shafer-Landau, Russ. 2012. *The Ethical Life: Fundamental Readings in Ethics and Moral Problems*. New York: Oxford University Press.

Silva, Tony. 2016. "Bud-Sex: Constructing Normative Masculinity among Rural Straight Men That Have Sex with Men." *Gender and Society* 31, no. 1: 51–73.

Simula, Brandy L. 2013. "Queer Utopias in Painful Spaces: BDSM Participants' Interrelational Resistance to Heternormativity and Gender Regulation." In *A Critical Inquiry into Queer Utopias*, edited by Angela Jones, 71–100. New York: Palgrave.

Small, Mario. 2009. *Unanticipated Gains: Origins of Network Inequality in Everyday Life*. New York: Oxford University Press.

Snitow, Ann Barr, Christine Stansell, and Sharon Thompson. 1983. *Powers of Desire: The Politics of Sexuality*. New York: Monthly Review Press.

Sontag, Susan. (1967) 2002. "The Pornographic Imagination." In *Styles of Radical Will*, 35–73. New York: Macmillan.

Steinblatt, Jacob. 2015. "A Popular Cam Girl Just Got Shut Down for Wearing a Nazi Uniform." *Vocativ*, August 3, www.vocativ.com.

Stryker, Susan. 2008. *Transgender History*. New York: Seal Press.

Taormino, Tristan, Celine Parreñas Shimizu, Constance Penley, and Mireille Miller-Young. 2012. *The Feminist Porn Book: The Politics of Producing Pleasure*. New York: Feminist Press.

Telles, Edward. 2004. *Race in Another America: The Significance of Skin Color in Brazil*. Princeton, NJ: Princeton University Press.

Tierney, Allison. 2018. "Sex Workers Say They're Being Pushed Off Social Media Platforms." *Vice*, April 2, www.vice.com.

Tompkins, Avery Brooks. 2014. "'There's No Chasing Involved': Cis/Trans Relationships, 'Tranny Chasers,' and the Future of a Sex-Positive Trans Politics." *Journal of Homosexuality* 61, no. 5: 766–80.

Trout, Christopher. 2017. "The Semi-nude Lives of Webcam Stars." *Engadget*, June 1, www.engadget.com.

Twigg, Julia, Carol Wolkowitz, Rachel Lara Cohen, and Sarah Nettleton. 2011. "Conceptualising Body Work in Health and Social Care." *Sociology of Health & Illness* 33: 171–88.

Utrata, Jennifer. 2011. "Youth Privilege: Doing Age and Gender in Russia's Single-Mother Families." *Gender and Society* 25, no. 5: 616–41.

Vance, Carole S., ed. 1984. *Pleasure and Danger: Exploring Female Sexuality*. Boston: Routledge & Kegan Paul.

Van Doorn, Niels, and Olav Velthuis. 2018. "A Good Hustle: The Moral Economy of Market Competition in Adult Webcam Modeling." *Journal of Cultural Economy* 11, no. 3: 177–92.

Van Eeden-Moorefield, Brad, Kevin Malloy, and Kristen Benson. 2016. "Gay Men's (Non)Monogamy Ideals and Lived Experience." *Sex Roles* 75, nos. 1–2: 43–55.

Vaughan, Liwen, and Rongbin Yang. 2012. "Web Data as Academic and Business Quality Estimates: A Comparison of Three Data Sources." *Journal of the American Society for Information Science and Technology* 63, no. 10: 1960–72.

Veblen, Thorstein. 1899. *The Theory of the Leisure Class*. Project Gutenberg, www.gutenberg.org.

Vehovar, Vasja, and Katja Lozar Manfreda. 2008. "Overview: Online Surveys." In *The SAGE Handbook of Online Research Methods*, edited by Nigel G. Fielding, Raymond M. Lee, and Grant Blank, 177–94. Los Angeles: SAGE.

Vidal-Ortiz, Salvador. 2004. "On Being a White Person of Color: Using Autoethnography to Understand Puerto Ricans' Racialization." *Qualitative Sociology* 27, no. 2: 179–203.

Wager, Meg. 2015. "Cam Girl in Nazi Uniform Makes $30,000 in Tips before Webcam Site Shuts Down Show." *New York Daily News*, August 3.

Walby, Kevin. 2012. *Touching Encounters: Sex, Work, and Male-for-Male Internet Escorting*. Chicago: University of Chicago Press.

Wallenstein, Gene. 2009. *The Pleasure Instinct: Why We Crave Adventure, Chocolate, Pheromones, and Music*. Hoboken, NJ: John Wiley & Sons.

Walters, Larry. 2013. "The Gold Standard: Why Foreign Webmasters Should Care about US Law." Walters Law Group, https://firstamendment.com.

Ward, Jane. 2015. *Not Gay: Sex between Straight White Men*. New York: NYU Press.

Weinstock, Jacqueline S., and Esther Rothblum. 1996. *Lesbian Friendships: For Ourselves and Each Other*. New York: NYU Press.

Weisman, Carrie. 2015. "Inside the Rapidly Growing Cam Industry That's Changing the Porn Industry as We Know It." *Alternet*, February 16.

Weiss, Margot. 2011. *Techniques of Pleasure: BDSM and the Circuits of Sexuality*. Durham, NC: Duke University Press.

Weitzer, Ronald. 2005. "New Directions in Research on Prostitution." *Crime, Law, and Social Change* 43, no. 4: 211–35.

———. 2010. "Sex Work: Paradigms and Politics." In *Sex for Sale: Prostitution, Pornography, and the Sex Industry*, 2nd ed., 1–43. New York: Routledge.

Welter, Barbara. 1966. "The Cult of True Womanhood: 1820–1860." *American Quarterly* 18, no. 2: 151–74.

Whitesel, Jason. 2014. *Fat Gay Men: Girth, Mirth, and the Politics of Stigma*. New York: New York University Press.

Williams, Valerie. 2017. "99% of MLM Businesses Lose Money, but Women Are Still Signing On." *Scary Mommy*, August 17.

Willis, Ellen. (1992) 2012a. "Feminism, Moralism, and Pornography." In *Beginning to See the Light: Sex, Hope, and Rock-and-Roll*, 219–27. Minneapolis: University of Minnesota Press.

———. (1992) 2012b. "Lust Horizons: Is the Women's Movement Pro-Sex?" In *No More Nice Girls: Countercultural Essays*, 3–14. Minneapolis: University of Minnesota Press.

Wolkowitz, Carol. 2002. "The Social Relations of Body Work." *Work, Employment and Society* 16, no. 3: 497–510.

———. 2006. *Bodies at Work*. Thousand Oaks, CA: SAGE.

Woodward, Kathleen. 2006. "Performing Age, Performing Gender." *NWSA Journal* 18, no. 1: 162–89.

Yarbrough, Marilyn, and Crystal Bennett. 2000. "Cassandra and the 'Sistahs': The Peculiar Treatment of African American Women in the Myth of Women as Liars." *Gender, Race & Justice* 3, no. 2: 625–57.

Zajdow, Grazyna. 2010. "It Blasted Me into Space: Intoxication and an Ethics of Pleasure." *Health Sociology Review* 19, no. 2: 218–29.

Zhou, Yanyan, and Bryant Paul. 2016. "Lotus Blossom or Dragon Lady: A Content Analysis of 'Asian Women' Online Pornography." *Sexuality & Culture* 20, no. 4: 1083–110.

INDEX

ableism, xiii, 10, 15, 61, 88, 249. *See also* disability
abolitionist, 246
accommodations, 93. *See also* disability
ace identities, 8, 22, 92
ACF. *See* AmberCutie's Forum
acting, 5, 153, 155, 192, 224
activism, 88, 133, 239, 241, 301
activists, 2, 10, 38, 87, 200, 239, 244, 247–248
Adult Video Network (AVN), 138–139
adultvideochat, 139
AdultWork, 93
advertise, 160, 164, 166, 190, 207, 230. *See also* advertisements; advertising
advertisements, 70, 73, 80, 230
advertising, 42,124, 230–231, 233, 236, 238, 305
advocacy, 135, 233, 235, 241, 247
advocate, 12, 20, 131, 245, 301
advocates, 2, 87, 231–232, 244–245, 248
affect, 15, 24, 61, 84, 117, 129, 138, 145,155, 163, 165, 173, 176, 204, 219, 232–236, 240, 244, 248–249
affiliates, 57
Africa, 49, 190, 198, 260, 265
aftercare, 218–219, 224, 227. *See also* BDSM; kink
aging, 158, 161
Agustín, Laura, 87, 297
Ahmed, Sara, 24–25, 297
algorithms, 189, 201
amateur, 5–6, 47, 52–53
AmberCutie's Forum (ACF), 137, 145–148, 150–151
apps, 57–58, 60, 69, 187
art, 12, 34, 51, 72, 89–90, 108, 183–184

artist, 184–185, 223. *See also* art; artistic
artistic, 65, 183–184, 240
asexual, 22, 35, 98, 252, 260. *See also* ace identities
attraction, 181, 200
Attwood, Feona, 48
audience, 49–50, 67, 70, 161–162, 164, 213
authenticity, v, 5–7, 9, 41, 44–47, 51, 53, 72, 110, 120, 155–156, 158, 160, 181, 201–202
autoethnography, 5, 9, 11–12
autonomy, 1–3, 16, 57–58, 60, 79, 86, 97, 101–102, 131, 248

Backpage, 230–231, 235–237
ban, 65, 127–130, 244–245, 248, 253–258, 260–263
Bangbroschat, 66
banhammer, 127–128. *See also* ban
BAYSWAN, 135
BBW. *See* big beautiful women
BBWcam (BBWC), 67
BDSM: blasphemy role playing, 206–208; bondage, 204, 222; collared relationship, 220; cuckolding, 206–207, 213–214; degradation, 211, 216–217; discipline, 71–72, 204; dominance/domination, 204, 207, 209, 225; femdomming, 198; fetish, 56, 76, 103, 138–139, 169–174, 192, 198, 201, 203, 205–208, 210–211, 213–214, 217–218, 220, 225, 227; humiliation, 206–208, 211, 215–217; incest fetish, 205–206; masochism, 204; race play, 202, 205, 207, 209–219; roleplaying, 205–208, 223; sadism, 204; small penis humiliation (SPH), 206, 208, 210, 213–215; submission, 204;

313

ABOUT THE AUTHOR

Angela Jones is Associate Professor of Sociology at Farmingdale State College, SUNY. Her research interests include African American political thought and protest, gender, sexuality, race, and queer methodologies and theory.

Printed in the USA
CPSIA information can be obtained
at www.ICGtesting.com
LVHW051739151223
766568LV00003B/227